The Ghosts of Happy Valley

The Ghosts of
Happy Valley

Searching for the Lost World of
Africa's Infamous Aristocrats

Juliet Barnes

Aurum
history

First published in Great Britain
2013 by Aurum Press Ltd
74–77 White Lion Street
Islington
London N1 9PF
www.aurumpress.co.uk

Front endpaper: © Illustrated London News Ltd/Mary Evans
Back endpaper: Nigel Pavitt

A catalogue record for this book is available from the British Library.

ISBN 978 1 78131 085 4

1 3 5 7 9 10 8 6 4 2
2013 2015 2017 2016 2014

Typeset in Fournier MT by SX Composing DTP, Rayleigh, Essex
Printed and bound by CPI Group (UK) Ltd., Croydon, CR0 4YY

For Solomon

Contents

Acknowledgements

First and foremost I am indebted to Solomon Gitau, both for showing me the old houses of Happy Valley and continuing to inspire me to visit and revisit, and for sharing his passion for the natural world. He earns my continued admiration for taking on the role of spokesman for Happy Valley's endangered colobus monkeys and threatened forests, and a percentage of my writing proceeds about Happy Valley will continue to assist his causes. Without Solomon, this book would not have been written, and I am grateful to him for sharing his handwritten autobiographical stories, *Born in Happy Valley*, *The Black Days* and *Face to Face with White Mischief Spirits*. I remain grateful to the late Jean O'Meara and Astrid von Kalckstein for their inspiration and support of Solomon's environmental causes, and for Astrid's continued support of him and his family, as well as for sharing her archive of letters, e-mails and documents regarding Solomon's conservation work.

I am also grateful to the UK team: my agent, Robert Smith, for believing in the book and for all his advice; to Graham Coster of Aurum Press, for taking it on and encouraging me with his enthusiasm and expertise; Steve Gove, my copy-editor for his tireless editing and endless patience; Melissa Smith, Lucy Warburton, Jessica Axe and Anne Bowman for their time and expert assistance, not to mention all those people in the London office who I don't see or meet, but without whose work the book would never have come into being.

My family are integral to this book: both my parents, Peter and Margery Barnes, for many stories and passing on their love of reading; my mother for her patience in reading early drafts and my father for firing me with his own enthusiasm for exploring the obscurer parts of Kenya, as well as teaching me to drive on appalling roads. My children, Michael and Siana, have grown up with a mum who disappeared periodically in an unreliable Land Rover on eccentric missions, and who can be snappy when disturbed during writing hours, but they have also taught me so much. I also thank my late grandmothers, Phyllis Platt and Evelyn Barnes; and my aunts, Sue Bremner and Rosamund and her husband Keith Watson for their stories.

I remain most grateful to Lord and Lady Delamere for renting to me my blissful home on Soysambu, where I can write in peace, as well as for telling me many entertaining stories over a whisky, and for their generous and unconditional hospitality and unlimited use of their library, including copies of Boy Long's Diaries.

I thank Nigel Pavitt for his photographs, and Veronica Finch for hers. I am also grateful to Janie Begg for being so generous with her time, for many entertaining stories and sharing old photographs. They and many other Kenyans or visitors have driven or accompanied me to Happy Valley and inspired my research, including Peter Mutua, Janey Ready, Alice Percival, Ben and Libby Hoskyns-Abrahall, Frances Osborne, John Heminway, the late Chris Orme-Smith, Leonie Gibbs, Sophie Walbeoffe, and Frank and Anne Daykin. My research has further been assisted by conversations and e-mails with Paul Spicer and Errol Trzebinski, while the latter's knowledge and advice has been especially valuable.

Many other former settlers of the Kenya highlands, or their relatives, have kindly shared wonderful stories and photos, contributing invaluably to my research. They include Bubbles Delap, Tobina Cole, Joan Heath, Giuliana Moretti, Dianella Moretti-Proske and the late Lyduska Piotto. I am also grateful for letters and e-mails from Belle Barker (who also lent photos and cine films), Jean Konschell, Mary Evennett, Angelique Armand-Delille, Bruce and Don Rooken-Smith,

Marge Nye-Chart, Caroline Hanbury Bateman, Linda Tomlin, Bryony Anderson, Sheila Begg, Sheila McLoughlin, the late Debbie Case, Alan Gray, Ray Terry, Maureen Barratt, Benjie Bowles, Richard Morgan-Grenville, Guy D'Olier, Sheilah Simons, Benjie Bowles and the late Mervyn Carnelly.

I thank Shel Arensen, editor of *Old Africa*, and Tony Clegg-Butt, editor of *Travel News*, for encouraging my historical writings; Ian Marshall, John Vaughen and Dick Moss for sharing their old survey maps; John Grimshaw, who read one of the first manuscripts; and Solomon's Canadian friend Suzanne, for use of her house. I am especially grateful to the late Monty Brown for sharing his library, archives and thoughts on the Erroll murder, and for lending me copies of Chapter 14 of Arthur Wolseley-Lewis's typed memoir, the part pertaining to the murder, and to both Monty and his wife Barbara for their kind hospitality and inspiring company.

I am especially grateful to the late *Mzee* Nuthu for his stories, wisdom, kindness and hospitality, and to the extended Nuthu family – but especially Grace, Peter, Paul and Elizabeth – who always welcome me like one of their own. I am grateful, too, for their kind hospitality to Solomon's cousin Jane and the late Esther Gitau; as well as to those many others who still live in Happy Valley and assisted with my research, including Alfred Githaiga, former caretaker of Slains, who lent me Malcolm Watson's typed memoirs, the old gardener at Nye-Chart's, Mama John and her husband, the Karanja family, Solomon's brother Njuguna, the late Danson Mwaura, Sister Teresa at St Peter's Polytechnic, Silas Karoga, Muma Maina, Amos and his late father at Kiambaga, Wahome at Morgan, Mrs Kanyoto in Limuru, and Nganga and Virginia at Kipipiri House.

Then there are the many elders I interviewed, including the *wazee* of Kiambogo: especially Ngugi, Karihe, Wanjiru, Kariuki, Kabiru and 'Major' Mururi; the *wazee* of Kipipiri who shared old memories of their former employers, including Njoroge, Muthoki and Njuguna; the Barkers' old cook and the men who changed my wheel without a jack; Mau Mau veterans Kamwambao, Mugwe, Njuguna, Mugwe and Wanjiru, who met me at Wanjohi; and the three old men who spoke to me on the slopes of Kipipiri, but especially *Mzee* Gachau, who has always kept in touch.

There are many more people in Happy Valley whose names I never knew, or have forgotten or omitted in error, who have shown me old houses, put me on the right road or shared memories and cups of tea. Then there are all those children at the schools and along the roadsides, whose smiles and waves rejuvenated me after a long day's drive. It will be up to them whether the old houses survive or if their children ever see a colobus monkey enjoying its freedom in the indigenous forest.

Chronology of Some Significant Historical Events

1844   Missionary Ludwig Krapf arrives in Mombasa, establishing first mission station at Rabai

1870   **Birth of 3rd Baron Delamere,** Hugh Cholmondeley, in England

1871   Stanley finds Livingstone at Ujiji

1883   **Birth of Sir Jock Delves Broughton** in England. Explorer Joseph Thomson arrives in Rift Valley

1888   Birth of Gilbert Colville in England

1890   **Anglo-German agreement:** partitioning of East Africa

1893   **Birth of Lady Idina Sackville** in England

1895   Interior (west of Mombasa) declared the **British East Africa Protectorate** in June

1896   Start of inland railway in Mombasa

1897   3rd Baron Delamere arrives in Kenya on foot from Berbera

1899   Railway reaches mile 327 (now Nairobi) and halts before ascent into highlands

1900   **Birth of Alice Silverthorne**

1901   **Birth of future Earl of Erroll, Josslyn Hay,** in Scotland

1902   British government extends protectorate boundaries into Uganda

1903   Railway reaches Lake Victoria. Delamere buys land at Njoro

1904   South African settlers arrive

1906   **Geoffrey Buxton arrives in Happy Valley**

1907 **Slavery abolished.** Gilbert Colville comes to Kenya

1913 **Birth of Diana Caldwell. Idina Sackville marries Euan Wallace**

1914 Birth of Idina's son David. **Start of First World War**

1915 Birth of Idina's son Gerald

1918 **Armistice, end of First World War**

1919 **Idina divorces Wallace, marries Charles Gordon and comes to Kenya** in April

1920 **Inland protectorate becomes colony**

1922 **Alice Silverthorne marries Comte Frédéric de Janzé in Chicago.** Kikuyu Central Association begins. Police break up political gathering led by Harry Thuku near Norfolk Hotel on 16 March

1923 **Idina divorces Gordon and in September gets engaged to Josslyn Hay** in Venice, and marries him on 22 September in London. Alice de Janzé's first daughter born in Paris

1924 **Idina and Josslyn Hay arrive in Kenya and build Slains.** Alice's second daughter born in Paris

1925 **Alice and Frédéric de Janzé invited to Kenya by Hays, arrive in December.** Ramsay-Hills arrive and buy farm in Naivasha

1926 Birth of Diana, Idina and Josslyn Hay's daughter in January. **De Janzés buy Wanjohi Farm in June. Hay having an affair with Mary Ramsay-Hill. Raymond de Trafford arrives and starts affair with Alice de Janzé**

1927 **Alice de Janzé shoots Raymond de Trafford and herself in Paris in March.** Alice divorces Frédéric in June. Alice tried and acquitted on 23 December

1928 Alice returns to Kenya in January, but is deported in March. Josslyn Hay's father dies on 20 February. **Jossyn Hay, now 22nd Earl of Erroll, runs off with Mary Ramsay-Hill to England** in March. 3rd Baron Delamere marries Gladys Markham. Edward, Prince of Wales, and Henry, Duke of Gloucester, come to Kenya on safari. Both have affairs with Beryl Markham

1929 Wall Street Crash, start of Great Depression. Slains up for auction in January and in June **Idina and Erroll divorce.** Jomo Kenyatta goes to London to promote the Kikuyu case. End of year Beryl Markham banished by Queen Mary

1930 **Erroll marries Mary Ramsay-Hill** in February and returns to Kenya that month on ship with Edward, Prince of Wales, and Beryl Markham. **Idina marries Donald Haldeman, buys and builds Clouds, returns to Kenya**

1932 **Alice de Janzé marries Raymond de Trafford.** Royal Commission, Carter Land Commission appointed for Kenyan native land grievances. **Oswald Mosley sets up British Union of Fascists**

1934 **Erroll joins British Union of Fascists.** Idina leaves Haldeman in March, returns to Kenya in July with new boyfriend, pilot Chris Langlands

1936 Beryl Markham becomes first woman to fly solo across the Atlantic from England. Edward VIII abdicates

1937 Erroll attends coronation of George VI

1939 **Idina marries Vincent Soltau** in March. **Hitler invades Poland** on 1 September, **start of Second World War. Death of Mary, Countess of Erroll**

1940 Soltau is posted to Cairo in mid-year. **Diana and Jock Broughton married in England** on 5 November, **arrive in Kenya** on 12 November

1941 **Erroll murdered** on 24 January. Euan Wallace dies on 8 February in England of stomach cancer. **Trial of Broughton** begins on 26 May followed by acquittal. **Suicide of Alice de Trafford** on 27 September

1942 **Suicide of Broughton** on 5 December in Liverpool

1943 Idina's son Gerald (Gee) confirmed missing. **Diana Broughton marries Gilbert Colville**

1944 Idina's son David killed in Medina in August

1945 **Idina Soltau moves to Mombasa** with boyfriend James Bird. **End of Second World War** in May

1948 Duke of Gloucester due to arrive to give Nairobi city status, prompting Kikuyu oath-taking ceremony at Kiambaa

1950 Kikuyu underground movement banned

1951 **Start of Mau Mau**

1952 **State of Emergency declared,** Jomo Kenyatta arrested. HRH Princess Elizabeth visits Treetops Hotel in Aberdare forest and becomes queen on death of her father

1953 **Charles Fergusson and Richard Bingley murdered** on New Year's Day

1954 Mau Mau burn down Treetops Hotel

1955 **Idina dies in October. Diana divorces Colville and marries Tom Delamere**

1963 Jomo Kenyatta addresses white settlers in Nakuru on 12 August. **Kenya becomes independent** at midnight on 12 December

1978 Jomo Kenyatta dies, Daniel Arap Moi becomes president

1987 **Diana Delamere dies**

1992 Start of multi-party politics

2002 Mwai Kibaki elected president of Kenya

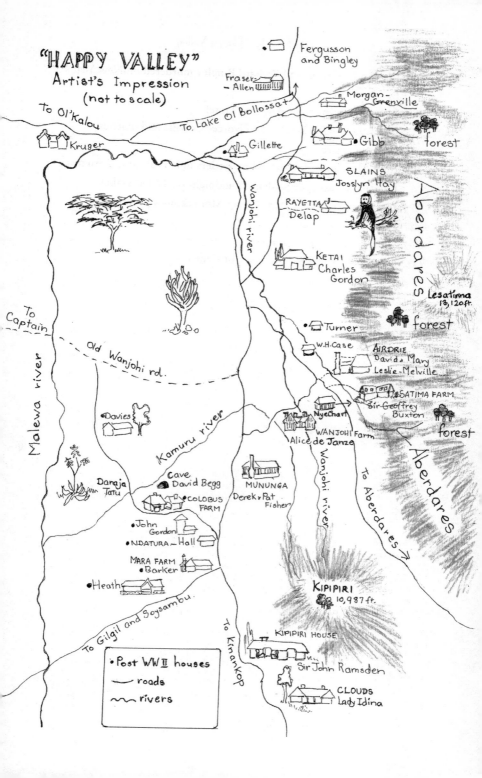

1

Clouds, Smoke and Mirrors

1

An Unexpected Escort into
the Centre of Scandal

My mother and several other women artists were painting flamingos beside Lake Elmenteita the day I first met Solomon. It was a hot afternoon in January 2000, and they'd all gathered for tea on the veranda of my cottage in the heart of Kenya's Rift Valley.

Solomon jumped up to open the gate, barely waiting for me to emerge from my Land Rover before shaking my hand with vigour. I looked curiously at this dark, tall man with his white teeth, black piercing eyes and slightly unkempt appearance. He seemed unfazed to be the odd one out at the tea party. The only man and the only black person, Solomon was dressed in a faded red jogging suit and worn canvas shoes, topped by a leather visor hand-painted with leaves and lizards. His surname, Gitau, is a Kikuyu name, but Solomon bears little resemblance to these characteristically short, light-skinned African people.

I'd heard a bit about Solomon from my mother: he's an activist in the area they used to call Happy Valley. Back in colonial days, various shady characters had made a name for themselves in this highland valley, but today it's the name of Solomon Gitau which is spoken with hushed cadences of scandal. His outspoken defence of the area's last remaining colobus monkeys and their vanishing forest habitat had incurred the wrath of his neighbours and the local authorities, especially when he interfered with a lucrative illegal poaching operation. He was called 'monkey man', branded mad by most of his neighbours. I knew that despite having no regular income, he battled to replant trees in the area lying between the Rift Valley and the Aberdare Mountains, while also providing a voice for the wild forest creatures. He'd been brutally tortured by the authorities because of his outspoken determination, repeatedly threatened and sabotaged, yet had continued undeterred, starting up conservation groups throughout the area and beyond, somehow maintaining his optimistic determination to succeed in saving a largely forgotten area's natural heritage. Today if occasional visitors drive through Happy Valley, it's usually en route to the Aberdare National Park, where most of the remaining wildlife fled as the area's human population grew massively after Kenya's independence.

A year previously Solomon had written his life story by hand and given it to my mother to edit, as he finds writing in English difficult. I'd glanced at the old exercise book with its grubby newspaper cover without much interest, but once I had opened it and read a few paragraphs, I had immediately felt compelled to finish the strangely gripping autobiography. Solomon was born in the heart of Happy Valley – just before the last of the white settlers left – and his story is extraordinary.

It's surprising that Kenya's table-like range of volcanic mountains are still commonly called by their British colonial name, the Aberdares, even though after independence they were officially renamed the Nyandarua Range. These mountains rise to 13,120 feet, while close by, a little further west, is the smaller, hunched-looking Kipipiri mountain, rising to 10,987 feet. Happy Valley is the high green valley tucked between the two, spreading out to encompass the surrounding area to the north and west. Now it is densely populated by African farmers, most of whom were born long after the departure of the hedonistic clique of white colonials who lived there for a mere handful of decades.

The British East Africa Protectorate, part of which became the Kenya Colony, attracted plenty of aristocratic, adventurous and rebellious white settlers in the first decades of the twentieth century.

A handful of them, Happy Valley's wife-swapping set, used the space and freedom of Kenya's breathtaking landscapes to behave with wild abandon, tarring their fellow settlers with the dubious reputation associated with one particularly promiscuous clique. This circle's transitory zenith of the 1920s and 1930s, with their sex, drugs and finally the murder mystery concerning the death of an earl in 1941, is framed enticingly by the surrounding century of dramatically colourful history, which also perhaps contributes to the continued seduction of world attention by this attractive former colony straddling the equator. There's the land question too. Kenya's Kikuyu tribe, feeling robbed of their country's best land, initiated and fought a guerrilla war in the 1950s. Known as Mau Mau, it made the headlines daily in Britain. The Kikuyu are the largest tribe in Kenya, albeit only one of forty-plus in the country. Kenya's first and third presidents were Kikuyu, and as it happens today's Happy Valley is populated by Kikuyu.

An indefinable mystique hangs about that dissolute clique of white settlers who tarnished the name of Happy Valley between the wars, their salacious antics supposedly taking priority over farming. But as Elspeth Huxley, that seasoned writer on Kenya, pointed out in her book *Forks and Hope*:

> Gin-soaked as they were, they enhanced rather than damaged the natural charms of their valley by leaving the native trees alone and creating gardens of outstanding beauty, by paddocking green pastures for butter-yellow Guernseys, stocking streams with trout and building attractive, rambling, creeper-festooned bungalows of local timbers with shingle roofs.

Besides, decadent behaviour wasn't totally restricted to Happy Valley. Aristocrats and royals from all over the world were joining in the fun. Edward, Prince of Wales, and his brother Henry, Duke of Gloucester, came to Kenya on hunting safaris in 1928 and 1930, their conquests not restricted to the animal kingdom. Dashing pilot and racehorse trainer Beryl Markham, the first woman to fly solo from England to America, probably scores best here. Her many lovers included Lord Erroll, professional hunter Baron Bror Blixen (married to Karen of *Out of Africa* fame) and the Hon. Denys Finch Hatton (also the lover of Karen Blixen, and an inspiration for her book). Tall, blonde and beautiful, Beryl – already on her second marriage after a bohemian upbringing in Kenya – managed to have affairs with the Prince and Duke simultaneously, eventually being paid off by Buckingham Palace to stay out of the way for life!

But it's on Happy Valley that interest still focuses. Scandal in Kenya had taken on a new dimension in 1923. It was in that year Lady Idina Hay arrived to settle in the area: she was twice divorced and eight years older than her latest husband, the attractive and aristocratic Hon. Josslyn Hay, 22nd Earl of Erroll. Idina was destined to become Happy Valley's Mistress of Ceremonies, while her third husband's penchant for sexual variety was no inhibitor. Add in Alice de Janzé, spoilt American heiress married to a French count, plus a few other moneyed undesirables, and here the real Happy Valley stories begin.

Happy Valley's heyday was brief, although it outlasted Idina's third marriage. In 1939, at the start of the Second World War, Josslyn Hay, now Lord Erroll – his second wife Mary, Countess of Erroll, having died from a lifestyle of excessive drink and drugs – was busy conducting his affair with another married woman, Phyllis Filmer. The affair terminated with the arrival in Kenya of the newly married Sir Jock and Diana Broughton at the end of 1940. They rented a house in Nairobi's leafy suburb of Karen, named in honour of Baroness Karen Blixen after she left Kenya in 1931.

Sir Jock Delves Broughton was thirty years older than his striking blonde wife. They had a written agreement that he would not hold her back if she met somebody else – which she immediately did. Diana fell madly and very publicly in love with Erroll – and he seemed to return her feelings. Idina, Phyllis and that other notorious flame of Erroll's, Alice de Trafford, formerly de Janzé, united in their dislike of Diana.

Two months later, in the pale light of dawn, some passing Africans found Erroll dead, with a bullet in his brain, tucked in the foetal position in the footwell of his Buick – which had almost toppled into a roadside murram pit, about a mile from the Broughton home.

After wining and dining at Nairobi's most popular colonial meeting place, Muthaiga Club, with Diana, her husband and a friend, Erroll had taken Diana dancing, had a quick romp with her at his Muthaiga house, and finally dropped her home in the small hours of the morning. Muthaiga is a suburb on the opposite side of Nairobi to Karen, but in the dead of night there wouldn't have been any traffic. Erroll had evidently begun driving back to Muthaiga when somebody had intercepted him. Or had his killer been hiding in the back of his car? Or perhaps he was shot at Broughton's house, then his body driven away by the murderer or an accomplice?

Sir Jock was arrested and charged with Erroll's murder, leading to the longest trial central Africa had ever known – three weeks. The world was at war, which made the headlines from the colony doubly embarrassing. Meanwhile, police evidence was patchy and poorly handled. In retrospect, this too was suspicious.

In preparation, Diana flew to South Africa to meet the ballistics expert and get herself an entirely new wardrobe – something eye-catching and different for every day of the trial. In Muthaiga Club, the atmosphere was charged with apprehension – would her cuckolded husband be the first white man to hang in Kenya?

During the trial, Alice, Idina and Phyllis dressed up in their best and sat together, glaring at Diana's beautifully clad back. No doubt plenty of other women in court fantasised about hurling invisible poisoned arrows at her too. If any of them knew anything about the murder, they never let on. Or had they simply all been too drunk that fateful night to remember what had happened?

Nothing was concluded and nobody was found guilty, but ever since there has been much speculation as to Erroll's killer and the motive, and endless research has gone into seeking the truth. The Happy Valley hype has also kept the stories alive: far more than if the victim had been just a hard-working, happily married settler.

Sir Jock killed himself the following year. Diana Broughton, meanwhile, grieved for two years before marrying the reclusive and rich landowner, Gilbert Colville. She even persuaded him to buy her the home where her late lover had lived with his wife Mary.

In 1955, fourteen years after the murder, Diana married a fourth time; this time the man she chose was Lord Delamere, Colville's best friend and neighbour.

Almost a century later, that irresistible intrigue still lingers on from the heyday of Kenya's infamous Happy Valley, two giddy decades that climaxed in the unresolved murder of Lord Erroll. Controversy remains, although many authors have come up with theories since the first whodunnit book, James Fox's *White Mischief* (1982) – made into a major feature film starring Charles Dance, Greta Scacchi and Joss Ackland – reignited interest in the case. The man (some say woman) who fired a bullet into the brain of the philandering earl died with his (or her) secret. Surprisingly, perhaps, none of the other members of the hedonistic Happy Valley inner circle ever kissed and told either.

Solomon was a small boy when Kenya became independent from British rule in 1963: white settlers were leaving and their farms were being divided up and allocated to native Kenyans. As the years passed, he watched the rapid population growth of his own Kikuyu people as they spurred on mindless destruction of the indigenous mountain forests. Today the continued demise of the trees causes formerly reliable rivers to alternately dry up and flood, washing down valuable topsoil into the lakes of the Rift Valley. Solomon's book has no happy endings.

After exchanging pleasantries with the other guests, I asked Solomon about his conservation work, carried out on an entirely voluntary basis. He talked without restraint, his husky voice rising and falling musically, fraught with conviction and emotion. His poor English surprised me – I'd expected this man, who very clearly intends to change things, to be more sophisticated. Rural Kenyan subsistence farmers tend to have more immediately pressing problems than saving trees or wild animals, which respectively represent bags of charcoal and pests. Like the majority of Kenya's rapidly growing rural population, Solomon has always lived in a simple homestead with no electricity or running water; there are few maintained access roads or other communications, and the inhabitants' educational opportunities are limited.

He gesticulated with thin, sensitive hands, smiling broadly as he talked passionately about monkeys and trees, but frowning suddenly when he mentioned the mounting threats to both. There was something dynamic about Solomon: his enthusiasm, winning smile and positive attitude were infectious.

We paused to listen to the sing-song bray of the zebra. A bachelor herd of impala were jumping through the thorn bush, kicking up the dust into a cloudless, blue sky. I asked Solomon about his 'book', whose story he had introduced with an unexpected comparison:

> If you don't know Happy Valley, try to visit the area. All around Happy Valley are many historic houses. The spirits of the dead white people who used to live in these houses are living on in the African people who live there now . . . As I read the book *White Mischief* I saw that there is no big difference between these white people and the modern African living in Happy Valley.

The air was dry and I could smell something dead – the hyenas and jackals would be out tonight. Apart from the indomitable scarlet bougainvillaea bushes, my garden was like a desert. I thought about how unlikely it seemed for a black Kenyan to display any interest in a set of colonial characters who appeared to have attracted posthumous fame by doing nothing constructive, yet our conversation over cups of tea and scones with Cape gooseberry jam (made by one of the artists) soon switched from Solomon's book to the old houses in Happy Valley.

Today's significant landowners in Happy Valley are vastly wealthy black politicians, in spite of constant low mutterings about the source of their gains. In the former farming lands dubbed the 'white highlands' – which surround and include Happy Valley – it's not uncommon to find a farm owned by a powerful politician, an absentee landlord with numerous other business interests. While his wife flies to Europe to buy designer clothes and his children are privately educated in Britain or America, his farm workers are seldom paid much above the minimum wage for unskilled labour, living on less in a month than their boss will spend on a bottle of imported Champagne at Muthaiga Club.

The passenger train, 'the lunatic line', originally built by the British at vast expense, no longer runs daily from Mombasa to Nairobi, nor on to Kisumu. The tiny station at Gilgil in the Rift Valley was once the stepping-off point for white passengers headed for Happy Valley and beyond, who usually paused at the Gilgil Hotel, opened in 1920 by Lady Colville, mother of Gilbert and briefly mother-in-law to Diana. Today few passengers disembark at Gilgil and none of them are white. The Gilgil Hotel, having changed ownership several times, after Kenya's independence became a brothel, is scathingly referred to as the 'Moulin Rouge' by Gilgil's white community. Today it provides squalid dwellings for many families in an expanding, increasingly scruffy roadside town which became flooded with internally displaced Kenyans during the post-election violence at the beginning of 2008. Up the various roads from Gilgil to Happy Valley, the land remains predominantly in Kikuyu hands. The population grows steadily, the farms become smaller, creating an intricate patchwork landscape, their edges blurred by non-indigenous fast-growing trees. The forest recedes, and the Aberdares and Kipipiri regularly burn.

'I can take you to the Happy Valley,' said Solomon, helping himself to another scone. 'You can write the story!'

I'd always wanted to explore the area: I'd read *White Mischief*, which told of a house called Clouds that had been the headquarters for wild sessions of carousing before you traded in your husband for a night with somebody else's. I was dubious about unearthing yet another who-killed-the-Earl-of-Erroll theory, let alone replaying what went on at those parties thrown by Lady Idina. But the prospect of seeing Happy Valley's old, abandoned homes was interesting. So was the idea of getting to know Solomon and finding out what had inspired him to follow so single-mindedly such an unusual bent. As Ralph Waldo Emerson once said, 'The use of history is to give value to the present hour and its duty.' But I'd add Goethe's view, that the 'best thing which we derive from history is the enthusiasm that it raises in us'.

Clouds was still standing, people said. Somebody had seen it from the air, but nobody knew how to get there by road.

'You won't see a white face there nowadays,' an elderly, retired white farmer had warned.

'All those roads are appalling!' another had cautioned.

'In this day and age, you'll get mugged in that area – it's all Kikuyu country now!' the farmer had continued. 'You mustn't go alone.'

'You ought to find somebody who has a gun to accompany you,' an even more twitchy old-timer had said to me.

Solomon certainly doesn't have a gun – I can't imagine him killing a cockroach. But his wanderings through the area on foot have familiarised him with the whereabouts of all the decaying ruins, once people's homes. And his native language is Kikuyu, making him the perfect guide.

'When you see these old houses of white people,' Solomon said conspiratorially, 'then you will want to write the *true* histories!'

I was less sure. At this point he was just a potential guide into an area which had always had some mysterious allure for me.

'There are some stories,' continued Solomon, widening his eyes. 'Terrible stories. You will be the first white person to hear.'

'You can write about the old houses,' suggested one of the artists, adding a few touches to her picture of flamingos.

A sudden gust of dry wind blew clouds of dust on to the veranda and we covered our teacups with our hands.

2

Destination Unknown

Early one February morning in 2000, I met Solomon at an uninspiring roadside village called Captain, a bumpy hour's drive from my home. 'After Captain Colville,' said Solomon. According to Gilgil old-timer Ray Terry, this was Captain Archie Colville, no relation to the Colville who became the third husband of Diana Broughton. Captain, the village, sprawls untidily along a junction off the main road from Gilgil to Nyahururu. The latter was formerly called Thomson's Falls after Scottish explorer Joseph Thomson first admired the waterfall in 1883.

Leaving the tarmac, we made a right-hand turn and headed towards the distant blue hulk of the Aberdares, the flow of conversation stifled by the protesting rattles of my old Land Rover as it jostled along the rocky, rutted road, marked on the map as the 'old Wanjohi road'. Solomon, shouting above the noise of the car, pointed out old settlers' homes, barely recognisable as such in this heavily populated country. Today's newer Kikuyu homesteads were an incongruous mix of one-roomed houses on small plots and larger farms – weekend pads flaunting large, tiled red roofs. Many of the latter homes were owned by wealthy politicians, whom Solomon named with a disapproving air. At that time no white people lived in Happy Valley except for one Dutchman growing flowers for a wealthy Kenyan. The occasional voluntary worker passed through, Solomon said, but in some villages we visited, the children I met had never seen a white person.

As we slowly drew closer to the blue hulk of the Aberdares, I felt a prickle of excitement and wondered if I had a pen and notebook anywhere in the car. I hadn't even taken a camera. This spontaneous Happy Valley tour was just supposed to be an interesting day out.

So it was to prove. I hauled my Land Rover over miles more of rocky, potholed roads, deep channels and gullies gouged out of their neglected surfaces by the previous years' long rains, which had included the torrential downpours and subsequent floods of 1997's El Niño. We stopped to look at some old tumbledown homes, hidden behind untrimmed cypress hedges 30-feet high, cedar fence posts covered in wisps of green 'old man's beard', remains of stores, cattle dips and bridges that Solomon said had been built in the 1920s. I paused to marvel at an old rose scrambling over a piece of wall: a reminder of some faceless, pale, foreign lady who would have ordered its planting. Undeterred by fifty-plus subsequent years of neglect, the bush had somehow survived, even without that meagrely paid 'garden boy' to tend it.

Some houses were completely intact. Others had vanished, leaving only a foundation stone or brick chimney. Some of these once-luxurious dwellings lay empty – allegedly haunted. Rooms of others were now homes for many local families, or poorly funded schools. Most of these people were extremely poor by any standards, and yet they offered us unconditional hospitality – we were invited in for tea, even expected to share their meal. An underpaid government schoolteacher said he was writing the history of the Mau Mau uprising in that area – could I publish it? Another white-haired, half-blind man to whom we gave a lift chuckled when he told us he remembered 'those white people' . . .

Our final destination near the end of that long, exhausting day was planned to be Clouds itself, which according to popular rumour had been the whirlpool of Happy Valley, the place where you got sucked in: the sexy and seductive Lady Idina had lived here and unashamedly thrown those decadent parties which supposedly titillated her guests to plunge into erotic adventures. 'Are you married or do you live in Kenya?' has always been considered a great joke, well tossed among the G&Ts and Scotch. Happy Valley has permanently been painted into Kenya's history, albeit with a British brush. The fascination lingers, fanned by its frequently rewritten legend.

The Anglo-German agreement of 1890 partitioned East Africa into British and German zones and the interior of Kenya became a British protectorate in 1895. Kenya's best farming land lies in the highlands, covering less than 25 per cent of a predominantly semi-arid country. The prime land with well-watered, fertile soil and two annual rainy seasons included what would later be named 'Happy Valley' – the area around the Wanjohi Valley and Kipipiri – invitingly unpopulated at that time, with only the occasional Dorobo honey hunter passing through the lush forests and green glades. It was also a route between grazing grounds for the nomadic Maasai, whose stamp was left in the names of certain features – Kipipiri is Maasai.

The first white settler in this area was Geoffrey Buxton, who arrived in 1906, building his mud and brick house a few years later: Happy Valley's first English-style house. The Soldier Settlement Scheme of 1919 saw further allocation of land in British East Africa, with 99- and 999-year leases being offered to settlers of pure European origin who had served in an officially recognised imperial service unit. This was an attempt to increase the white population, while bringing economic development to the area. But it was also about protection: there was the new threat of African unrest after African troops who'd fought in the First World War had seen how easily white men could be killed.

The scheme attracted plenty of old Etonians. The war had interrupted the careers of a whole generation, but their settlement in Africa eased their passage to peace and gave them the added attraction of retaining their status among uneducated Africans. Kenya, proclaimed a colony in 1920, was already acquiring a reputation as 'the Officers' Mess'. The Africans, meanwhile, now had taxes thrust upon them by Britain, coercing them to take paid work as labourers in Nairobi or on white farms. Nor were they allowed to grow crops for export in case they lowered the standards.

There followed the fleeting era of Lady Idina and her like-minded pleasure-seeking friends, their indulgent lifestyle swept away by the

Second World War. Afterwards things changed fast. There was a further influx of white settlers escaping Britain's post-war austerity, high taxes and the Labour government. By the beginning of the 1950s the old Happy Valley crowd had faded away: most of the larger estates had been divided up into smaller farms, albeit still large by British standards. The houses where earlier settlers had partied with reckless abandon were now homes for different sorts of families. On the whole these white settlers were not aristocratic or affluent and were working hard to make a living out of sheep and pyrethrum – the latter a cash crop that grows well in Kenya's highlands and whose flowers are used in the manufacture of insecticides. Now settler wives tended to be too busy teaching their own children, market gardening, tending English flowers and making jams and pickles, to parade around in designer gear casting lascivious glances at neighbours' husbands. But their lifestyle wasn't destined to last any longer than that of their predecessors.

Back in 1907 Winston Churchill had warned, after visiting Kenya, 'There are already in miniature all the elements of keen racial and political discord.' Almost half a century later no black man even had the right to vote, let alone claim his sacred, ancestral land. The banned underground resistance movement that had begun in the 1940s as the Kikuyu Central Organisation was by the early 1950s showing strong aversion to British rule, its members taking oaths in secret to pledge solidarity. In 1952 a state of emergency was declared. The eight-year Mau Mau uprising was a threat to the existence of white farmers and Happy Valley was right in the thick of it.

Settlers now lived in terror of their formerly loyal staff turning against them and collaborating in their murder. Cows were hamstrung; Kikuyu people were disembowelled and hacked to pieces if they did not pledge loyalty to Mau Mau. Several white farmers were viciously attacked: on the Kinangop, not far from Clouds, the Rucks and their young son were butchered, the child in his bed. Then there was the grisly murder of two white farmers, Charles Fergusson and Richard Bingley, as they sat down to dinner in their home on the northern edge of Happy Valley. As Kikuyu freedom fighters continued to whip up an atmosphere thick with fear and mistrust, the formidable new generation of Happy Valley *memsahibs* slept with guns under their pillows in fortified buildings to protect them from nocturnal attacks, while their husbands joined the Kenya Regiment and went off to fight the determined, fearless men hiding in the impenetrable forests of Mount Kenya and the Aberdares.

Long-haired and unwashed, the Kikuyu freedom fighters knew their way through the thickets and managed to sidestep danger in ways that flummoxed the British. Even RAF bombing of the mountain forests failed to dislodge them or sabotage their teams of supportive women who delivered food and messages. As Elspeth Huxley points out in *Nine Faces of Kenya*: 'British soldiers in boots and smelling of soap and cigarettes had little chance of success against forest gangs in league with local fauna.' Increasingly the Kenya Regiment was forced to rely on 'pseudo gangs' of white settlers, heavily disguised, venturing into the heart of the forest.

Times had to change and Jomo Kenyatta, Kikuyu leader of the Kenya African National Union (KANU) party, was released from detention in 1961 to become the country's first Prime Minister when Kenya's flag was raised at midnight on 12 December 1963 amidst jubilation and fireworks. It was time: India had shed British rule in 1947 and ten years later Ghana had become the first independent African British colony. As Jeremy Murray-Brown records in *Kenyatta*, the new Prime Minister (whose title was to become President the following year) said: 'This is the greatest day in Kenya's history and the happiest day of my life,' smiling when the Duke of Edinburgh whispered: 'Do you want to change your mind?'

Kenya was the first white-settled colony to achieve African rule. Four months before independence Kenyatta had addressed a crowd of several hundred sceptical and nervous white settlers in Nakuru, his main theme being forgiveness on both sides. They still had a future in independent Kenya, he assured them – but they could, if they wanted, sell their farms. He had British financial backing: a £20 million land-resettlement fund to purchase farms for black Kenyans, with assistance from West Germany and the World Bank providing the balance.

The launch of the 'million-acre scheme' saw more than that amount of land owned by 780 white farmers bought to settle approximately 35,000 Kenyan families by the end of 1971.

No white farmers stayed on in Happy Valley. According to Richard Cox in *Kenyatta's Country* (1965) the resettlement scheme in the area near Clouds, which lay at an altitude of 8,200 feet, was not going well. He describes it as 'high, cold, sour land that forty years ago bankrupted its share of white settlers' and was now blighting the Kikuyu's maize, beans and potatoes. The co-operative milk scheme was accepting milk that had been watered down with muddy river water, and cows were dying because smallholders could not afford to dip them against ticks.

Some European settlers foretold doom and gloom, and left Kenya for supposedly greener pastures: Australia, South Africa, New Zealand – even the UK if they were really brave. Those who stayed had to embrace change, often painful for them to watch, as African owners and politicians ran things their way, dividing up farms, leaving formerly beautiful old homes to fall into a state of disrepair.

Most of Solomon Gitau's life has been played out against this backdrop of rapid change in the decades since independence. Solomon's 'work' is never done and nor is he paid by anybody to do it – yet he gets on with it as if his life depended on it. I had begun to understand this a little better, having read his handwritten autobiography.

Solomon titles his story *Born in Happy Valley*. It's a humbling tale of an unusual young boy's struggles with poverty, cruelty and misunderstanding. Solomon's father, Gitau, was a well-known freedom fighter who was killed by the British. Solomon's family don't even know where he's buried. The Aberdares were his hunting ground: he was a deeply respected elder whom people nicknamed *Nya Ndarua*. After independence, Solomon explains, the area was named after him. But, Solomon says, Gitau was not his real father – a fact that does not endear Solomon to his older brothers.

Mrs Gitau already had more than enough sons to support, but on 29 December 1959, Solomon was born in her small, circular, mud-walled hut. Solomon's mother and elder brothers were full of hope and excitement back then in the 1960s as they set about building their grass-thatched hut on their newly allocated plot of land.

Kenya was heading towards independence, *Uhuru*, which literally means freedom. Solomon writes how strongly this impressed itself on his young mind:

> It was a time when all the people were whispering: 'Uhuru is coming'. Everybody was preparing for freedom ... saying white men must return to their home because they had brought conditions of slavery to this country. People carried black, red and green flags or wore black, red and green robes. Political parties addressed different meetings, mixing truth with lies, like men wooing women. Politicians were shouting like bull lions. When I saw all this I asked my mother: 'What is Uhuru?'
>
> She said: 'No muzungu [white person] will be allowed to stay in Kenya. They killed your father. We shall take their houses and shambas [farms] and everything belonging to them.'
>
> I heard the name Kenyatta, son of Muigai. When he was appointed as the first Prime Minister of Kenya, people celebrated. They made beer. Now nearly all the women and men were drunk every day. I saw men and women stagger along the paths pissing, women walking with untied dresses, producing strange smells, men knocking women down on the way.
>
> I said to my mother: 'I don't like Uhuru, because I am afraid people will behave like this forever.'
>
> My mother whipped my buttocks and said: 'You're like a devil. Go home now.'

As he grew older, Solomon was to remain out of step with his siblings and peers, irritating his mother not least with what she saw as his perverse interest in the natural world. He remembers from an early age watching colobus monkeys and marvelling at the forest in which they lived. As a result of his parentage and unusual interests, he found himself first being sent away and then running away from home, his young life already setting the pattern for regular future altercations with authority. After his mother died, his brothers united in opposing all that Solomon did – particularly his marriage to Esther Wairimu, the girl he loved. Having nowhere else to go, Solomon followed rural custom and built a small hut on his family land, where Esther raised the children while he went away to work. His life was to hit rock bottom when, one day, he had a message from home. The news was devastating: in his absence, his hut had been burnt down, chasing away Esther and their two small daughters.

Solomon spoke about this incident on our first Happy Valley safari. I was exhausted from a long day of terrible roads, but was suddenly compelled to listen to him above the noise of the Land Rover: his voice shook and he leaned forward suddenly. I glanced at him and saw his face was streaked with tears. 'I can still not believe this,' he said – and from what he had been saying, it seemed there might have been some kind of family connection to this horrifying event.

He changed the subject suddenly: 'They remember the white people in their names, you see!' Solomon pointed as we passed various signs to Mawingo DC's office, Mawingo Clinic and Mawingo School. *Mawingo* is Kiswahili for 'Clouds'.

I looked without enthusiasm at the unappealing and noisy jumble of Mawingo town, wondering how far we still had to go. A *matatu* – Kenya's answer to public transport, which involves cramming as many people as possible into a minibus and transporting them at terrifying speed to ensure maximum profit – with 'Heaven can wait' painted in large letters across its rear was hooting for passengers. It waited impatiently outside the Lady Diana Hotel, from which the distorted shouts of a rap artist issued vigorously. This wasn't the infamous Diana, Lord Erroll's mistress, but the beloved and beautiful princess from the same country as those earlier colonials. Previous generations of British royals are generally revered in Kenya, the late Princess of Wales above all.

None of this untidy, tin-roofed sprawl would have existed in Idina's day: today's fast-growing town of Mawingo was probably still under forest, or certainly under a dairy herd.

We turned left at Mawingo. Finally there remained a track that would have been easier to navigate on foot, the red forest soil slippery after rain. On our left the denuded hills and valleys receded upwards into the dark hulk of Kipipiri. The soil continued to bleed into the streams and rivers, its rich nutrients leached by deforestation.

A few miles on, Solomon pointed right towards a bicycle track, insisting that I drive down it. Less than a quarter of a mile later we halted before padlocked gates, through which I could see a dark avenue of towering eucalyptus trees, a glimpse of a mossy roof, covered with the cedar-wood tiles known as shingles, and a grubby white wall.

'That is it – Clouds House!' Solomon said triumphantly.

'Will we be allowed in?' I began, but Solomon, to whom few obstacles are insurmountable, scaled the barriers and vanished while I sat in the car, barely able to believe this was it: Clouds! Could we really get any closer? I hardly dared share Solomon's optimism.

Africa teaches patience: hours of waiting allow time to observe and prepare. The afternoon was warm, but something made me shiver. I'd struggle to find my way out of the confusing maze of tracks and roads without Solomon. What if he never came back? That was a ridiculous idea: this place was spooking me into fearful imaginings.

I was comforted by the gentle grunts of cows and bleats of sheep in neighbouring fields. Pedestrians passed by: women bent under the weight of piles of firewood, men of various ages ambled up, cast their eyes over my Land Rover, and either wandered on or sat down nearby to wait and see what would happen next. A man rode up on his bicycle, but leapt off when he saw it was a white woman in the stationary vehicle. He pushed his bicycle past extremely slowly to get a longer look. Everyone greeted me politely, some asking where I came from and where I was going. Barefoot children in ragged, ill-fitting school uniforms shouted: 'Howareyou!' It was a statement rather than a question.

Clouds, lying on the south-western shoulders of Kipipiri, isn't in Happy – or any other – Valley. The valley proper is on the other side of Kipipiri, the River Wanjohi (Kikuyu for 'river of beer') bisecting it. The Wanjohi – which white settlers pronounced the 'One-Joey', but Kikuyu residents today pronounce 'Wan-jaw-he' – once an ice-cold, crystal-clear river into which early settlers introduced trout, has become increasingly sullied thanks to deforestation, as torrential rainfall spews topsoil into its waters.

Eventually a youngish Kikuyu man with a slight limp approached from the other side of the gate, accompanied by Solomon who wore a triumphant grin. I walked over as they came out of a side gate. We shook hands – his handshake was limp – and introduced ourselves. He was Paul, second son of *Mzee* Nuthu, owner of the house.

'You can leave the car and walk inside to tell my father your business,' said Paul.

The swelling crowd of spectators on the other side of the gate all assured me they would look after my car. For a fee, I suspected.

We walked through a chilly avenue of towering gums, these non-indigenous trees serving as a reminder of the pale stranger who'd had them planted. At the end of the dark, damp tunnel we emerged between two solidly square gatehouses with decaying roofs. Their faded elegance retained a beauty of its own. We were facing what seemed an enormously long, low house with no resemblance to any photograph of Clouds I had seen. A white-haired Kikuyu gentleman who spoke perfect English received us in the gentle sunshine, and after introductions to various members of the family, whose usage of English deteriorated considerably as we got down to the grandchildren, he looked at me shrewdly and said: 'Well?'

I tentatively explained my fascination with old houses.

'What do you want to see? This is *my* home now,' he said with a tolerant smile.

There were some old roses growing along the edge of the house: did Idina once supervise her *shamba* boy planting these? Of course, I longed to see the house – inside and out – but it seemed rude to ask. I had sensed his displeasure at what I guessed were the discourteous attitudes of previous visitors.

'May I see the front of the house?' I asked hesitantly. In up-country Kenya the 'front' of a house is where the veranda, garden and view are. You usually approach from the 'back', where you drive in and leave your car. Orchards and vegetable gardens are at the 'back'. At this point so were we.

Mzee sombrely led the way around the outside of the house, smiling suddenly and broadly when I admired his fruit trees.

'This is my own orchard,' he said fondly. 'The original fruit trees were around the back.'

I'd heard that Lady Idina loved her fruit trees, and continued to tend her more tropical varieties when she finally moved to the lower-lying, hotter Kenya coast in her latter years.

The old house seemed to watch us through dark grimy windows: eyes from the past. It emanated decadence and decay, tinged with sadness. The front of the house, in grey stone, was suddenly recognisable as the Clouds in old photographs. A tangle of overgrown weeds and scrambling Kikuyu grass had blurred the edges of the old stone steps and terraces. An untidy barbed-wire fence had been erected just below the steps to keep cows out of the cabbages, beans and potatoes that now covered Idina's once flourishing flower beds. Solomon was ecstatic to see the mununga tree that he pointed out (younger and smaller) in the old photograph of Clouds reproduced in the battered copy of *White Mischief*, which he suddenly produced from deep in his coat pocket. An evergreen belonging to the mahogany family, with a pale greyish-brown trunk and generously leafed crown, the attractive mununga grows up to 30 metres tall and is often planted in gardens for shade. Watching out of the corner of my eye as Solomon hugged it to measure its girth, I attempted to woo the old man: 'Do you grow high-altitude mangoes?'

'Mangoes could not grow here!' he replied.

'My mother grows them in her garden at over 7,000 feet above sea level, so they might survive here?'

'I have not seen one of those, but I'd like to try . . .' He was warming to me now, even if he was still a little wary of Solomon. I'd already observed that Solomon's colobus and forest ardour wasn't going down well with Paul.

Storm clouds were brewing, the brief play of sunlight on the sagging roof had vanished and it was time to brave the slow road home.

'But you may not leave,' the old man said regally, 'until I give you permission!'

'May I have your permission to leave?' I asked, a touch nervously. Were we going to be allowed to leave this strange old house – ever? An icy wind swept through the dark tunnel of eucalyptus, hissing at us threateningly as it rustled the waxy leaves.

'Yes, you may leave,' said *Mzee* Nuthu, with a sudden twinkle. Then he added: 'You are welcome to return – you can come to sleep for a night!'

'Thank you, I'd love to visit again,' I replied, realising that this was indeed an honour.

I could have the pleasure of Idina's room, I was told with a wry smile. He knew the house's history: he'd read *White Mischief* too. I smiled back, but I did wonder what that might be like: to brave eleven hours of darkness inside a house which felt haunted all the way from the gate? I'd noticed there were no power lines.

Elizabeth, the daughter of the house, who had accompanied us on our grand tour, put a large bag of pears into my hands. 'What year were you born?' she asked. At my reply she clasped my hand and said: 'So! We are age mates! Which church do you attend?' Solomon had receded into the background, and I couldn't think of a tactful reply, but luckily she seemed to forget the question, and asked how many children I had. Luckily I could answer this one honestly: 'I have two!'

She beamed: in rural Kenya a childless woman is cursed indeed. 'I have four,' she told me proudly.

Thanks to this unusual day out, Solomon had managed to inspire me with his own enthusiasm for Happy Valley. I'd glimpsed the bigger picture, from its history to its present: a kaleidoscope of extraordinary scandals, tragedies, grievances and conservation issues. I began to read more about it, puzzled that the Erroll murder hadn't been solved: why not? If I looked deeply enough into the history of the whole area, would I find any clues about what really happened to him? I felt almost possessed by it all. And yes, I was definitely going back for a night at Clouds!

3

A Night at Clouds

'Welcome to Clouds!' said *Mzee* Nuthu with a genteel incline of his white-haired head. 'You are the first white lady to stay here for many years!'

I felt deeply honoured to be an invited guest to the Clouds of the twenty-first century, where the gates remained locked and curious visitors were not necessarily welcomed. I stood on an unkempt sprawl of bright green Kikuyu grass by the back entrance and imagined the infamous Lady Idina receiving her guests right here: although allegedly in Idina's time you came for drink, drugs and sex, and stayed much longer than planned. The back lawn would have been manicured then too: laboriously cut and weeded by some underpaid, hard-working Kikuyu servant.

I was about to get inside Clouds! *The* Clouds of all the incredible stories. And now perhaps I was about to discover some more about it all.

What *would* Idina have said? Clucked disapprovingly, I suspect. Going to stay with an African family just wasn't done in her day. But then again Idina was, by all accounts, liberal and eccentric in so many ways that, had she been around today in the early twenty-first century, she may well have joined us on this curious mission.

Paul had opened the gate and signalled me to drive up the avenue on to the soft green grass behind the house. The *mzee*, Elizabeth, his first-born son Peter, who is a teacher, and half a dozen children who gazed at my pale complexion in horrified fascination, were there to welcome us as if we were old friends.

I had brought cigarettes, newspapers and a high-altitude mango tree seedling for the old man, metres of material for Elizabeth who'd said she enjoyed sewing, sweets and biscuits for the children, and tea and sugar for the house – and of course I'd come with Solomon.

Three-quarters of a century ago, had I been a guest of Lady Idina's, I might have brought a bottle (or case) of good claret, and most certainly a man or two, but definitely not a black one. At Idina's X-rated parties, the guests were expected to have swapped spouses or partners certainly by the end of the weekend, if not by nightfall on the first day. Blowing a feather across a sheet held over the table was a popular after-dinner method of divining who was to sleep with whom. Then, it was rumoured, there was the choosing the keys game, using the numbered keys to each locked room. Ending up in Idina's bed at some point of the day or night was apparently par for the course for male guests.

I still had cold feet about sleeping here . . .

'Let us proceed to Lady Idina's rooms,' said the old man solemnly, although humour spilt from his eyes.

We walked through a wide entrance where a car lay disintegrating, all four tyres cracked and flat. There was a volley of hysterical barking from inside a wooden structure on legs, no bigger than a rabbit hutch. 'We need dogs here – for security,' explained Paul. It's an African thing, locking up dogs all day so they are insanely ferocious by the time they are let out at night, and will attack intruders. Animals aren't beloved pets (unless you're Solomon, who has a fat, brindled dog called Hippo – originally rescued by Esther from a neighbour who'd been badly mistreating it) and it's something I've never been able to get used to.

As we walked through a large crumbling courtyard, where chickens pecked beneath the washing lines, I suddenly realised how much smaller the house was than it seemed from the outside; most of the imagined space was actually this open square. A narrow veranda edged the chipped and browning walls of the surrounding house, although most of its cedar roof tiles had dropped and rotted away and the remaining moss-covered wooden roof supports were concave or broken. Rows of closed doors led off into what I imagined were Idina's guest rooms where, as the stories say, you never knew who you'd end up in bed with. Now some of these rooms provided cramped homes for the Nuthu sons and daughters along with their spouses and children. Others were empty, or were used as stores.

Mzee noticed me glancing at the wooden, shield-shaped plaques on the walls, and explained, 'They used to be mounts for stuffed animal heads.' (Perhaps he sensed I had been wickedly imagining the leering heads of conquered husbands.) Directly across the courtyard a scarlet rose bush bloomed outrageously, rising above the rubbish chucked indiscriminately around the courtyard.

Mzee unlocked the double doors and we stepped into a long, wood-panelled room, its wooden parquet floor partially covered by drying maize. In the muted light filtering through the grimy windows I made out a fireplace at each end, and window seats. *What* a room for grand parties: ample swinging space for at least three eightsome reels! At one end among dusty cobwebs were marks left by the removal of what must once have been many bookshelves.

Solomon suddenly elbowed me, pointed with his chin at a dim corner of the ceiling and whispered hoarsely: 'See how many spirits of white people are hanging.' In the gloom I could just make out, clustered together, the little inverted bodies of numerous bats, before we passed through a dark doorway into a spacious, empty room with another fireplace.

'Here is her ladyship's bedroom,' said the old man, with a knowing smile.

The front of this dark, panelled room had been crudely partitioned off with plywood. 'The Canadian Hunger Foundation Water Project rented part of the house ten years previously, and made these bedrooms for their staff,' explained Peter, 'but they never used them.'

The lonely iron bed on which Elizabeth laid my bedding roll was the only furniture.

The procession moved on to the bathroom. A tarnished lion's head glowered over a green bath, above it a handle that must have once forced hot or cold water through its roaring mouth. Across the room was a dust-covered bench seat: was this where her guests swigged cocktails while watching Lady Idina bathe, apparently part of the pre-dinner rituals at Clouds?

The small room, with a green toilet, was powdered with dust and swathed with cobwebs. 'There is no water now,' explained the old man, 'but Elizabeth can bring a bucket so you can wash.' Then, with a mock bow, he said, 'Now you are the Lady Idina and I am your servant! You will need some food?'

I looked at Solomon, who said, 'Oh yes!'

The old man smiled: 'You may come to my room to eat when you are ready.'

After the family left us, Solomon opened the door to one of the many cupboards lining the bathroom and stepped inside with the air of a man searching for a corpse. Nothing dead, but the cupboards were as wide as corridors and I wondered suddenly if this was how Idina's guests had traversed their way from bedroom to bedroom in secret. After a moment's silence Solomon answered my thoughts by colliding loudly with each end of the cupboard in turn.

'This place feels bad,' he said, emerging from the dark cavity and making me jump. 'There are many spirits here!'

I kept silent. I'd already been wondering whether driving home in the dark through unknown *Mungiki* territory would be more frightening than braving the whole night here. The *Mungiki* are an illegal Kikuyu sect whose secret operations include the extortion of 'protection' money. They've been known to leave enemies' heads in places for all to see – and be warned. Solomon knows a bit about the organisation because one of his brothers is involved.

Dusk was edging through dirty windows, and the crickets beginning their nightly whirrs and cheeps. Solomon seemed extremely jumpy as we crossed the darkening living room and courtyard. He clutched my shoulder as Paul appeared from an almost invisible doorway and conducted us into *Mzee*'s living space, another large panelled room at

the rear of the courtyard, which had presumably been a guest bedroom.
Thankfully it was warm with firelight and the smells of food, and felt
light years from our dark, echoing quarters.

We were shown to wooden chairs beside the Formica-topped
table, where the paraffin lamp lit up a circle of the smoke-blackened
ceiling. There was no sign of any of the original furniture. *Marula*
reed matting lined the walls and the windows were covered by thick
cardboard and large, heavy pieces of cloth, protecting us from the
night's chilly darkness.

Mzee introduced us to his wife: an elderly woman in a headscarf,
her bare feet gnarled and twisted like tree roots. She greeted us in
Kikuyu before returning to the adjoining room, which I guessed had
once been an en suite bathroom. It is not customary in rural Kikuyu
society for women to eat with their men. Kikuyu men traditionally
had several wives and if a wife was not obedient or hardworking it
was acceptable to beat her. Neither idea has entirely died out in many
parts of Kenya today. My impressions of *Mzee* Nuthu as a modern
gentleman, however, were confirmed when he said: 'My wife does not
speak English or even much Kiswahili. She is a simple woman, but I
love her. I have never seen the need to take another wife.'

Elizabeth brought a basin of warm water to wash our hands before
Mzee said grace, thanking God for new friends and this food. After
the prayer, Elizabeth left and I was the only woman at the table, but
I was a guest and it would not do to question my 'right' to be there.
We ate African style, with our hands, while the old lady retired to sit
by the fire, and Peter chatted from a nearby sofa with a worn cover
of an indiscriminate brown resulting from many years of decay. His
wife would be preparing his meal for him, so he declined to share
ours. *Mzee* and Paul shared with us the bowl of *irio*: mashed potatoes
with beans, maize and nettles ('Good for diabetes,' said *Mzee* when
I expressed surprise that something with such a vicious sting should
taste so delicious), all washed down with tin mugs of sweet tea. Kenyan
tea, known as *kinyeji*, is stewed on a fire with plenty of milk and sugar,
pleasantly tainted with wood smoke.

Feeling perfectly well fed, we moved to sit beside the fire that would once have warmed Idina's overnight guests. Clouds actually has nine chimneys, although judging by what they got up to nobody should have been cold.

The old man smoked the cigarettes I'd brought him and told us about himself. He came to Clouds in 1967, having been a political detainee during the state of emergency. It is likely that he had contacts in the right places, plus he was of the 'right' tribe, maybe even a friend of Kenyatta's. Thus he ended up getting a valuable piece of land during the redistribution. He told us that he used to be an accountant in Muranga (known in colonial times as Fort Hall). Solomon, who is given to expressing admiration loud and often, was told by *M₎ee*: 'It is easy with accounts! You give with the right hand and take with the left and that is called debit and credit.' *M₎ee* smiled and continued. 'Now I have twenty-five grandchildren and I am happy to be retired. We can live off the land: money is short so unfortunately we cannot repair the old house, and also we have medical expenses for Elizabeth.'

'I'm sorry to hear that,' I said. 'I hope it's not serious.'

The old man looked at the fire. 'She is frequently sick: she has the fits and falls down. So she cannot work. And Paul, he does not work, but Peter is a teacher at a government junior school, forty minutes' walk away.'

'It pays badly,' Peter explained. 'It is difficult for everyone. The school is supposed to be free, but parents have to pay for books, uniforms and *harambee* funds, so not everyone can afford it. Primary education is compulsory, but if you have no money for these *harambee* meetings what do you do?'

Harambee is Kikuyu for 'let's all work together', once a seasoned chant of Kenya's first president, *M₎ee* Jomo Kenyatta. But by the time of our visit the word had become charged with apprehension: a school *harambee* usually meant that parents must donate money or risk their child being thrown out. Peter explained that the combination of lack of government funding and mismanagement of what was available, due to the corruption of many of the Kenya government's educational employees, compounded the problem.

Numerous small, scruffy grandchildren with bright dark eyes and winning smiles came into the half-lit room to be fed leftover *irio*. They took turns to stand between their grandfather's knees, until they grew drowsy, eyed by the skinny cats mewing from the shadows.

'So now,' concluded the old man, 'you can return to tell your friends that you spent a night at *the* Clouds.'

I asked him what he thought of the carryings-on in Clouds in those early days. He shrugged: 'Who really knows the truth?' Then he added, 'In those times there was much injustice in the white man's treatment of Kikuyu men: they were employing them as house servants when it is against Kikuyu culture for men to serve women; and also the white people were calling them "boys" – even if they were old men. This is a terrible insult to a Kikuyu who has been circumcised.'

Jomo Kenyatta, in his book *Facing Mount Kenya*, explains some of the *Gikuyu* (Kikuyu) customs and the importance of land to his people, Bantu agriculturalists at heart: rendering the earth sacred. He recounts how the Kikuyu lost their best lands: they looked upon the new Europeans as 'wanderers who had deserted their homes and were lonely and in need of friends', so they helped them out, while believing they would finally get tired of a restless existence and return to their own lands.

Before the first white people even arrived, Mugo Wa Kibiru, a Kikuyu visionary, had foreseen the arrival of these pale strangers with their curious clothes and killing sticks. He'd also predicted a vast iron centipede, breathing fire and stretching west to the big inland water. He prophesied that these newcomers would strip his people of all they possessed, but more happily that they would depart again.

'Of course when these white men came,' the old man said evenly, 'there was nothing in this area except thick forest, wild animals and a few Maasai passing through. They bought this land incredibly cheaply – two cents an acre!'

Solomon was shaking his head sympathetically. I thought about how impossible the imposition of the British on Kikuyu culture must have been. Traditionally the Kikuyu didn't mention things in exact numbers as it would bring ill omen upon that which was being counted. The British saw this as shifty. The Kikuyu have a complex naming system which the British also failed to understand. Kikuyu boys were circumcised at about fifteen and girls before menstruation started, at about twelve. Female circumcision was an old and valued custom in many tribes, perhaps not handled sensitively enough by early missionaries. Aside from the many justifiable arguments against it, the fact that it still happens in parts of Kenya today shows how embedded it is in ancient cultures.

Respect for elders is paramount in Kikuyu culture, so the idea of an old man being ordered around, often abusively, by a young *memsahib* was reprehensible. Traditionally Kikuyu men hunted, fought, tended fields and looked after cattle, while women attended to the house and food, and the vegetable garden around the house. Swapping roles made you a laughing stock, yet suddenly men were cooks and 'houseboys' – as they were condescendingly called then (and extraordinarily still are, even by the Kenyan Africans themselves!) – in white households. Everything had worked fine with bartering, and the occasional inter-tribal skirmish, but suddenly with the arrival of the white people it was all about money and the increasingly pressing need to earn it.

As for adultery – if a woman strayed she was returned to her parents and the dowry was paid back. Honestly, what had the Kikuyu thought of Idina?

It was time to return to my gloomy quarters to pass an uneasy night. I thought of women in poor African households where the entire family will sleep cosily in one bed. By all accounts Idina wouldn't have slept alone in a cold bed either. It was chilly up here at over 8,000 feet above sea level, and whistling draughts crept through the broken glass of my window. I put my head inside my sleeping bag to muffle the creaks of the rickety roof and moaning of the wind, and thought about why I was here . . .

4

Thoughts, Words and Misty Memories

Houses have always fascinated me. To me they are imbued with laughter, sorrow and myriad feelings in between, left behind by the people who have lived in them, slowly distilled over the years into powerful energies, some peaceful and happy, others disconcerting: even totally terrifying, as I was to discover on future explorations in Happy Valley.

I especially love old houses. In Kenya an eighty-year-old house is *really* old: very few permanent buildings have survived that are much older. As it happens I rent a relatively old, mud-walled house on Lord Delamere's Soysambu ranch. Over a century before, the 3rd Baron Delamere had arrived, dedicating his foresight and fortune to the country he'd fallen in love with. Now his grandson was my landlord.

But why Happy Valley? Perhaps I was inspired by my own family history: my paternal grandmother used to ply my young mind with colourful stories. As the gin in the bottle went down, her memories of working at Nairobi's well-known New Stanley Hotel grew wilder. She was behind the reception desk when Lord Erroll and his mistresses, including Diana Broughton, flitted through; she remembered the night he was shot.

My mother's family had farmed at Dundori, north-west of Happy Valley, at an even higher altitude. From the back of their bamboo house they could see the peaks of Mount Kenya behind the hump of the Aberdares, the latter's lower slopes protecting the secrets of Happy Valley, almost always shadowy and dark, often obscured by cloud. My mother's older sister, Susan, now in her eighties, wrote from England: 'I do remember my mother pointing out Lady Idina sitting on a chair on the veranda of the Stag's Head Hotel in Nakuru. It didn't mean a thing to me, I just thought she was another *memsahib*.'

Then there was the tragedy of my maternal grandfather's cousin, rooted in a later Happy Valley scandal. In 1942, when my mother was eleven, news of her Uncle Rowley's tragic death finally reached her at boarding school in Molo, many hours away; initially they'd feared it was her father because the paper only reported the surname – Platt. Rowley, apparently a kind and gentle soul, had married an 'unsuitable' Irishwoman. They'd farmed in the Subukia valley, on the equator, 30 miles north of Happy Valley, and Rowley's wife, Mary, had been swept into what remained of the Happy Valley set, her antics contributing to his despair and ultimate suicide. It was all hushed up at the time but my maternal grandparents used to speak of it with deep sadness.

'He only had one ball,' my grandmother once told me, with a slight twinkle. 'But he was a darling, sweet man – while *she* just couldn't keep her clothes on! She used to swim naked in their pool and cavort with *that lot*.'

'She wore the most hideous purple hat . . .' retorted my aunt.

Still unable to sleep, I began to scribble in a notebook by torchlight. There had been plenty written on Happy Valley, so ultimately what was left to say? Was there any hope of my solving a murder which had continued to create speculation for half a century? And here I was chasing after any lingering memory or whiff of past antics in the home where Lady Idina – first wife of the murder victim – had stayed the longest, and by all accounts played the hardest . . .

I'd read a few more books on the subject by this second visit. Almost every historian writing about Kenya's colonial past touches on Happy Valley and its colourful cast. The most astonishing thing is how the murder mystery continued to ignite theories, beginning in the 1980s when James Fox's *White Mischief* implicated the cuckolded Sir Jock Delves Broughton. In 1969 Fox and Cyril Connolly had discovered that nothing written on the Erroll murder since 1941 had solved the mystery. They teamed up to investigate it for the *Sunday Times*, their research stimulating their fascination with the saga as they unearthed new evidence.

White Mischief is a riveting read and probably remains the best-known book on the Erroll murder. But critics claimed that Fox's final and concluding 'evidence' was hardly tenable. It was taken from the mouth of a teenager, daughter of one of the least likeable Happy Valley characters. Young Juanita Carberry was not renowned for being truthful – and no wonder, considering her lonely, abusive upbringing, which she wrote about in her autobiography, *Child of Happy Valley*.

Then in the 1990s, in *Diana, Lady Delamere and the Lord Erroll Murder*, Leda Farrant used Diana Broughton's supposed 'admission' to seal her guilt. Diana is another character who arouses intrigue, although her connection with Happy Valley, the place, was non-existent. Her final stamping ground, apart from her Kilifi home by the sea, was her fourth husband's: Lord Delamere's cattle ranch beside Lake Elementeita. This is the same ranch on which I live, a mere 3 miles from the home that was once Diana's. From the dusty field beside my house where one of the late Diana's retired racehorses grazes beside a tattered, rescued donkey, I look across the scorched plains to the distant blue outline of the Aberdares. With the setting sun at my back, and if there's no cloud masking the mountains, it's easy to distinguish Kipipiri rising in front, slightly to the right as if providing an opening for the imagination to slip in. Happy Valley feels closer than it really is. From my parched lawn, I can see if it is raining at Clouds . . .

Meanwhile, Alice de Janzé's biographer had just been in touch with me with questions about the area. Alice was a friend and neighbour of Idina's and her life is another tale of carousing, love affairs and eventually tragedy, for she committed suicide in 1941. Like Idina and Diana, she retains that sexually charged, magnetic power to invite people to wonder about her long after her death.

Lots of history, I thought sleepily: what about the present? And what of a murder left unsolved?

*

I finally slept astonishingly deeply. My dreams were bizarre: I was at a party, chain-smoking marijuana through a long cigarette holder. The women were in the sleeveless, waistless dresses, with shockingly high (at the time) hemlines, characteristic of the streamlined 1920s designs that had been straightened and simplified from the curvy, bosomed, long-skirted, quintessentially feminine styles favoured before the war. Fashion in the 1920s had made women's lines more masculine and simple, yet somehow sexier. The short hairstyles and long, swinging strings of pearls added to this powerful new image.

I seemed to know the people at this party and there were many I wanted to talk to, but I couldn't get my feet to touch the ground, so had to be content with being ignored while floating about at head level. Perhaps potatoes grown at Clouds have magic-mushroom-like powers, I thought, between restless dreams.

I was relieved when the sky paled and the melodious song of the orange-breasted, white-browed robin chat dispersed the stillness. Solomon was pacing about outside in the early sun, complaining of a very disturbed night too.

Before we left, laden with generous, home-grown gifts, we warmed our hands with mugs of steaming tea, while *Mzee* proudly showed me Idina's rose bushes he'd continued to tend, including several varieties he had grafted.

We said our goodbyes behind the kitchen, which extended out on one side from the house. In most colonial set-ups, the kitchen (from whence servants produced astonishing feasts from wood-burning stoves, conjured up in the gloom cast by smoke-blackened walls and without any refrigeration or other mod cons) would have been a separate wing, designed with outside entrances through which the servants could come and go without disturbing the *memsahibs* and *bwanas*. Clouds was unusual with this attached kitchen, now a shed for the cows and sheep, tiles missing from its roof: the animals must huddle at one end when the rain lashed in.

As we drove home Solomon complained that he had been 'visited' by bad spirits all night. 'I will write a poem!' he declared. Arguably

Solomon's 'visions' were influenced by his repeated reading of *White Mischief*, although it was odd that we'd both had somewhat parallel dreams.

The next time I saw Solomon he presented me with an exercise book, in which he had laboriously written out his 'visions' that night at Clouds. *Face to Face with White Mischief Spirits*, he titled it. I read on, the poor English paling into insignificance as I took in its increasingly extraordinary contents:

> It was on 16 March 2000 that my friend Juliet and I decided to spend the night at Clouds House . . . My friend was the first white woman to sleep there after the white mischief departed, therefore I was fearing to see the ghosts of white mischief coming for us.
>
> After sleeping I started dreaming and it was not like a dream, it was like a vision. There were smells of smoke. I saw very many white people drinking and shouting to one another.

Solomon dreamt that Alice de Janzé approached him, questioning who he was and where he came from. She demanded to know who had invited him to come and sleep at Clouds. When Solomon explained that he used to live on Alice's farm and that his late mother, Juha, used to work for her, she softened and said that yes, she'd seen Solomon's mother recently.

Among the other bizarre conversations, Solomon dreamt that while he'd talked to Idina herself, a male guest sitting at the fire had pointed at him and said: 'Where does that monkey come from?' Idina had then further questioned his right to be there, as well as mine, for I featured in the dream as well. But Solomon explained that he was a colobus monkey, which fascinated all the other guests, who wanted to come and hear the monkey talking.

Studying old photographs in various books it's very evident that Idina had sex appeal oozing from every pore – and women probably found her attractive too, as the shot of her and Alice de Janzé both wearing velvet trousers and holding hands – reproduced in Errol Trzebinski's biography of Lord Erroll – suggests. Comte Frédéric de Janzé (Alice's first husband) wrote his own story about his time in Happy Valley, called *Vertical Land* (1928). He hints at Idina's sexual power as she stood before the fire wrapped in a golden kikoi: 'Her half-closed eyes waken to our mute appeal. As ever, desire and the long drawn tobacco smoke weave around her ankles, slowly entwining that slight frame; around her neck it curls; a shudder, eyes close. Contentment! Power!'

My curiosity now fully aroused by my Clouds visits, I asked some of the elderly white settlers who'd stayed on in Kenya after independence in 1963 what they remembered about Idina. Before he died in the early 2000s, Mervyn Carnelly spoke to me on his sunny veranda overlooking the placid, acacia-fringed Lake Naivasha.

'Everyone adored Idina,' Carnelly said with feeling. His wife added that every *man* in the colony probably did, even if they had to keep it from their wives. Carnelly smiled: 'The army used to visit – officers headed from Abyssinia straight to Clouds and several were having affairs with her.'

Many people spoke very highly of Idina. She'd been such fun, by most accounts, as well as clever, witty and an excellent hostess. 'There's been too much going on about her exploits with men,' complained one friend who'd been a distant neighbour in the 1940s, 'and not enough said about what a fabulous person she was.' In a letter published in *White Mischief*, Albert Andrew – who had visited Kenya in the 1940s and later read Cyril Connolly's murder account – wrote to him about Idina: 'Nobody could have been kinder or more thoughtful, and she was most certainly not snobbish. She was willing to be nice to anyone and the last thing she thought about was class. She was exceptionally nice to her servants.'

Others were less complimentary. Lady Grigg, wife of the governor of the time, was horrified on visiting Clouds to find Idina's clothes and pearls scattered over the floor; while Eileen Scott wrote critically in her diary of Idina's setting the trend for ladies to wear shorts, which she saw as 'ugly and unnecessary'. Lady Scott, a well known and respected settler, also accused Idina of doing 'a lot of harm in this country'. The

new breed of more conventional Happy Valley housewives after the
Second World War, who had less time (or inclination) to waste on
attending wife-swapping parties, further criticised Idina's carryings-on
in front of the Africans, some going so far as to say that she might have
contributed to Mau Mau and the murder of Europeans by undermining
the servants' respect for their white employers. One even said Idina
had African boyfriends (simply not done in those times).

On one of my Happy Valley safaris I stopped beside a white-haired,
toothless *mzee* hobbling along the road from Mawingo back towards the
town called Machinery. This road sweeps through and around a series
of steep valleys while slowly descending from the lower shoulders of
Kipipiri. The deaf old man was apparently walking all the way back to
the roadside town of Miharati. 'Surely that would take him all night,'
I said to Solomon, but the *mzee* didn't seem bothered and hadn't waved
us down, although he accepted a lift. Climbing into the Land Rover
proved quite a mission.

'We have been visiting Clouds House,' Solomon said loudly
in Kiswahili.

'Oh yes! I know that house very well . . .' The old man, it turned out,
remembered Clouds back in the forties. If he'd been about fifteen in the
late 1940s, he would only be in his mid seventies now. It was common
practice to have a kitchen *toto*, a young boy taken into the kitchen to
be apprentice to the cook or 'houseboy'. I didn't ask the old man his
age. It's not rude, as it is in western society, because traditionally in
Kenya the older you are the more respect you command. However,
these elders tend to have no idea of their date, let alone year, of birth.

'So you must have known Idina!' I bellowed, also in Kiswahili, as
the old man didn't speak English.

That made him laugh: 'Oh yes. She was on her own then, without
any one husband, but lots of people came and went and there were
big parties! One *mzungu* [white person] played on the *marimbo* and the
other *wazungu* [white people] sang and drank a lot of *pombe* [beer, or
alcohol] from strange glasses with stalks!' (Alice had played a ukulele,
although she'd died in 1941, which would make the *mzee* very, although
not impossibly, old.)

'Was she a *very* bad lady?' asked Solomon, hoping for some more scandalous details, while I smiled to myself at the perfect description of a wine glass.

The old man's eyes grew even mistier, his voice even more cracked. 'No,' he said firmly. 'She was a very good lady! She was kind to us all.'

Lord Delamere, stepson of the late Diana who'd married his father, the 4th Baron Delamere, told me that Josphat, his old cook who'd died in the 1980s, had also been a kitchen *toto* at Clouds from the age of about thirteen.

'This poor lad was permanently in trouble for never knowing which bedroom required morning tea, and which fresh orange juice. How could he when those who had made their orders had ended up in the wrong rooms?' asked Lord Delamere. 'And as for returning their clothes, including some rather skimpy undergarments, which Josphat poetically compared to "ribbons of mist", to the right rooms – it simply wasn't possible to get it right!' Presumably Josphat and his peers enjoyed great sessions of gossip in the kitchen, which tended not to be an area much visited by colonial *memsahibs*.

'Josphat was well trained at Clouds: he became loved by all, the real old-fashioned butler type,' added Lady Delamere. 'He will always be remembered for his blissful cooking, which he taught to many others. Sadly he died of a heart attack about twelve years ago – he was only eighty-five.'

I asked Lord Delamere what he thought of the Happy Valley crowd.

'Unfortunately it was just a dozen or so people who were bored, sniffed copious quantities of cocaine, injected heroin and drank too much,' he said. 'They gave the colony a bad name, while the majority of farmers, including my grandfather, were working extremely hard and had nothing whatever to do with them.'

He was astonished to hear of my visits to Clouds. He'd known many former settler houses when he'd worked in the Lands Resettlement Offices in the early 1960s. Like most people, he thought Clouds would have fallen down after years of neglect. I imagined that Lord Delamere would get on well with *Mzee* Nuthu, both being old-fashioned

gentlemen with a sense of humour, both interested in plants. Neither
had any racial hang-ups either.

'When you come to visit us again, you will be welcome!' *Mzee*
Nuthu had told me when we left after our overnight visit. Thus over
the next two years we continued to visit Clouds, often accompanied
by other visitors, although unfortunately Lord Delamere's failing
health prevented his ever accompanying me. Alice Percival, a
friend's cousin from England, wanted to revisit the old house:
she'd stayed there as a child, accompanied by her grandmother.
On the drive up, Alice was shocked how fields of maize and beans
now replaced the thick forest she remembered. She and Solomon
discovered a mutual concern for the environment and debated the
future of Kenya's rivers and lakes without their vital forests as a
water catchment, acting as a slow filter for heavy rain, allowing it to
drip gently into the water sources.

The long rains had been heavy and Clouds was surrounded by
verdant growth. As we stood on the front steps carpeted with blue
periwinkle, surrounded by overgrown baby-blue hydrangea bushes
and a tangle of nettles, purple salvia, tiny white daisies and pink
fuchsias, we imagined Idina's original gardens, buried somewhere
beneath today's cabbages and beans. Most of Kenya is too hot and dry
for such non-indigenous varieties – it takes the high-altitude, cold, wet
climate of Clouds to produce these very English flowers.

Alice pointed – through a ragged line of high, concealing cypress
hedge – towards what had once been a wonderful view: one that had
contributed towards plenty of giddy behaviour. The heady view had
once influenced one of Idina's American friends too. On safari in
Kenya, Rhoda Lewisohn had fallen in love with French pilot Gabriel
Prudholme, fifteen years her junior, abandoning her husband in
America to come and search for her dream home in Kenya. Having
stayed at Clouds, Rhoda wanted her own version. Gabriel tirelessly
flew her over Kenya's plains, valleys, hills and mountains, until she
spotted a love nest that had been built on the slopes of Mount Kenya
for another American woman, who finally agreed to sell her precious

home. Rhoda restyled this with no expense spared – and called it
Mawingo, after Clouds. After the Prudholme love story soured, the
house had a stint as the Mawingo Hotel and then became the Mount
Kenya Safari Club, where millionaires hobnobbed with film stars – and
celebrities still luxuriate today.

'We used to have breakfast here on the terrace and look out over
the Rift Valley below,' said Alice. It occurred to me, as we soaked up
the sun on the same terrace, that none of the Happy Valley houses had
verandas, unlike most other colonial houses in Kenya. It was obvious
why, of course – it was simply too cold. You sat in the sun to keep warm
in the early morning or late afternoon, but closer to midday its rays
were harmful at that altitude. When the chill of evening descended you
moved to your indoor fire, laid and lit by the servants.

Alice was saying: 'Idina was very slim, clever and well read. You
sparkled in her company.' Here was the other side of Idina again: the
gracious hostess, impressing a young girl with her elegance, and no
mention of orgies being instigated at the dinner table.

That day *Mzee* and Paul had gone to the nearby town. Peter was
also away, teaching. The younger children had noticed us admiring
the flowers, so they picked us every bloom in sight, thrusting forth
their offerings with increasing boldness and muffled giggles. The old
mama, *Mzee*'s wife, together with Elizabeth and Peter's wife, escorted
us, exchanging news. *Mzee* had been suffering from a bad cough for
a while, they said. One of Peter's younger sons watched us from the
doorway: he held a tiny Siamese kitten, a worm-infested throwback,
perhaps, to more aristocratic feline blood, many generations ago.

Peter's wife invited us to tea in her home, which was one of the
rooms at the back of the courtyard where I had not been before. It was
very similar to *Mzee*'s room, with its fireplace and a room leading off
it which would once have been a bathroom. By chance it turned out to
be the very bedroom where Alice Percival had slept all those years ago.
'What an extraordinary coincidence!' she exclaimed, as we sipped very
sweet tea out of tin mugs. 'It makes me feel quite strange!'

I usually wrote to warn *Mzee* of our arrival, but letters often didn't
arrive. Yet somehow important news does get through in Africa. One

day in 2002, I arrived to stay at a friend's house near the small and scruffy town of Gilgil.

It took Solomon at least two hours to walk from his home to Gilgil, and I have no idea how he knew where I was staying that night. The area above Gilgil Club's golf course, once farmland, is now subdivided into smaller plots where plenty of retired Europeans live, many of them ex-farmers. There were various houses I could have been staying in, but Solomon, prone to unnerving psychic bouts, visited the right one and left me a note before I'd even arrived. It was sad news – and had astonishingly reached me within twenty-four hours of the event. He wrote, without bothering about punctuation:

> *dear Juliet, how are you I am fine Now I think you are okey and the children. Now I had from one of my friends today that Baba Nuthu had died do you know that because I just told with doubt your friend Solomon Gitau*

Having finally worked out what it was telling me, I stared at the crumpled page torn from an exercise book. Now two long-term owners of Clouds had grown old and died in its lifetime.

Peter had written to my Delamere Estates address and invited me to the burial, but his letter arrived well after the event. I wrote back to the family, expressing my sympathies as well as my admiration for their late father, but later discovered my reply never got there . . .

'History,' said Lord David Cecil, 'is only interesting as long as it is strictly true.' When I first visited Clouds in early 2000, having only read *White Mischief*, I thus believed, along with most people I had spoken to, that it had been Idina's home from the outset, when she was married to Josslyn Hay, more fondly known as Joss. Fox subtitled his photograph of Clouds 'Joss and Idina's home in the Aberdares'. First, though, it isn't in – or even beside or below – the Aberdares, it's on the far side of Kipipiri, and second Joss never lived there anyway. According to Fox, Idina arrived in Kenya with Joss in 1924, moving to Clouds – 'a thatched mansion' – in 1925, the venue for all those wild parties. Thatch is the traditional roofing material in Kenya, but Clouds was never thatched – the pitch of the roof was too shallow to prevent thatch leaking during the heavy rainstorms that prevail in the Kenya highlands. Clouds is roofed with cedar-wood shingles.

Charles Hayes in *Oserian, Place of Peace* (1997) further compounds the confusion when he writes that Idina and Joss started off at a farm called Slains, but also bought a second home called Clouds in 1925, describing the house as being alongside a river flowing from the Aberdare Mountains (such a river would actually have to flow uphill again to get to Clouds). He also mentions a waterfall and a green cement bath at Clouds. Fox mentions a bath too, in the centre of the room. Having seen the bath at Clouds, I knew it was green, but it certainly isn't cement, nor is it in the centre of the room.

Errol Trzebinski's book *The Life and Death of Lord Erroll* (2000), besides thrusting forward a revolutionary murder theory that MI5 had ordered his assassination, confirms that Idina and Joss arrived in Kenya in 1924. Trzebinski explains, however, that they lived at another home called Slains, which Idina sold before her divorce from Joss was made absolute in 1930, building a similar property – Clouds – where she lived without him. She further clarifies the situation with her description of a green onyx bath in the centre of the majestic bathroom at Slains where Idina would wallow in Champagne.

Having established that Idina's first marital home was not Clouds but Slains, I hoped her first Happy Valley home with Joss, if we could find it, might give some more clues about the life – perhaps even the death – of the enigmatic Earl. But where on earth was Slains? During those early Clouds expeditions it had become apparent that nobody on this side of Kipipiri mountain seemed to know where Slains was – or if the house still existed.

Several visits after our unforgettable night at Clouds, we had been jolting our way home in the late afternoon while children raced behind the car and shouted '*Mzungu!*' Captain's profusion of roadside plastic bags shone in the slanting rays of the sun and even the familiar-voiced ring-necked dove seemed to be purring '*mzungu*' at me in somewhat agonised disharmony with the stutter and drone of the Land Rover's engine.

'We can go again soon to the Happy Valley,' Solomon said optimistically, as he disembarked with his bag of eggs and potatoes from Clouds. I'd switched off the engine but the doves, the shouts and the engine were still competing in my head. 'I have heard about some very old men who remember so much about these Happy Valley white people,' he continued, sticking his head through the passenger window. 'I think at last we shall find this Slain house of Lord Erroll!'

5

The Search for Slains

Even though the much desired, loved, talked about and written about Josslyn Hay only lived a handful of his years in Happy Valley during his brief stint as number three of Idina's five husbands, his murder seems doomed to be eternally linked to this headily high-altitude spot on the map. This is probably in part because the hedonistic Happy Valley cast spilt their promiscuous reputation colony-wide, encompassing the Rift Valley when the Djinn Palace on the shores of Lake Naivasha became Joss's second marital home. But it was certainly in Happy Valley, at Slains to be precise, that Joss's reputation as seducer of other men's wives and heartbreaker took off.

Josslyn Hay, 22nd Earl of Erroll – Joss to those who knew him – came from an old and grand Scottish family. Adoring women always featured in his life, beginning with a doting mother. At the age of fifteen he was caught having sex with a maid and expelled from Eton. Eloping at twenty-two with the thoroughly unsuitable Idina, he escaped to Kenya in 1924. Already not the faithful type, newly married Joss was almost caught by the husband of the woman who was pleasuring him in her boat cabin.

English gossip columnists pounced on Idina and Joss's affair: she was twice married and eight years his senior, and his family weren't delighted to discover they'd married on the quiet. It also sabotaged his budding career in the Foreign Office; after his father had pulled the right strings Joss had gained valuable experience in the diplomatic service, including three years as private secretary to His Majesty's Ambassador to Berlin, perfecting his German and making him some good German friends. It was on his travels through Europe that he met Idina – hardly suitable as a potential future diplomat's wife. While engaged and on a visit to Venice, Joss and Idina were introduced to Sir Oswald Mosley, who would become a good friend and whose Fascist movement would later attract Joss.

There's a well-known picture – the original decorated the cover of *Tatler* in 1923 – of Josslyn Hay and Lady Idina hand in hand and barefoot on an Italian beach. Idina had tiny feet and a girlish figure; the clement Kenyan climate would provide opportunity to display both more often.

When the couple headed to Kenya, it was hardly into obscurity, for they quickly became infamous in Happy Valley and beyond. The freedom of life in the colony certainly provided space for Joss's womanising talents to expand. Kenya's white female population (married or not) continued to adore him and compete for his favours. Idina and Alice de Janzé apparently seemed content, as close friends, to share him, although by 1926, after Idina had given birth to their daughter, the marriage was not thriving: Idina launched into an affair with 'Boy' Caswell Long, a manager for Lord Delamere before he married Genesta (later the wife of Lord Hamilton). Meanwhile, Joss was enjoying a sexual liaison with wealthy, married Mary Ramsay-Hill (Molly to her friends), who'd only been in Kenya a year.

By early 1928 Joss and Mary had hatched a plan to run away together. He'd been home to Happy Valley to collect whatever he needed, which didn't include his young daughter. Mary was to secretly board the train at Naivasha to join him. Her husband, Cyril Ramsay-Hill, discovered she'd gone, loaded his pistol and rushed to Naivasha station. Finding he'd just missed them, he drove fast and furiously to Nairobi, arriving at the station before the train, which had to heave its carriages up the steep walls of the Rift Valley. He thought better of using the pistol, borrowed a rhino-hide whip (with the excuse he needed to 'whip a dog') and gave Joss a flogging in front of anyone lucky enough to be on the train that day. According to Charles Hayes in *Oserian, Place of Peace*, Ramsay-Hill's parting shot was to cable the ship on which his wife and Joss were travelling: 'You've got the bitch. Now buy her the kennel.'

Mary married Joss in 1930, returning with him to Kenya, the same year Idina returned with her new husband, Donald Haldeman, a British-born American divorcé who had already been a white hunter in Kenya. This was when Idina bought Clouds. Mary, who'd clinched the title of Countess of Erroll, had managed to retain a very grand kennel – the exotic Djinn Palace, built by Ramsay-Hill. Living thus in style in Naivasha, Joss was busy with politics. In 1934, on a visit to England, when Kenya was struggling economically, he became a member of the British Union of Fascists. Joss, who believed settlers needed more power, told the *East African Standard* when questioned on his return, that the Blackshirts believed in action, not just words. He went on to give a series of talks on Fascism to settlers. But he also attended to lighter matters – he was commodore of Naivasha Yacht Club and chairman of Naivasha Club.

As the years passed, Mary fell prey to her addictions, and she died aged forty-six of excessive drinking and use of hard drugs. It was 1939, the same year Hitler invaded Poland and Idina married husband number five.

It's debatable if Joss ever fell for any of his women for any length of time. His boredom threshold seems to have been extremely low. Diana Broughton simply wasn't on the scene long enough for Joss to have tired of her. She supposedly fell for him, but their short and intense affair never had the chance to stand any tests of time.

Joss was shot in the small hours of 24 January 1941. Later that same morning Broughton arrived at the mortuary, puzzlingly obliging: he wished to place his wife Diana's handkerchief on the body. Alice de Trafford and the current Lady Delamere were already there. James Fox relates in *White Mischief* how Alice had put a branch on Erroll's body, and another among Joss's many female fans, Gwladys (as he gives her first name) Delamere – the 3rd Baron Delamere's second wife, though by then his widow as she'd been many years his junior – had asked for his identity disc.

Nobody did an aching heart count after Joss's murder, but the list of suspects must have been just as impressive. Many friends and admirers attended his funeral, although Diana was supposedly too distraught and instead sent her husband with a letter to bury with her lover. The hearse was draped with the Union Jack, three volleys were fired and a bugler sounded the last post and Reveille.

Inspector Arthur Poppy, who handled the murder investigation, returned at midnight with six convicts supposedly to 'plant a rose bush', but actually dug a very deep hole and retrieved the envelope – only, says Fox, to find it was a scrap of paper on which Joss and Diana had scribbled adoring lines to one another. Had Poppy really been hoping for an apology from Diana to Joss for murdering him? Or even a revelation of who did?

Erroll's remains lie in the Kiambu churchyard beside those of the Countess. St Paul's, fifteen minutes' drive from Nairobi's upmarket suburb of Muthaiga, is a small pinkish-red stone church, English in style with its stout wooden door adjacent to its bell tower. A plaque in the entrance tells visitors that its construction dates from 1911. In the nearby graveyard, the oldest grave has a weathered stone cross in memory of a ten-month-old boy who died in 1914. In a forest of crosses and headstones in varying shades of grey, I found Erroll's marble headstone standing out, pale and square, the pebbled rectangle above his bones scattered with leaves and a wilting frangipani flower. Its inscription (and Mary's) read: *Thy will be done*. Looking at it made me wonder exactly whose will had been done.

Erroll has been on the receiving end of plenty of bad press, including allegations of unkind treatment of his servants. But he was liked and respected by many people – as a farmer and a friend. Genesta Hamilton wrote in her memoir *A Stone's Throw*, when she heard of his death: 'I was miserable. So few friends and so precious they are. And Joss, such fun, so loved life, so quick and bright, with a wit like sparkles on water.' She had been less fond of Idina, understandably considering Idina's affair with Boy Long, her second husband.

Errol Trzebinski writes in *The Life and Death of Lord Erroll* that Joss was a serious and respected farmer as well as good to his staff, as asserted by his Kikuyu valet in court; and that his generosity extended to the families of all his workers every Boxing Day. Many Kenyans, however, do have a well-meaning, benign manner of saying exactly what they believe their interrogators want to hear. The truth often remains to be guessed. And nowadays we might not have the same concept as in the colonial era of what being 'good' to employees entails.

Erroll's unsolved murder having begun to intrigue me, it was time to focus on the search for Slains. Perhaps the old house held on to some hitherto undiscovered secrets.

Solomon arranged meetings with elders of the Wanjohi region and we asked about old settler homes. One old man remembered Idina's neighbour, although only by the single name Ramsden, and had heard of Erroll. 'He was the son of Ramsden,' he insisted. Others only came up with their versions of names of people who had lived in the area later on: 'Ceaserone', 'Dushka' and 'Dilap'.

Looking for clues, but still with nothing much to go by, we visited an old settler home which Solomon had discovered on one of his foot patrols through the area while investigating the plight of the colobus monkeys. 'It is the house of Dilap,' he said.

Nestled between the steep sides of the Aberdares and the gurgling waters of the Wanjohi River, the former homestead was reduced to an old cedar cottage with a shingle roof. The use of cedar was not restricted to roofs: it would have provided cheap, easily available building materials in those days – and termites don't eat it. A red rose bush scrambled up one corner, clutching at gaps in the roof tiles with unkempt talons. Further away a brick fireplace and stone chimney stood, bizarrely isolated. Presumably the main house had either burnt down or been dismantled for timber. The only other sign that anything, or anyone, exotic had left their mark here was an ornamental palm, looking equally out of place. The grinding howl of chainsaws disturbed the chilly air as Solomon suddenly grabbed my arm: 'Colobus!'

There were four bewitchingly beautiful, long-haired, black and white monkeys watching us from where the dark line of forest suddenly opened into cultivated fields. Colobus are dependent on indigenous trees for their food, homes and protection. Unfortunately, as fast as they are forced out of their receding forest environment they raid these subsistence farmers' vegetable patches, where they are trapped and their valuable skins sold.

Solomon launched into a fiery lecture on conservation – aimed at half a dozen women of varying ages who had paused from digging the adjacent field to stone the monkeys. 'So you must not harm them! They are my friends and brothers,' he concluded.

'They steal my potatoes,' returned an elderly woman.

In the silence that followed, the chainsaws paused as if in silent mourning for a brief moment, before a splintering crash heralded the falling of a tree that had probably taken several hundred years to reach its magnificent size. Solomon winced. The women bent again to tend their fields. A rare tacazee sunbird flew over their heads, a regal flash of purple, green and gold. A turaco called from the forest behind, a large, indigo-crested bird that reveals ruby wings in flight. In the far distance I could see the Mohican profile of the long-crested eagle. All these birds depended on the trees too . . . did anybody round here ever notice these exotic feathered creatures?

The colobus had gone, taking flying leaps between high branches. Around us were encroaching acres of brown earth, their nakedness broken by fat tree stumps. The new fields were enclosed by fences, roughly built from those destroyed trees. The high backdrop of the Aberdares was pitted with black and brown scars where fires had left brittle groves of dead trees. Its rich, green shawl of mountain forest was losing its daily battle for survival; Solomon's unvoiced thoughts and my own were probably similar, as we wondered how long the shrinking forest could continue to provide life and shelter for so many plant, insect, animal and bird species. How much longer could its roots hold back the rich topsoil from washing away down Kenya's rivers, affecting the shorelines of the Rift Valley's lakes and upsetting yet more fragile ecosystems?

Solomon was sorrowfully examining an old tree stump, 4 feet in diameter. 'Look!' he said, brightening as a giant green grasshopper marched stiffly up his arm. 'So beautiful!'

The demented drone of the chainsaw tore through the air again. Some wealthy and influential outsider would benefit from the sale of the endangered hardwood. But these people living in tin-roofed houses made of cedar off-cuts, relying on firewood for fuel and selling their charcoal for a small amount of cash to buy school books and uniforms for their many children, had no inclination to save trees either. If the forests were gone in a couple of decades, so what? It wasn't *their* problem. *Shauri ya mungu* – 'the problem is God's' – as many Kenyans say.

Nobody here had heard of Slains or Lord Erroll. We negotiated the washed-away track running north along the base of the mountain range. This had been Solomon's idea and I was not convinced that we shouldn't have gone back to the roads we knew went somewhere. A man on a bicycle with a full sack of giant cabbages strapped on to his carrier actually overtook us. To our left the yellow-grey plateau country stretched out: spiky clumps of highland grass, the umbrella-shaped acacia abyssinica trees and dark grey rocks mottled white with lichen. Once fields of golden wheat had grown here, while sheep grazed on the grasses as far as the eye could see. Now fences criss-crossed the expanses and tin roofs flashed fiercely in the sun: even traditional thatched roofs were slowly becoming extinct.

We eventually passed an old-looking red-brick building beside some towering gum trees. An unused metal container lay by the entrance like a giant's milking pail. We stopped in the narrow road – surely no one else would be insane enough to drive this way – and a man emerged, introducing himself as Alfred, the caretaker. 'There is a historic home not far away,' he told us. 'This used to be for cooling the milk,' he indicated the brick building, 'now it is my home!'

Alfred led us through a field past a pit-latrine, behind which lay a much older, albeit broken bath, discarded amongst the weeds. 'Follow me,' he said, heading on up the hill. 'It is not too far . . .'

I suddenly felt a profound peace and a rich sense of the unknown, as though the wind was laden with stories. Solomon, who has an unlikely fund of information, mused: 'I think this can be La Dushka's house. The *wazee* remember her as a famous lady who lived near Dilap.'

What house? I wondered as we walked on towards the towering Aberdares through this strangely tranquil field, with no sign of any house anywhere. I asked our guide if he knew who had lived here.

'Lord Malcolm,' he said firmly. 'His daughter, she visited, and left some papers . . .'

We walked through two lines of closely planted, gigantic cypress trees, now well over 50 feet high. 'This was the hedge,' said Alfred, standing beside one of the trees, its circumference as thick as several men, 'and this was a stream, here a pond.' He pointed out dry depressions in the ground. 'And *here* the old house!'

In the thick undergrowth I could just make out something like a large anthill, but as we ploughed our way through the nettles and tangled bushes, crumbling mud walls emerged. Solomon, who has absolutely no fear of snakes, vanished and later reappeared on a window ledge beside what was just recognisable as a corner of the house – there was even a determined patch of white plaster clinging to a vestige of wall. 'There are rooms,' enthused Solomon, 'a fireplace too. This is a big house!'

'Was,' I said.

'When I arrived in 1963,' said Alfred the caretaker earnestly, 'the house was beautiful. But the natives they come and destroy everything – they pull down the roof and all the wood. They steal the furniture.'

I blinked at him. Nobody nowadays uses the word 'native'. It has the smack of colonial superiority.

The sun was slanting through the high eucalyptus that lined the track below us. We had to get back to a real road before darkness confused us further. Before we departed, Alfred presented me with a thick wad of typed sheets left by a mysterious, elderly lady called Diana who had visited the house because, Alfred said, her father once lived here. Could this be Diana, Countess of Erroll? She'd be in her late seventies now . . .

My excitement was short lived. The memoir turned out to be written by a pioneer farmer who described his life in another area altogether, near Thomson's Falls, on the northern shoulders of the

Aberdares. Several months later a friend of my mother's, who'd also grown up in that area but now lives in Australia, identified the writer as Malcolm Watson – she'd been a bridesmaid at his wedding. The mystery Diana's addresses were on an attached page: Diana Watson, care of a man in Germany or a monastery in England. I wrote to both addresses but never had a reply.

Malcolm Watson had at one point worked for Delamere at his other farm Manera, in Naivasha. The typed sheets described their many guests, including those who were less than welcome and whom he called the 'remittance men, who had been given a remittance from their families as long as they kept well away from the UK and shaming their relatives'. This was the Happy Valley lot. Watson probably sums up the feelings of many settlers of the time with his comments: 'The capers of this group were notorious for their utter immorality. Africans were afraid of working for them and Europeans avoided them if they could.' He recalls how they arrived at his Manera home, claiming Lord Delamere had said they could stay: 'Lord Delamere of course knew of these people, but had little in common with any of them.'

Although this had been a false lead, it spurred my mother into remembering that she'd had a sweetheart she used to write to when she was about fifteen. He'd been called Alan Wisdom and she even recalled his address: Aberdare Milk Products, Slains Farm, Wanjohi. 'He used to mention some neighbours called the Delaps,' she said. 'I taught the Delap children at Nyeri School in the fifties. I remember little Susan Delap saying: *My mummy's name is Bubbles.*'

Perhaps at last we were getting warmer . . .

I found Bubbles Delap, whose real name is Maureen, in the Charles Disney home for retired people, just around the corner from Muthaiga Club, where she can't afford membership. This charming and amusingly eccentric lady was delighted to share her memories, and even more delighted at the idea that I had a car and might take her out. So I took her for a curry lunch, which seemed to be a great treat as no family members appeared to live nearby. 'And I *love* curry, it's my favourite,' she said in a stage whisper, having mountaineered her way up into the passenger seat of my Land Rover, which still had vestiges of Happy Valley mud clinging to its flanks.

'Needless to say I'm a bit of an exaggerator,' she laughed over the spiced dishes of mutton and chicken between us in the almost-empty restaurant.

I was dying to ask about Slains, but first Bubbles wished to tell me her own story. Her mother, Doreen, had run away from Roedean School aged sixteen and come to Kenya. Doreen was apparently an attractive and spirited girl; she served as a dairy maid at Windsor Castle during the First World War, before arriving in Kenya to work for Lord Delamere, who didn't expect – or want – a female employee. Doreen – who, eccentrically for the times, always wore shorts – persuaded Delamere to take her on, but soon left to marry Ernest Hay 'Sandy' Wright, sixteen years her senior. Having given birth to Bubbles, Doreen was to divorce and remarry Wright, also later marrying Dickie Peel, an army major, and a professor in South Africa whose name Bubbles had forgotten. But, most famously, she had a child with Ewart Grogan, the highly intellectual and adventurous pioneer settler renowned for walking from Cape to Cairo to win the hand of his beloved Gertrude, who also happened to be an heiress – though the story's romance is somewhat tainted by Grogan's many affairs.

In 1929, Doreen, by then among the 54-year-old Grogan's conquests, gave birth to a daughter, June. Both possible fathers, Wright and Grogan, amicably stood by her bedside after the birth, joking about the child's paternity. June grew up looking remarkably like Grogan, who was happy to fill the gap left by the non-maternal Doreen. He remained a dutiful parent, often taking June out from school, and built her a house at Taveta near the Kivoto springs, irrespective of the fact that Doreen had by then divorced and remarried Wright.

Meanwhile, Bubbles Wright had grown up, and was in her late teens when she went to a ball at Muthaiga Club 'with some Earl who talked politics'. He bored her, she said, but then she met the handsome Bill Delap, who shared her love of dancing. He was already married to Rosemary Montgomery, but later divorced her to marry Bubbles, now nineteen, in 1946. Bubbles remained 'good friends' with Rosemary, although inevitable tensions arose over the two sons of the first marriage – Bubbles was only eight years older than her eldest stepson. Rosemary, who according to Bubbles was very attractive and part of the original Happy Valley set, died of nephritis – a renal illness – at the age of thirty-nine. 'She was very attractive and *very* wild,' said Bubbles (who wore faded but unmistakable signs of beauty herself). 'She said Bill beat her.' She paused and added: 'He never beat me.' Plenty of women, she claimed, had been 'after Bill'. Then she laughed, 'One woman was always chasing him and she had a perfectly good husband.'

'Idina?' I suggested.

She ignored this and said, with a touch of envy, 'But by this time Happy Valley's heyday was past and no one had what it took to recreate it. It's a sort of glamour that goes with money and title.'

'But you knew Idina?' I asked.

'Oh yes! Everyone knew her.'

'And what was she like?'

Considerably younger than Idina, Bubbles would have known her briefly in the 1940s. She smiled, with a hint of triumph. 'She wasn't a bit good looking, but she was small, dainty, elegant – like a bird – and she dressed beautifully.'

'And what about her wild reputation?' I asked.

'Oh yes, she had lots of army boyfriends,' confirmed Bubbles. 'So many people tried to restart Happy Valley and failed,' she explained. 'But Sunday lunches at Clouds were still memorable occasions: Idina was a great entertainer. Once she announced "I feel like a swim" and got into her sunken bath fully clothed!' As Idina was living at Clouds by then where there was no sunken bath, Bubbles may have been referring to one of the ponds in Idina's much-admired water gardens, her memory blurred by whatever they were drinking. Bubbles added: 'She never had much education, she learnt from her husbands – and of course she adored books . . .'

I showed Bubbles my recent photographs of the remaining wooden house. 'That was the original house Bill built,' she said. 'When I married Bill an Italian POW built us a stone house. He used to sing on the roof. It had four or five bedrooms and was L-shaped.'

I produced the next photograph of the lonely chimney and she raised her eyebrows: 'I'm surprised there's nothing left of it. I have some photos somewhere . . .' She concentrated once more on using her naan bread to polish off the mutton curry, afterwards managing a kulfi ice-cream and a spiced masala tea as well. I got the impression it was a very long time since anybody had wined and dined Bubbles, and was grateful for the privilege.

When we got back to her rooms, she couldn't find any of her photos anywhere, so she sat down again and described her former home in Happy Valley, with its lovely view across the crystal-clear trout stream at the bottom of the garden: 'The Wanjohi River – we used to swim in it . . .'

The rich soil had been ideal for market gardening, as well as supporting their Jersey cattle, pigs and ducks. The Delap farm was called Rayetta Estate. 'It's a Maasai name – I can't remember what it means,' Bubbles said vaguely. 'It was 15 miles to Ol Kalou, along the worst road in Kenya! Once it took us twenty-four hours . . .'

I remembered seeing a sign for Rayetta Primary School near the old home. Another old name lingering on.

Bill had written a weekly column, *The Shamba Man*, for a local newspaper. 'He was also a prize-winning photographer. And he used to take people up the Aberdares,' explained Bubbles, her train of thought tumbling from one subject to another. Bubbles' two stepsons had gone to school at Pembroke House in Gilgil. She and Bill had three daughters.

In 1963 the Delaps had left for Australia, 'but we returned after a few months to sack a dishonest manager', Bubbles said. 'By then we had six hundred acres: three hundred under pyrethrum, a school, a *duka* [basic shop] and plans to build a church. But when we left at independence we got a rotten price from the British government – only £4,000!'

Bill Delap died in 1982 and was buried according to his wishes at Point Lenana, the third-highest peak on Mount Kenya and the highest that can be reached on foot. Bubbles smiled: 'I have some pictures of him skiing up there! Nobody else did that, you know . . .'

It had been hard to glean the information I wanted as Bubbles was actually very deaf. As I was leaving, I asked about her neighbours. Bubbles remembered an Italian neighbour. 'She was called La Duska – I think she was a duchess – and she made gorgonzola cheese. They had a red-brick dairy. She threw marvellous parties and was very wild and attractive – a very good cook. She lived in a lovely old whitewashed mud house with parquet floors, full of beautiful furniture. After that she had some manager there for a bit . . .'

'Was the manager called Wisdom?' I asked excitedly and very loudly. She confirmed that he was.

'So the farm was called Slains?' I shouted.

Bubbles thought so.

I asked around about an Italian duchess who'd lived at Slains after Idina. One elderly ex-settler thought she was a countess. The *wazee* in the area had mentioned 'La Dushka'. Somebody else vaguely remembered an Italian count living 'somewhere up there'. 'Count Cesaroni,' confirmed another. 'Oh yes, that is Ceaserone,' said Solomon. But nobody knew if the duchess and the count were connected in any way.

The former's name is spelt variously by historians. Elspeth Huxley mentions in *Pioneer Scrapbook* that Liduska Hornik's excellent gorgonzola cheeses made the area famous, while Tim Hutchinson's *Kenya Up-Country Directory* lists Ladiska Hornik under 'Thomson's Falls', also mentioning gorgonzola cheese. A retired farmer, Tim has laboured away for years to provide a *Who's Who* of Kenya's white settlers, who lived where – and sometimes when. A real work of love, it often relies on people's memories, so it inevitably fails to be totally accurate all the time. Under 'Gilgil' in Hutchinson's book there is a 'Cesaroni, Maj Count A, Kipipiri 1931', who had one daughter and, once again, the gorgonzola connection.

Solomon had introduced me to Janie Begg, adding that she knew 'much history'. Janie's late father, David Begg, once lived near Gilgil, where he met his wife Lily who'd worked as barmaid at Lady Colville's Gilgil Hotel. They married and had three daughters; Janie is the middle one. Eccentric, independent and unmarried, she speaks Kikuyu fluently and dowses with a pendulum. It was Janie who put me in touch with the mysterious 'La Duska'. Mrs Piotto, as she was now called, lived in the Nairobi suburb of Karen, just round the corner from the spot where Erroll was murdered on the junction of the Karen and Ngong roads, beside St Francis' Church.

I waited at the locked gate with its sign 'Piotto'. It took a long time, and several trips on foot from the gate along the lengthy drive to the house, for the gardener to persuade Mrs Piotto to let me in. She eventually agreed after protracted explanations that I had just visited her old home and really wanted to talk to her. 'But she's in a hurry,' he told me warningly as he finally opened it.

An elegant lady with navy slacks, grey hair and a long string of pearls over a pastel sweater met me and called to an elderly manservant for chairs to be set out in the garden. I explained I was a writer, interested in Happy Valley, which was definitely the wrong thing to say.

'A *writer*? Ha! They all write rubbish, all of them,' she cried in an engaging Italian accent. 'Dina and all these people they are dead. Why not leave them in peace? It is not interesting anyway,' she admonished. 'They were all just people!' She stood up, ready to see me leave. 'Everything said about them is lies,' she added fiercely.

'I have visited Slains,' I said tentatively. 'I could show you some photographs.'

I'd dug myself an even deeper hole. She let rip at me now. Why would anybody want to visit an area now ruined by the Africans? Who would want to look at destruction and ruins, at wasted farmland? Anyway, she wanted to cook lunch now . . .

As I hastily prepared to leave she gave me a second look. 'If you want to visit me again,' she said very severely, 'telephone me so I can prepare something. Here is my number.'

It took me some time to muster up the courage to call Mrs Piotto. She wasn't sure she even remembered me, but she invited me to tea at four o'clock sharp.

Having tea with the duchess, who wasn't actually a duchess, I discovered that her real name was Lyduska – she spelt it out for me. She was very much the charming hostess today and happy to talk to me, although I didn't dare mention anything about Happy Valley, let alone any murders.

Lyduska Piotto's mother was Italian-Austrian and her father was a Czech in the Austrian army, she explained, as we enjoyed a beautifully prepared afternoon tea: anchovies and capers on bread, almond biscuits, and tea in bone china cups. It was a warm afternoon, but we sat beside a crackling fire – transporting us back to another life many decades ago. It would have been cold enough to need that early evening fire at Slains, nestled in the lap of a high plateau where chilled air dropped down from the Aberdare Mountains.

I tentatively explained how much I loved houses, and the sensation of déjà vu I felt experiencing the wonderful ambience of Slains.

Lyduska Piotto gave me a searching but gentle look. She had astonishing, brilliant-blue eyes. 'Yes,' she said, 'I always felt that beautiful atmosphere there too.' She told me the story of finding this, her present home, how she had fallen for its 'feel'. It had been a wreck of a place, but it attracted her because it was right out of town and had many beautiful trees. Her husband had thought her mad, but then he'd only lived here a very short time. She mentioned a car crash, then changed the subject.

Lyduska told me she had been incredibly happy at Slains, perhaps the happiest ever in her life. She'd been strictly brought up. As a child, her birthday present might be a single rose. 'I was always called a silly goose,' she laughed, suddenly gesturing out of the window at her honking gaggle of geese, 'so there are my sisters who live with me now!' She smiled: 'I love my dogs and horses too. They are friends – if you are sad you can go and be with them.' She looked at me hard, as if suddenly reading my own thoughts: I was emotionally reeling after an unpleasant divorce, and as it happened I was sobbing nightly into the nearest cat or dog. 'Everyone has problems,' she said quietly, going on to tell me that her parents had separated when she was young – largely due, she believed, to her maternal grandmother's hatred of her father. Thus she barely saw her father and when she tried to visit him before he died, it was the war and the Germans wouldn't let her. 'But I abused them strongly – in German,' she added. I believed her: she'd already displayed her fiery Latin temperament on my first visit. I almost felt sorry for the Germans.

The fire was becoming too hot now, but I didn't want to move as Lyduska had begun talking about Slains. In 1938, aged seventeen, she first came to Kenya to live with her uncle on her mother's side, who'd bought half of the farm. 'You see my aunt had first met Dina in the smart circles of Venice,' she explained, 'and so she came home saying she had met a very pretty woman who lived in some funny place called Gilgil. That was how it began.'

'Idina?' I asked.

She nodded, smiling fondly.

One of Lyduska's first social engagements in Kenya was a ball at Muthaiga Club, where she saw the Happy Valley set for herself. 'Dina was flirting with everyone and dancing,' she said dreamily: 'I didn't like Erroll – an *artisan praticco* – but Dina was madly in love with him. I loved to watch her.' This puzzled me, as Idina and Erroll certainly weren't together at the end of the 1930s. However, with the way they all carried on, it was perfectly possible that Idina still had her dalliances with her ex-husband.

Lyduska continued with an affectionate smile: 'Dina was not beautiful – frail looking but not frail at all, small bones but well covered in flesh, naughty but a lovely person.' She paused, then suddenly frowned: 'She should be left in peace. All those people should be. Writers write such rubbish about them!'

I'd been about to ask her who she thought had murdered Erroll, but remembering her angry comments about writers on our first meeting, I asked instead about her early days in Happy Valley, which she seemed glad to talk about for hours. The young Lyduska, who I suspect was a great beauty herself, adored running wild in this exciting new and untamed country around Slains. It worried her aunt, who used to reprimand her intrepid niece: 'She said to me, "If you don't stop your wanderings a Maasai will rape you out there in those lonely places!" I did not listen to her, I loved this wonderful country,' Lyduska laughed.

When her aunt and uncle had left, Lyduska had stayed on, running Slains, which she had come to love deeply. 'It was a beautiful house.

There were waterfalls and a stream running past. The house was built of cedar tree posts, with mud in between, and it was very big – you could sleep seven or eight guests: there were chimneys in all the rooms. The main fireplace was copied from the El Greco house in Venice . . .' She made a serpentine motion with her hand. 'The walls were wavy – like this!' She laughed: 'Dina and her contractor were drunk when they built it.' Her eyes shone with remembered happiness. 'You liked my house too?'

It would have been unkind to elaborate upon the state it was in now. 'Yes,' I said simply, but truthfully. 'It's a very special place.'

Idina had moved away, Lyduska thought, in about 1929, leaving some silver, a few pieces of furniture and lovely French carnations in the garden. She indicated the black and white photograph of Idina in its silver frame on an elegant table. 'She was a wonderful person, so why do they write such bad lies about her?'

She remembered all the old Happy Valley crowd: Alice and her neighbour, a woman called Pat. She also remembered Bubbles: 'She was a very good-looking young lady . . .' They'd seen one another frequently as Slains and Rayetta were within reasonable riding distance of one another, the track running directly between them more negotiable to a horse than my Land Rover. I gleaned that they'd enjoyed something of a love-hate relationship. 'She was your best friend one minute and shouting at you the next,' Bubbles had said, adding that she enjoyed going to lunch at Slains as Lyduska was an excellent cook and entertainer: 'She had a very pretty house, but then we fell out!' Fifty years on, I'd noticed how both these women, each retaining a certain faded glamour, were still inclined to snipe at each other, as well as their neighbours.

Lyduska was warming up now, relating some of the spicier stories. They all had 'party lines' in the 1950s: this was to do with telephones rather than drugs. There was one shared line, but each user had their own ring. So when somebody wound the handle of the telephone receiver to dial the exchange, they would ask for a certain person, and that person's signal of, say, one long and two short rings would echo through all the houses. The person whose ring it was should have been the only one to pick up, but of course anybody could listen in, which was presumably how the exchange workers passed the long, tedious hours. Lyduska remembered listening in to one call, probably along with the rest of the valley, and hearing a breathless male voice asking:

'What are you wearing?'

'My nightie,' purred a soft female voice.

'I wish I could squeeze you . . .' he began, before an explosive, masculine sound warned him that somebody was listening and the line went dead.

Meanwhile, Bubbles, just to secure Happy Valley's reputation, had told me that Bill's first wife Rosemary (who'd been a friend of Alice de Janzé's) and her friend had 'carried on and entertained soldiers in a high-society brothel'. As second wives tend not to look kindly on their predecessors and Rosemary Delap wasn't around to defend herself, I took the accusation with a fistful of salt. Bubbles also told me – on two separate occasions with an air of revealing a scandal – that Lyduska was *very* wild and had *lived with* her Italian boyfriend.

During the war Lyduska and her boyfriend had gone to Italy, which was when the Wisdoms managed the farm. But they were back, Lyduska said, in 1948 and soon afterwards came the first mutterings of Mau Mau. People no longer trusted faithful servants with their house keys. Reports of murders on isolated farms or cows being hamstrung circulated wildly, deepening fear throughout the white settler community. Happy Valley was right in the danger zone.

Lyduska recounted a night when there was a disturbance outside and some of the staff had alerted them: 'My husband rushed out to the fields to check on the cattle and I just ran out in my nightdress without thinking.' She paused and shook her head slightly. 'I was about to go down the front steps, you know the ones?'

I nodded, having ascended and descended those same steps.

'. . . but it was as if an invisible arm held me back. I couldn't go any further. My angel was pushing me away from the danger,' she said softly. 'There had been Mau Mau hiding in the orange trees at the bottom of those steps – seven or eight of them.'

She had experienced something similar when she was young, in front of a German firing squad. She was the only one who wasn't killed. 'It was not my time then,' she said, 'And it was not my time at Slains to be killed by the Mau Mau either. My time will come, but not like that.

'But who could you trust?' she suddenly asked. She had known the victims of the notorious murder in the north of the region: 'Fergusson told me that his boys loved him and would never hurt him. A week later he had been horribly murdered!'

Lyduska had eventually sold the property in the early 1960s when the British government were buying up farms to downsize and allocate for native settlement. She sighed, 'We only got £10,000 for nearly three thousand acres.'

It had been a delightful tea and I didn't want to outstay my welcome. I hadn't discovered anything more about Count Cesaroni, nor had I asked Lyduska who she thought had murdered Erroll, but I vowed to come back and ask her again one day.

6

Slains Unearthed

I couldn't wait to go back to Slains. Alfred the caretaker had written to me in pencil, on lined paper that looked as if it had been torn out of a school exercise book, sealed in a grubby airmail envelope: 'It is my sincere hope that you and your family have managed to cross the boundaries to this new year as we did,' he wrote, asking after my research on the old, crumbling house. He added: 'It is my hope that you have gone deeper as per the bone.' Then he related how the sons of the owner of the farm had arrived with a pack of casual labourers and cut all the trees down: 'Here is nothing but a total destruction,' he lamented.

Solomon shook his head at the news. 'They do not care!' he raged.

When we returned to the ruin, six months had passed, and the vast cypress hedge, as well as every other tree in the vicinity, had been reduced to corpulent stacks of drying logs. We crossed the naked, newly ploughed earth where Idina (or her garden 'boys') must once have grown pansies, roses and probably even daffodils at this altitude, while Solomon delivered a sorrowful eulogy for the trees.

But the plough had circled the old house with unlikely respect, even though it could have easily given it back to the earth. Now it was easier to see its layout and compare it with the old photographs. Even if the walls were only knee high in places, there were the stone steps descending in front of the door. And there was the cleft in the Aberdares behind, where a waterfall once dropped down. The shape of the land and the position of the house were exactly right. There was no mistaking Slains!

I suddenly smiled at the unkind irony that Malcolm Watson's wad of memories had somehow ended up in the original home of two of the people he really could not abide, and whom he incorrectly named as 'Jocylyn Hay (sic) who became the Earl of Errol' and 'Lady Diana Hay-Gordon-Haldeman'. In fact, few of those who've written about Slains seem to have been there. Even Errol Trzebinski, the most comprehensive of researchers, says that the house faced Lake Ol Bolossat and Thomson's Falls, and was built at an altitude of 5,500 feet. It's actually closer to 7,800 feet and would have faced Gilgil, with Ol Bolossat over to its right.

As I stood on the steps of Slains I recalled Trzebinski's luscious descriptions of the Hays' life here with a French maid and European manager among the retinue of employees – and streams of guests. Apparently, after Joss and Idina's early morning rides, Joss changed into a kilt before enjoying a breakfast of porridge and cream. In spite of the Champagne-cocaine-morphine-tainted reputation of the Happy Valley clique, Joss was a non-smoker, an extremely moderate drinker by Kenyan standards and the first farmer to breed high-grade Guernsey cattle in Kenya. Unusually for the times and his background, he apparently didn't like hunting, shooting or fishing either.

But Slains played only a small part in Joss's life; after leaving Idina he maintained his philandering lifestyle regardless of whether he was married or divorced, or whether his current wife was dying or dead. As well as affairs with Phyllis Filmer, Diana Broughton and Gladys Delamere, he seduced wild child Beryl Markham. Beryl was one of the very few women who wouldn't have wanted to murder Erroll: she'd had no shortage of love interests, including her flings with royalty. It's surprising nobody murdered her: she was not Karen Blixen's favourite person, particularly as she was allegedly having an affair with Denys Finch Hatton, Karen's lover, when he was killed in a plane crash in Tsavo in May 1931. Another great friend of Beryl's was Frank Greswolde-Williams, who as Trzebinski says in *The Lives of Beryl Markham* (1993) apparently kept the Happy Valley set happy by supplying them with cocaine.

From the front steps of Joss and Idina's first home, the views expanded across the high plateau country, to the hazy Rift Valley, dropping away towards the pale blue wall of the distant Mau escarpment which forms its far side. In the foreground was a row of agapanthus lilies, clearly sturdy survivors. I had a strong feeling that this house and farm had been loved and that people had been happy here – and an even more powerful sense that I'd been here before, even if only in a dream.

I thought about Joss. In the photographs he's a slightly podgy man with those effeminate looks that had been fashionable in the twenties. He doesn't look attractive in black and white – you evidently had to meet him in the flesh to experience his fatal charms. He'd been a 'pretty boy' as a child, not helped by the fact that his mother, as was the aristocratic fashion of the times, grew his hair and dressed him as a girl. There were mutterings of homosexual affairs at Eton, while later on his good friendship with the openly homosexual Fabian Wallace in Happy Valley days led to speculations that he could have been bisexual. He even allegedly wore women's perfume.

It's possible that Joss, in spite of supposedly sexually awakening many women, was never satisfied with any of them himself, thus his serial infidelities. Or was he just a misogynist who needed to create a safety net of multiple women to ensure he would never be alone? Some psychologists say that men who have affairs are working out childhood needs, fears and conflicts. Nowadays they call them sex addicts. But whatever Joss's secret reasons for bed-hopping, his female following was not to be underestimated. Nobody is still around to verify stories of his incredible skills in bed, nor can any woman alive claim to have penetrated that charming, heartless veneer to discover a soul mate. Skills between the sheets aside, many women get their 'fix' from imagining they will be the one who changes their man, stilling his roving eye in a fantastical, fairy-tale ending. At the end of the day Joss probably just slept around because he could: after all, plenty of women made themselves readily available.

*

Solomon suddenly called me from behind the house, where the tearing out of roots and toppling of layers of soil had unearthed something. Among the broken clods lay a rusted cartridge, a piece of a knife blade, stained dark as if somebody had been stabbed with it; then, as we began to dig around, a blue glass perfume bottle and many fragments of broken china and glassware, one of them proclaiming it had been 'made in England'. There was a piece imprinted with 'Grindley', one with a Chinese design, another hand decorated, a cracked fragment of a floral painting on glass. We had stumbled upon the old rubbish dump.

Our pockets full of pieces of plate, the blue perfume bottle in my handbag, we returned to Alfred, who invited us into his home. Inside the cool dairy with its stone floor and heavy wooden doors, I sat on a large, scratched, leather-covered chair with hardwood armrests: the type that would cost plenty nowadays in an antique auction.

'*Utirere!* [Kikuyu for 'listen!'] From the historic house I rescued this chair – and these.' Alfred showed me a wardrobe and a dresser – now painted red. They were not elegant enough to be Idina's prize pieces, unless they had been in a corner of a dark room, I decided. 'I'm a bit modern,' Alfred grinned, sensing my aversion to the paint. 'There were also grape vines, fruit trees and so many flowers all around the house, but everything went. And the roof, windows and doors, all taken. The people around here do not value history!' He was sitting in a newer imitation-leather seat, above which hung a two-year-old calendar proclaiming the President's support in eradicating polio and AIDS, and a plastic picture of a pagoda with formal gardens. 'East or west', read the inscription, 'home is best'. The remaining wall space was papered with old newspaper cuttings and outdated election posters of an ex-MP.

I pictured parts of Slains strewn far and wide: a bit of roof on a chicken house here, a solid wooden door on a goat house there, the smoke of valuable old furniture and cedar window frames used as firewood dispersed everywhere.

Alfred's eldest daughter served us generous platefuls of chicken, potatoes, carrots and rice, with mugs of soup, heavy with fat. Solomon swigged soup while extolling the colobus monkeys' rights, outraged at Alfred's story of one recently being trapped and killed in the area. He leant forwards in his seat beneath a line of gaudy Christmas decorations. A shiny picture of a green lawn with fountains, flowers and peacocks hung behind his head. 'The great thing in this world', the bold writing at the bottom told me, 'is not so much where we are but in which direction we are moving'.

Our host was more interested in discussing his financial problems: he had five children, 'one is stranded from school because of no money'. He shook his head. His landlords were not paying him his due 500 shillings (around £4), his monthly wage, and the river was drying up because an aborted water project upstream had blocked its passage.

The radio, in between crackles and fizzes, was playing 'When the going gets tough the tough get going'. '*Utirere*, we all want better for our children than we have,' said Alfred sadly. He talked about his father, Githuku, who'd worked for Bill Delap as cattleman alongside Kenya's leading freedom fighter, Dedan Kimathi. When the British were grappling with the problem of Kikuyu terrorists melting into the forests without trace, Kimathi had been their most wanted man. He'd also been Delap's milk recorder, Alfred explained, and Githuku had been one of the first men to go into hiding in the Aberdare forest with Kimathi soon after Mau Mau started. Ian Parker in *The Last Colonial Regiment: The History of the Kenya Regiment (TF)* states, with no mention of Delap or Wanjohi, that Dedan Kimathi was a milk recorder in Subukia until six weeks before the state of emergency.

I told my grandmother's story. She'd been on a farm on the edge of the Dundori forest with a dozen young live-in pupils from neighbouring European farms who attended her home-based school, which necessitated boarding because everybody lived too far apart to work it otherwise. My grandfather had been called up, so he was away tracking Mau Mau fighters deep in the Aberdare forest. One morning, when the cook brought in the tray of early morning tea, he seemed agitated and the cups were rattling like castanets. 'What's the matter?' my grandmother had asked. The cook had tremblingly stuttered that 'a man' was by the kitchen door. My grandmother went out in her dressing gown and found a freedom fighter, his hair in unkempt dreadlocks and his clothes ragged and filthy. 'His eyes were like a wild forest animal's!' she'd told me.

The man had shown her his finger, badly severed at the joint, and she had cleaned, treated and bandaged it for him. Some hours after the man left, the schoolchildren had discovered a strange structure below the garden, at the edge of the forest. It was designed to catch the wind, which would clash two sturdy sticks of bamboo together.

'Don't touch it,' warned the African staff. 'That man was Kimathi himself and he has left this symbol to tell others to leave this house alone . . .' This was at least 40 miles from the Aberdare forest, but Kimathi was apparently able to cover long distances at a run.

'Utirere!' said Alfred. 'When he died Kimathi was missing one finger!'

My grandmother, by the sound of it, had failed to save Kimathi's finger, but their home remained untouched throughout the state of emergency.

Alfred himself had been born on the Delap farm in 1954 – a year after his father had been one of three freedom fighters to launch one of the first attacks on British settlers. Together the three men had crept up on the home of Charles Fergusson, the white settler-farmer who'd been in Kenya for thirty years. As the elderly man sat down to dinner with his young student farmer, Richard Bingley, they were attacked and murdered.

I thought of the coincidences: one of Delap's servants had done the horrible deed – and now I'd met his son. Perhaps Githuku had even been one of the men who hid at the base of the steps at Slains that night Lyduska had run out in her nightdress.

'Slaughtered into pieces,' concluded Alfred, waving a chicken bone. 'Then after many years when Kimathi was killed by the British my father went back to work for Delap and they all became friends again.' The song on the radio had switched to 'It's a Beautiful Life'.

7

Soccer After Suicide

The pupils of Happy Valley School had spotted us through the windows. They streamed out of their classrooms, surrounding us on the playing fields: at least 400 wildly excited children between the ages of five and fifteen. They pushed around us, pressing in close enough to touch our skin and hair. I had a friend from France with me – also blonde – and we were both feeling uncomfortable. This invasion of our space was becoming threatening. The noisy, undisciplined mob around us made it impossible to see beyond the thick wall of dark faces.

'These children are very rude!' Solomon appeared, brandishing a large stick, causing them to scream and scatter. 'Many of these children have not seen a white person before,' he explained. We were visiting the former home of the third member of Happy Valley's notorious triumvirate, the beautiful, colourful Alice de Janzé, later de Trafford. Portrayed by different writers as unbalanced and unpredictable, Alice was also irresistible: before taking her own life, she not only played the ukulele, but sang seductively, mixing wicked cocktails in between popping drugs. In photographs she always looks exotically sultry, even eccentric: with a lion cub on her lap, or posing with the Happy Valley brigade on the front steps of rambling bungalows. But she never smiles.

Alice's former farm lies roughly halfway between Slains and Clouds, on the western shoulders of Kipipiri. Her house would have faced Lake Ol Bolossat, now a glistening sheet of water to the right of the many new tin roofs of Ol Kalou town, although then there would have been no houses to mar Alice's view. The Wanjohi River flowing to our right would have provided her water supply. All that remained of Alice's home now were a few foundation stones, half buried under a sprawl of Kikuyu grass. Solomon pointed out the one surviving walnut tree in the middle of a field, looking as if it had come under frequent assault from an axe. There were some long, low buildings at the back: the old servants' quarters. Meanwhile, at the side, where the road circled round and crossed a small ravine, was Alice's manager's house, built out of dark-stained cedar wood with a tin roof, although parts of it still had patches of older shingle.

Solomon knew this area more intimately than any other corner of Happy Valley. 'Harris [as he pronounced Alice – the Kikuyu tend to mix up their r's and l's] was buried somewhere around here.' He indicated a football goalpost close to the river. 'And I was born just there!' He pointed at the nearby hill. Perhaps his own roots accounted for his particular fascination with Alice: of all the Happy Valley crew, she's the one he talked about most.

I'd read a bit about Alice, plenty of sensational stuff unravelling a story of drama and despair. James Fox, in *White Mischief*, along with various other writers on Kenyan colonial times, provides a kaleidoscope of detail that seems to shift with every turn of the page.

American born and a wealthy heiress, Alice Silverthorne, who'd lost her mother at a young age, had an early introduction to the 'good' life, drinking cocktails with her father in European night clubs, paraded as a pretty young accessory in unsuitable venues. She grew into an eye-catching young woman, exuding powerful sex appeal with her short dark bob and wide, innocent eyes. In the glamorous circles of Paris she met and married the young French aristocrat Frédéric de Janzé, a count, politician, racing driver and aspiring writer, who also moved in high circles.

After Alice and Frédéric had produced two daughters, Nolwen and Paola, the couple visited Happy Valley. They already knew Idina and Joss, who'd enhanced their high-flying Parisian circles with wafts of the exotic. Now the de Janzés could sample the Hays' thrilling lifestyle. Enamoured, they decided to join it, buying a farm and moving to Wanjohi.

Alice, like Idina, added a shot of scandal to a colonial farming community, where most settler wives lived challenging lives, creating homes and farms out of virgin territory, getting their hands thoroughly dirty while dressing for comfort and practicality. Idina and Alice could afford to hire others to do the boring work while they pursued their other interests. Between them they introduced a new fashion of soft, slinky trousers – offending those more conservative *memsahibs* even though trousers were so practical for chilly Wanjohi. Their freestyle sex lives wouldn't have improved their image: Joss was soon commuting between Idina or Alice in Happy Valley and Mary Ramsay-Hill on the shores of Lake Naivasha. Meanwhile, if Alice disappeared for several days with Idina's wandering husband, Idina herself could ride over to Wanjohi Farm and find solace with Frédéric, whose poetically erotic descriptions of her in his book, *Vertical Land*, might well suggest that the pair found comfort in each other's arms.

Alice's pet lion cub, presumably a more exciting accessory than anything to be found in Paris, came into her life one morning when the de Janzés were out riding. They spotted a family of cubs near some rocks but left them alone, assuming their parents would be around. Later two young Indian princes, passing through on a hunting safari, invited the de Janzés and Hays to dinner at their camp. There the de Janzés noticed that two of the trophies were fresh lion skins: Alice, seemingly more sentimental about animals than children – hers had been left in France – immediately worried about the cubs. She was proved right the following day when they found the newly orphaned cubs: one was already dead, another died that night, but Samson survived, becoming as notorious as his new, adopted mother for misbehaviour at parties. No doubt stories of his antics also circulated amongst the Parisian cocktails.

Frédéric de Janzé, although he liked lions, wasn't particularly complimentary about the inhabitants of Happy Valley in general. He accused them of being restless, nomadic types rather than colonists;

'indefatigable amusement seekers' as well as misfits with nervous debilities, 'who lacked the courage to grow old, the stamina to . . . build anew in this land'. He prophetically wrote in *Vertical Land* of his wife Alice: 'No man will touch her exclusive soul, shadowy with memories, unstable, suicidal.'

Then, as Ulf Aschan describes in *The Man Whom Women Loved: The Life of Bror Blixen* (1987), came a disruptive new arrival 'in the demon form of Raymond de Trafford', who plunged into a turbulent affair with Alice. Coming from an old and aristocratic English family of wealthy landowners, de Trafford knew the 'right' people, including Idina and Delamere. He slotted beautifully into the Happy Valley set – a dysfunctional philanderer who drank too much and argued even more, even daring to try (without success) to outclass the erudite Frédéric de Janzé on literary subjects. When Raymond's older brother Humphrey offered him £10,000 to be castrated, Raymond, broke as usual, said he would have one ball removed for £5,000! Ulf Aschan documents Evelyn Waugh's description of Raymond, whom Waugh met in Kenya in 1931: 'something of a handful, very nice but so BAD and he fights and fucks and gambles and gets disgustingly drunk all the time'.

Frédéric was less delighted with Raymond (or Raymund, depending on which book you are reading). He whisked Alice back to Paris, but she remained unrepentant, demanding a divorce. Raymond followed them to Paris and moved in with Alice. It was early 1927 – it had taken just over a year of living in Happy Valley to wreck their marriage. Frédéric appealed to the Vatican for an annulment, with custody of the children. Alice, who'd devoted more quality time to a lion cub anyway, didn't fight for her daughters. Raymond was to be another matter.

After a visit to England in March 1927, Raymond returned to Paris to tell Alice the sobering news that his strict Catholic family forbade their marriage. If he imagined he could simply see her off at the station after a nice lunch, then move merrily on, he was underestimating her: there at the Gare du Nord, Alice pulled out a gun and fired at Raymond, hitting him in the chest, kidney or groin (books also vary over this), then shot herself. The incident was reported in the international press; the news reached Idina and Joss, who hastened from Kenya to France, visiting Alice in the women's hospital of the Saint-Lazare prison. Raymond licked his wounds in England, while his family must have been basking in relief at his dual lucky escapes, from both marriage and death.

On 23 December this true femme fatale was tried for attempted murder. Alice claimed she'd intended suicide, but acted on impulse. Raymond agreed it was an accident. It seemed that the Parisian judge had also fallen under Alice's spell: she got off with a minimal fine.

Alice went back to Kenya, but was deported in March, an action engineered by a bristling Lady Grigg. She couldn't abide Alice's very public affair with Joss, as if the French station scandal had not been enough. Thus labelled a wicked and disreputable divorcee, whose tarnished reputation would certainly not enhance that of the colony, Alice found herself back in Paris. One of her first visitors from Kenya was Joss, en route to England after the death of his father. He now had Mary Ramsay-Hill in tow – presumably she'd already worked out that her new paramour was not the faithful type. Raymond, who'd been drinking and womanising back in Kenya and was running short of money, was another frequent visitor. In 1932 Alice married Raymond: he needed her money and she wished to return to Kenya, which she could do as a 'respectable' married woman. Lady Grigg, mercifully, had moved elsewhere.

It can't have surprised many when, after three months, the de Traffords separated. Alice resumed life in Happy Valley with her pet eland and a dachshund called Minnie, who must both have been pleasantly easy company after de Trafford.

By the late 1930s, Alice was administering drugs with a silver syringe to quell her pain, be it emotional or physical – the latter an unkind reminder of her own bullet. In Naivasha, Mary, now Joss's wife, was addicted to morphine. But now there was the less frivolous influence of the war.

When Erroll was murdered, Alice came under suspicion. Her 'houseboy' had apparently found a revolver on her land, by a bridge under a pile of stones. The car in which he'd been shot reeked of Chanel No. 5 – her perfume. Above all she'd had a practice run in the Gare du Nord. Another male admirer of Alice's, Julian Lezard (known as Lizzie), brought her to the mortuary where she laid her erotic memories to rest. According to James Fox in *White Mischief*, Lezard claimed that before putting a tree branch on Erroll's body, Alice kissed him on the lips, pulled the sheet back, smeared it with her vaginal juices and told the dead Erroll that now he would be hers 'for ever'. Lezard was another who suspected Alice of murder, his suspicions sealed by this incident.

Alice wasn't arrested this time: she'd supposedly been in bed with Dickie Pembroke when the murder took place. Pembroke, a young major, was apparently obsessed with Diana Broughton, who thought him boring – probably just as well considering the several complicated love triangles raging. Evidently Pembroke didn't mind a roll in the hay with another attractive female, while this conquest might have amused Alice, who hated Diana.

Alice frequently visited Sir Jock Delves Broughton in jail, taking supplies and books. Many of her friends said she never got over Joss's death, believing this intensified the unhappiness that shadowed her remaining years. According to her letters Alice was still visiting Erroll's grave just before she died. Meanwhile she had health problems and had to undergo surgery, her precious dog, Minnie, was ill and Dickie Pembroke was posted to Cairo.

Alice finally put her little dog down herself and then took an overdose, but was resuscitated by a friend and a doctor. According to friend and neighbour Pat Fisher, she was very depressed and had developed a preoccupying interest in the occult.

Alice had written to Pat after this first suicide attempt, saying: 'Life is no longer worth living when you no longer care whether you are wanted or not.' She asked her friend for discretion, saying in a letter published in the 'Letters from Wanjohi' chapter of *White Mischief* that it would be better if people thought she was suffering from post-operative depression: 'It is kinder towards Dickie and my children and better for you and Flo and William.' William was Dr Boyle – her surgeon and lover, father of Alice Percival, who had visited Clouds with us. Flo was her housekeeper.

Alice finally shot herself on 27 September 1941, after marking her furniture and all her possessions for distribution amongst her friends, then tidying her bedroom, filling it with flowers, dressing up and making up the bed with her best bed linen, embroidered with the de Janzé crest. Stories vary: some say her bloody corpse was found by a lady guest who'd returned after shopping, while others say she was discovered, not quite dead, by her housekeeper. Alice had apparently requested that a cocktail party be held at her grave. Nellie Grant, a pioneer who arrived in the protectorate with her husband in 1912, wrote a fitting epitaph in a letter to her daughter Elspeth Huxley: 'Alice de Trafford shot herself the other day – with surer aim, poor thing, than she applied to Raymond at the Gare du Nord. She was very miserable, did about one mile to the gallon on gin, and had had a major operation and lost her beloved little dachshund.'

The first time I visited Alice's former home, its dark atmosphere affected me. I somehow sensed that a lost and lonely soul had lived here. I'd imagine her to have been plagued by buried fears and feelings, perhaps to the point of paranoia. She'd had a strange childhood, treated as a 'grown up' by a father who has been portrayed as unbalanced himself: I couldn't help wondering if Alice had been sexually abused. It also seemed likely that Alice was suffering from a depressive illness, which back then would not have been understood or even recognised.

Or was I reading too much into her? Was Alice just bored by it all, determined to drop the stage curtain with a dramatic flourish?

When I took Alice Percival to Clouds, she had talked about Alice de Trafford. As we headed along the old Wanjohi road and crossed the Malewa River, just before today's newly erupted village called Demi, Alice said, 'This was where Noel and Tom Eaton-Evans lived; I stayed there with them.' She glanced off to the right at some ruins that might once have been farm buildings beside the curve of the river. 'But I can't see the house,' she continued as we slowly navigated our way around rocks and chasms in the muddy road. 'Noel Case, she was originally. She was Alice de Trafford's manager, when she was in her late twenties.

Alice never paid her staff – or Noel, who had to pay them all for her.'

I asked if Noel had been around until Alice's death. 'Yes indeed. A sobbing runner called Noel after Alice's suicide. Noel said that Alice had still been screaming inside the room, but by the time Noel had broken down the door Alice was dead.'

Alice Percival's father, Dr Boyle, who was by all accounts an extremely attractive man, once had a fishing cottage near Ol Kalou, Alice now told us, although he actually lived at Muthaiga. There were no signs of any fishing cottages now. Presumably they too had been smothered by today's noisy, busy and rapidly spreading town – once just a village with a church, one *duka*, a branch of the Kenya Farmers' Association and a post office.

Alice de Janzé had plenty of friends: according to Beryl Markham's biographer, Mary Lovell, Beryl enjoyed parties with Alice. Karen Blixen's published letters record that she also liked Alice, well enough to invite her to stay while sorting matters out before her expulsion from Kenya. On another occasion, Karen relished the discomfort of some of her more strait-laced, highly disapproving guests when Erroll came to visit 'for a bottle' and brought Alice. The 5th Baron Delamere and many other friends were also said to be very fond of Alice. Then there was Idina: there was something puzzling about Alice having regular sex with the man Idina loved. Equally strange, Idina apparently condoned this liberal arrangement with the justification that Alice was her 'best friend'. There was no mention in any books of Idina attending Alice's funeral.

I asked around Alice's former neighbours. One told me that Alice had to have a policewoman living with her all the time. 'You see she was an alcoholic and she owed money. And she had black irises grown especially for her funeral, you know!' she added in hushed tones. Lyduska Piotto said: 'I remember Alice; she had a deep voice and talked a lot. She adored her dogs and she had a pet cheetah. She had a parrot who said "Hole in your bum"!'

It seemed ironic that Alice, who abandoned her own two little girls in France for the Happy Valley life, now lay beneath the pitter-patter of many thousands of little feet. I listened to the sound of the Wanjohi, gurgling unseen below Alice's unmarked grave. Francis Bacon once compared time to a river, 'bringing down to us things which are light and puffed up, but letting weighty matters sink'.

The schoolchildren had backed off and now they just seemed like a bunch of rather bumptious kids in torn, ill-fitting uniforms – blue shirts and crimson sweaters, and shorts for the boys, crimson skirts for the girls. Hemlines were ragged and most of the children's uniforms looked at least seventh-hand. Some wore worn-out shoes, but most had walked to school barefoot. One child, I noticed, seemed much paler than the others, as if his ancestry was rooted somewhere in Happy Valley's heyday. The others had been pushing him forward as if they suspected something amiss too.

The Kikuyu headmaster, who wore a thick black trench coat, welcomed us, asking if we would like to see around the school. I accepted, hoping to find more clues about Alice lurking under desks or behind a door. 'Happy Valley School' was chalked in large letters on the wooden back door of Alice's old manager's house. Exuding wafts of the past, an untrimmed pink rose rambled up one corner of the dark cedar wall, while a stiff parade of white arum lilies grew alongside. The rest of the school buildings – newer, cheaply constructed classrooms of grey stone with tin roofs and wooden shutters – were set to one side, covering what would once have been Alice's front lawn. Someone had more recently planted daisies and marigolds in rows along the paths and around the school offices.

While I avoided stinging nettles on the way to the wooden hut built over the pit-latrine, Solomon had managed to acquire a handful of large, yellow-fleshed crimson plums from the staff room. Had one of Alice's 'garden boys' once planted the plum trees, I wondered, as plum juice ran down our chins. We ate them round the back, like naughty, pilfering schoolchildren.

Solomon suddenly said: 'I can arrange a meeting with some local *wazee* who can remember Harris. They can tell us the real history.'

8

Recollections and Dreams of Alice

Solomon kept his word. Some weeks later we left Gilgil at first light, arriving at Happy Valley School by mid-morning, pausing on the dirt track just below the school to collect Paulo Ngugi, an old man who lived in a tin-roofed mud house beside the Wanjohi River, a few rapids down from Alice's old home. A thin boy who looked about ten, but was probably a malnourished fourteen, watched us with a beaming smile, carrying a trout fingerling threaded on to a reed. 'But there aren't many fish in this river now,' said Solomon sombrely. 'They kill them too fast and no more are coming!'

My Land Rover wheezed its way up a steep, deeply rutted road on to the southern shoulders of Kipipiri to a village called Kiambogo. We parked outside a wooden shack. 'This is the *hoteli*,' Solomon announced, as proudly as if we'd just arrived at the Hilton. The hotel had one cramped room, one small window with a wooden shutter and a narrow door looking out across Alice's former home: grey stripes of the tin roofs of Happy Valley School beside the snaking river. Behind that, the view extended north over a densely populated plateau, stretching all the way to Lake Ol Bolossat and the house where the grisly murder of Fergusson and Bingley had taken place. Kipipiri's highest peak rose up behind our backs, its dark folds still concealing a few secret pockets of forest. To our right the smoke of huge forest fires obscured the mauve-blue walls of the Aberdares.

'You are most welcome,' said a young man in a white T-shirt

advertising an American basketball team. He could have been the hotel manager, the chef or just a friendly passer-by. As he never reappeared, I never found out.

We stooped through the wooden doorway into the relative gloom of the one-roomed hotel where we joined a group of very old men and one old woman, seated on hard benches beneath a ceiling of plastic sacking. The ones who weren't blind peered at me with great interest.

I ordered *chai* (tea) and chapattis all round. There wasn't much else on the menu (not that an actual menu existed) and Solomon said they needed food that was easy to eat: true enough, for most of them had no teeth.

'It's best not to confuse them with too many questions,' he explained. 'I have just asked them to remember things and we shall just listen.'

I listened as the *wazee* took pinches of snuff and reminisced in a mixture of Kikuyu and Swahili. I understood the Swahili, but Solomon had to act as translator for the curious cadences of their native tongue.

Ngugi spoke first. He was already used to my pale and alien looks, having come in my car. 'I was born in about 1928 and I was Alice's cookie. I was doing ironing and housework for Alice,' he told us. 'She was a kind woman – she loved her dogs.' He added that he used to be left in charge of the dogs when she went to see 'Mr Boli' (presumably Dr Boyle). 'Then one day we were instructed by Alice to dig a hole before she shot her dog, then herself,' he said in a matter-of-fact way, as if announcing part of the kitchen routine. 'Then many *wazungu* [white people] came and they buried her. She even left a note on her table saying no one should be blamed!' Ngugi would have been around thirteen when Alice died, which means he must have been the kitchen *toto*.

The old woman, Wanjiru, told us that she'd picked pyrethrum for Alice and helped with her tree nurseries. 'She was a very good woman,' she said firmly, repeating this to nods from the others. Her husband, Kariuki, now totally blind, had looked after Alice's cows. Alice had been very good to her staff, the old couple insisted: she protected them and gave them medicines when they were sick. They called her *wacheke*, which Solomon explained is Kikuyu for 'thin'; in their eyes at least, Alice was underweight, and a thin woman, to a traditional Kikuyu man, is a useless woman.

'The area still keeps Harris's nickname,' Solomon added fondly. 'The people around there call it *Wacheke!*'

I'd imagined we might get a few less complimentary stories, but all the *wazee* kept agreeing that Alice had been a very 'good' woman – perhaps the Kiswahili words *mzuri sana*, meaning 'very good', were also becoming lost in translation.

There were ears to our walls. The volume of voices rose as the curious crowd swelled outside. The one window and door had been firmly shut, so presumably they were waiting for us to emerge so they could get a better look at us, or more probably me. Blonde white women were a rarity up here.

'These young people have no respect!' admonished the only *mzee* who spoke English. 'Happy Valley has become Problem Valley.' He spoke about the pressure on land in this now poor area, and how some families still have ten children. Without hope of a sound education or job prospects, many youngsters escape from their unhappy situation by using alcohol, marijuana and even heroin. He told us with a sigh: 'Our young people copy foreign styles. They become Rastafarians, go to the disco and dance to reggae.'

Solomon launched suddenly into a speech about the forests being destroyed and rivers drying up. 'Yes,' agreed the English-speaking *mzee*, 'even the forest guards are cutting the trees and selling the wood, because you see their salaries are too low to survive on.'

'But they would still do the same if their salaries were very high,' said Solomon sadly, 'because the problem is just greed and corruption everywhere.'

A few *wazee* hadn't spoken yet. 'That one knows no other place than here,' said Solomon, indicating one old man who was staring absent mindedly into his tin mug. Actually, Kabiru seemed oblivious of anything, including our presence.

Karihe, who had no teeth at all, suddenly told us that he blamed the population increase today on the young, unmarried girls. 'They have children too young and they are refusing to listen to their parents!'

'You remember Harris?' Solomon prompted: '*Wacheke?*'

After a vacant stare at me, as if somehow trying to make the connection, Karihe nodded. '*Wacheke*! Eeeeh! She had a car, but she transported her pyrethrum in carts.' He shook his head, then took up a new thread. '*Wacheke*! She had pet gazelles, three ostrich and even a lion. She had a lot of cows.' There was a pregnant pause before he suddenly looked at me, almost accusingly. 'She shot herself at five in the evening and her staff called the manager of the neighbouring farm. She was buried by Murango, Gatitu and another man. Eeeeh! They were each given a cow as a reward. They were sad when she died because they were very devoted to *Wacheke*.' Having made this contribution, Karihe relapsed into unbroken silence.

I asked about drinking and drugs and wild parties. But the elders shook their heads. No, *Wacheke* didn't smoke or drink.

'She closed her door and was completely isolated from other people,' said one.

'She had no husband, but she had lots of white friends,' added another.

'She didn't shoot animals,' explained a third.

'She was very good to everybody . . .'

The swelling crowd outside occasionally became too noisy. Solomon would then stride out and order them to keep away and keep quiet. It was briefly effective. A shaft of light fell across our table as the young girl who seemed to be in charge of kitchen affairs came in through the back door. I could see a skein of blue sky above a small square of golden wheat. A pair of wet trainers were drying on a post in front of a pit-latrine, absorbing the smell of woodsmoke that issued from the kitchen. The kitchen was a simple affair: there was a fire, flanked by several large stones with a blackened *sufuria* (aluminium pan) balanced on top. This arrangement was sheltered from the elements by sheets of tin on three sides, and a low tin roof. The girl who worked in the kitchen had to stoop to go in and stir the *sufuria*. Our refreshments seemed to be taking their time, but the door had been left open, which offered hope.

Occasionally someone would slip through the back door, trying to appear inconspicuous, but Solomon would have none of it: they would be thrown out immediately. We appeared to have exclusive rights to the hotel. One man was admitted; he turned out to be Solomon's eldest brother, Njuguna, who looked well into his sixties.

'*Wacheke* died in 1940,' said Kariuki. 'After her death another white man who we called *Ngororo* came to live there, then John Ring from India, then a man called Sterling.' A 1954 survey map, published by the British War Office and shown to me by veteran land surveyor John Vaughn, shows Alice's home on the river – a church beside it – with the name not of 'Ring' but 'Laing'. Joan Heath, who lived below Clouds in the fifties, remembered 'John Lang' living there. 'Ring', again, was a slip of the Kikuyu tongue.

Kariuki thrust a large pinch of snuff into a nostril that looked almost raw already. He sniffed dramatically and said, 'In those days we were paid thirty shillings a month for our work. Women were paid twenty.'

'Some of us were paid *fifteen* shillings,' grunted Ngugi. 'It was still tough after the Mau Mau, but thanks to Kenyatta we were each given seven acres of land. Some people were given more.'

Having divided up that land for their many children and grandchildren, most of them are now on less than a quarter of an acre. Land, so precious to their people, is in increasingly short supply.

The third round of tea arrived, accompanied at last by the chapattis, and I produced the tin of jam Solomon had suggested I buy back in Captain's only shop. In spite of its startlingly scarlet appearance and synthetic, slightly perfumed smell, it was met with hearty approval and the elders fell silent as they tucked in to the feast. Solomon demolished his jammy chapatti, while relating to the gathering how as a child he had found caves in this area full of bones and human skulls.

The elders nodded: they knew those Mau Mau caves.

'There was also an old cedar tree – the tree of Kimathi,' Solomon added, 'and people carved their names there – including Kimathi!'

'Happy Valley was the best land so it was given to us Kikuyu as a reward for our fighting,' Njuguna added. 'The government also gave us building materials, fertiliser, seeds, gum-boots, *pangas* [machetes], coats, cows and money. You had to repay these loans in thirty years to get your title deed, so now most people here have no title deeds!'

The old men were tired. A few of them began to wander outside and away. Karihe had nodded off and Kabiru had somehow found his way to the door and headed off in an indeterminate direction. 'Somebody will take him home,' said Solomon.

He was right and I felt foolish for being concerned. Everyone knew everyone else and Kabiru would be gently steered home by a passer-by. There were no institutions for the elderly up here, just extended families who still upheld old traditions of revering their elderly members, looking after them until they passed away. Traditionally, when elderly Kikuyu were close to death, they were left outside the hut to die and for the hyenas to dispose of. Nowadays they are buried – usually on their land.

We'd been hours inside the hotel, eating and drinking mountains of delicious chapattis and extremely sweet tea stewed with milk, but the entire bill came to less than 200 shillings (about £1.50).

As the tea party drew itself to a natural end, I watched the old men hobble away and wondered whether they had courteously told us good things about Alice de Janzé because they thought that was what we wanted to hear. Or had she simply been very discreet in front of the servants, as one was in those days? Nobody in that era had African friends, let alone entertained Africans in their houses – apart from the 3rd Baron Delamere, who invited the Maasai into his home to talk cattle. It was a habit not always palatable to his fellow white settlers, who would object, when dropping by, to find half-naked warriors squatting companionably in his living room. The settlers further muttered behind Delamere's back because he tolerated their frequent thefts of his stock and 'overpaid' them.

That night we were to stay with Solomon's cousin Jane, who lived in a small and basic but comfortable stone house that seemed the height of luxury beside its many mud-walled neighbours. Jane lives next door to Solomon's old family home, built on the plot allocated to Solomon's mother in the early 1960s: all once part of Alice's 600 acres.

Jane's husband was away – delivering vegetables to town in his lorry (judging by the state of the roads that could take days) – but Jane hardly ever seemed alone, as numerous visitors and relations all seemed to be staying too. Dozens of children sat around the fire in the separate wooden hut that served as a kitchen. Tea was brewing and a tiny ginger kitten peeped at me from under a stool. I was on my way to the outdoor pit-latrine, watched by rows of bright, black eyes, my every gesture offering great amusement. When I said *'jambo'* in greeting, the kids dissolved into giggles, failing to smother their laughter behind their hands. When I emerged from the small, wooden building that reminded me of Grandpa Potts' flying hut in *Chitty Chitty Bang Bang*, a very thin, quiet girl of about thirteen brought me a bucket of hot water to wash in. She averted her eyes when I spoke to her, did not reply and certainly did not giggle before she slipped away with nervous deference. Often, in very poor Kenyan families, a girl will be sent off to relations to work in exchange for food and basic lodgings. It's an arrangement open to all forms of abuse.

Later that afternoon, Solomon and I walked over a saddle that Solomon called 'the flyover', down a path between steep cultivated fields. We looked below us, across fields of beans, potatoes and maize, at Alice's former home. 'We are at the place where Harris found the lion cubs,' said Solomon. 'I remember this area with so much forest and so many animals!' he added sadly.

Numerous passers-by stopped to greet us and shake hands. All were puzzled to see a white woman in the area, so Solomon was enjoying spinning out the explanations. I was in my own world, looking east across a sweeping, spectacular view that had changed so dramatically in forty years. But soon the screen of smoke from the burning Aberdares blurred much of the detail.

Walking back and climbing higher on another dirt track, we were heading to the smallholding owned by Solomon's brother, Njuguna. 'I was born here, right on this *shamba*, in 1959,' Solomon said, extending his hand towards the field of beans. We walked up a path, trying to ignore another fiery backdrop of fiercely burning forest on Kipipiri. Solomon briefly pointed out the site where his hut had been

burnt to the ground, then turned his attention to the larger fires that
silently erased our view of the mountains. As we joined a buzzing
cloud of flies and more relatives of Solomon's in Njuguna's simple
mud house with its earth floor and wallpaper of old newspapers, I
marvelled at Solomon's evident and astounding capacity for leaving
the past behind.

At Solomon's cousin Jane's that evening we were generously fed with
irio and mutton stew. Afterwards the two young boys who seemed
to live there too, although they weren't Jane's sons, struggled with
their homework by the dim light of a solar bulb. The night was cold
and, after the local drunk had visited to watch a football game on the
solar-powered TV, I was happy to roll up in a blanket in my allocated
bedroom. I was concerned that I was taking somebody else's room and
felt certain the family had only butchered a sheep for our benefit, but in
rural Kenya – or certainly Happy Valley – unconditional hospitality is
the norm. Back in the twenties I'm sure Idina's and Alice's hospitality
knew no bounds, but then they could well afford it.

It was a noisy night, thanks to the heart-shaped clock outside my
bedroom door: it welcomed each hour with a shattering wail, every
note rising in anguish, followed by chimes reminiscent of a cat being
skewered. It chimed ten at one in the morning – and so it continued
through the night until it yowled at me fourteen times. I gave up on
sleep and sat up in bed.

The window pane glowed and flickered orange – I could see the
jagged lines of forest fires as they danced along the length of the
Aberdares, some turning back on themselves, forming angry red rings,
flaring furiously against the dark mountainous bulk. I imagined the
many creatures fleeing in terror from those flames.

At six in the morning the jubilant clock exploded into a sound that
was a combination of a shriek, a howl and a wail – fifteen times. Solomon
hadn't slept much either, he told me as we cradled steaming tin mugs of
tea in the crystal dawn, sniffing the smoke from the burning mountains.

'I had many conversations all through the night and I could not rest
because I was then thinking about them,' he explained.

'Conversations?' I asked, imagining he'd sat up putting the world to rights with his relatives.

'Dreams,' he said gloomily, 'with dead people. But I was not asleep!'

I moved stiffly into the morning sun, too weary to hear his dreams. I changed the subject to forest fires and we both turned to face the eastern sky with its innocently slim spirals of smoke, signalling doom when the later morning winds began to brew around these mountains.

II

Monkey Business and Murder

9

Into the Heart of the Valley

I n his autobiography, Solomon nostalgically recalls the thick forest all around the simple, one-roomed hut where he grew up, just above Alice's old home. It was here that Solomon developed his love of colobus monkeys: 'I was fascinated to watch them and I used to think of them as another tribe of people living in the forest. I tried to listen to what they were saying to one another.'

Solomon's interest in animals, birds, insects and plants convinced his peers he was mad. His mother, certain he was possessed by a bad spirit, sent her youngest son away to live with relations, miles from home. First he lived with a senile grandmother, and then a cruel aunt who used her hut floor as a toilet at night and made Solomon clean up after her, with his hands.

Solomon, the nonconformist, refused to accept this as his lot. Hungry and thin, but not cowed, he escaped, stowing away on a Rift Valley-bound *matatu*. When he was discovered, with no money to pay his fare, he was thrown out in the Rift Valley farming town of Nakuru – closer to home, but still too far to walk. The young Solomon begged for a while and when the white *memsahibs* doing their weekly shopping didn't spare him a few shillings and the Indian shop owners had no scraps to throw to him either, he stole food from kiosks. Survival was risky: he was low in the pecking order of street children, who were regularly rounded up by the police and driven away, some of them never to be seen again. One day Solomon was caught, thrown roughly

into the back of a police van, then locked up in a stinking cell with so
many other boys and adult men that there was standing room only.
For his 'crimes' he was thoroughly beaten before being thrown back
amongst the criminals.

Small, skinny, wily and lucky, Solomon managed to escape and
run like the wind to the nearest main road, which happened to be the
one heading towards Gilgil. A *matatu* stopped and a fellow traveller,
who felt sorry for the strange, wild-eyed little boy, paid his fare to
Gilgil, then gave him enough money for the next leg of his journey
from Gilgil to Wanjohi. Thus Solomon made it back home, the final
miles completed on foot. He writes proudly that the return of Happy
Valley's 'lost boy' was even announced on the local radio. Luckily his
mother seemed relieved to see him too.

Solomon's local fame spurred him on to follow his dreams: at his
primary school his tree-planting activities grew into an environmental
club. By the time he had finished his primary education Solomon
had earned the respect of a kind teacher, who decided he was worth
sponsoring. There's no such thing as a free secondary education
in Kenya, so Solomon was one of the lucky few able to head off to
boarding school, where he worked hard in hope of a bright future.
But after finishing school, like so many other young Kenyans, then
and today, he had little hope of affording any further education or
even finding employment. Thus Solomon began his voluntary youth
conservation groups and tree nursery projects, slowly building up a
following of other unemployed young people.

For Solomon, our trips provided opportunities to check on his tree
nurseries all around Happy Valley, as well as to find out how many
more colobus monkeys had been trapped, killed or chased away. He
said it gave him extra credibility to be seen in a vehicle, albeit rather an
old and dirty one. I, meanwhile, was becoming ever more aware of the
area's conservation issues, alongside the history of the settlers who had
once fleetingly occupied this troubled area.

On one of our very early Happy Valley safaris, we'd stopped
beside a sprawling muddle of roadside kiosks, their signboards always

innovative: from the London Hotel to the Cheerful Shop. While Solomon went to find one of his colobus-friendly assistants, I watched a chicken wander nonchalantly into a bar. It was kicked out of the way by an emerging drunk – though not too drunk to spot me and cross the road, where he collapsed on the bonnet of my Land Rover and broadcast his financial problems and the woes of having seven children to anyone who wanted to listen.

'White mischief has become black mischief,' complained Solomon as he materialised on the passenger seat, having removed the drunk, who had begun to bang his head on the bonnet.

In my rear-view mirror I could see the smoke from the neglected fires of charcoal burners, running loose, eating deep into the forest, destroying yet more trees and expelling those remaining wild creatures.

'But we can return soon,' said Solomon, 'to the house of Harris's neighbours, Mary Miller and Major Bogosta. His house is very old.'

'Bogosta?' I asked, puzzled.

Solomon wrote it down. 'Bockostone'.

'Ah! Buxton,' I said.

Geoffrey Buxton was the first settler in Happy Valley – before Mau Mau and both world wars; before Idina and Joss. According to a mysterious somebody who'd once lived there and drawn a very wobbly looking map by hand, then sent it to a friend of a friend who'd recently sent it to me, Major G. Buxton's Satimma (sic) Farm was 2,500 acres. Next door, heading north towards Ol Bolossat, following the edge of the Aberdares Forest Reserve, was David Leslie-Melville's Airdrie Farm of 5,000 acres, and bordering both was Ketai Farm – which, the artist had noted, was 'bought in 1927 from Hamilton Harrison and Matthews Solicitors, previously Charles Gordon's'. He'd been Idina's second husband, with whom she'd run to Kenya on the rebound from her first marriage. Then, still heading north, there was Delap's farm Rayetta, and beyond that Slains. This area, then, could have been Idina's initial Happy Valley home. Meanwhile, on the other side of Buxton's, towards the Kipipiri forest, the map marked Alice de Trafford's Wanjohi Farm, which was 600 acres. Apart from the fact that the map is upside down if you put in the poles correctly, the rivers were right and the names tallied with my research.

Our next safari took us into the heart of the valley to visit the old homes of Alice's former neighbours. It was the dry season and the stony road from Ol Kalou to Wanjohi was flanked by flat, dusty beige country, its spikes of grass interspersed with the red-orange blooms of the hardy aloe plants. The blue bulk of the Aberdares ran alongside, to our left. Our progress was bumpy, dusty and slow, affording us plenty of time to make out a patch of old roof or wall, or a sudden flash of colour from an exotic flowering tree or shrub hiding behind the newer, concealing rows of fast-growing, non-indigenous trees. This was a safari planned to last several days and we were in no hurry.

We stopped at a grey-stone, red-roofed house, built in Cape Dutch style – the first surviving house we'd reached on the right. The man who lived there, Solomon said, 'used to whip his people!'

'A very cruel man,' Bubbles Delap expanded later. 'He used to beat his staff.' She used to ride over to see him (several hours away, but to young Bubbles it was presumably rare entertainment). 'He was always very pleasant, inviting me in for tea. His wife would disappear hastily into the kitchen,' she explained. 'But then once he told me not to ride there again unless invited. He was up to no good!'

A few months before independent Kenya's new flag was raised at midnight on 12 December 1963, J.M. Kruger from Ol Kalou wrote to the *East African Standard*, complaining of the increase in violent crime, concluding it couldn't be stopped because there were so many unemployed, hungry and landless people in the area waiting for their free gifts of promised land. Kruger ended his letter: 'In these circumstances, some of us have decided to sell our loose assets and leave the country before independence.' Presumably Kruger joined the many disillusioned Boer farmers on their trek back to South Africa, following the footsteps of their ancestors in reverse, just over half a century after they had first arrived to carve out a living in fresh lands. These dyed-in-the-wool men were not prepared to live under black rule.

An avenue of chopped-looking jacarandas lined the drive to Kruger's former house. The place felt eerily uninhabited as we wandered around the dry, empty pond, past an overgrown cypress hedge and round the back of the house to the many outbuildings, one of which would have been an outdoor kitchen. There was a locked door and a sign saying that this was the Land Settlement Office. The window panes were painted white, some sealed with newspaper from the inside, making it impossible to look in, although one broken window revealed a stack of files under the dust and cobwebs. Although it was a weekday, the silence was all-pervasive, as if the house had found peace at last and simply frozen into the bliss of it for ever.

'Where are the people who work here?' I asked Solomon, who smiled at me kindly as if I'd asked a stupid question.

When our car refused to start, a man suddenly appeared, rubbing the sleep out of his eyes. 'I am the land settlement officer,' he announced without enthusiasm, although presumably we did not look like anyone who would be asking him to find our file. He had been here three years, he added, as if that might excuse his exhaustion. We explained the car situation and asked for assistance in push starting it. After a despairing glance around at the surrounding emptiness, which failed to conjure up any help, the man looked at the heavy Land Rover wearily.

'It will just need a small push,' I said brightly.

I was wrong, of course, and after we'd driven away from the poor man, who looked as if he would rather fall asleep under one of the jacarandas than walk the distance back to wherever he'd emerged from, Solomon said: 'He is just staying here to rest!'

After inhaling plenty more dust, we came to another house on the left that Solomon said was 'Gillett's house'. This tallied with the 1954 survey map, which differed from the hand-drawn version in showing the names of more recent settlers. John and David Gillett were two brothers about whom stories varied. 'They used to go and visit Idina,' said Bubbles. But Joan Heath, a Kipipiri resident in the fifties, told me, 'John and David Gillett weren't very sociable. We occasionally saw them at Ol Kalou.'

Tim Hutchinson's *Up-Country Directory* told me that Major David Weham Gillett married Myra, was at Ol Kalou in 1948, and was second-in-command in the Kenya Regiment, after being in the King's African Rifles from 1939 to 1946. His brother, Captain John Stuart, married Moerag. Ian Parker recorded in *The Last Colonial Regiment* that David Gillett ended his war service in the senior ranks and rejoined the Kenya Regiment as a private, but was immediately recommissioned.

Gillett's stone house, with a mossy, green tin roof and various outbuildings, was built on a tongue-shaped spit of land, surrounded by an almost circular bend in the river. The place seemed deserted until a gaggle of small barefoot children in ragged sweaters appeared on the other side of the gate and climbed through the fence to get a better look at us. They didn't speak English – except for one word: 'Sweet!' they chanted, holding out dirty hands. I managed to find a grimy half roll of mints in the car before we drove on.

A little further along the road, Solomon instructed me to turn left again. 'To a very big house,' he promised. 'It was the house of Gibbs.'

Lieutenant-Colonel Alistair Monteith Gibb was the son of a Scottish engineer, Brigadier-General Sir Alexander Gibb, founder in 1922 of the British engineering consultancy Sir Alexander Gibb & Partners. Amongst its many designs was the 1936 Kincardine Bridge across the Firth of Forth. In 1927 Alistair married Rosemary, daughter of the Earl of Lovelace; they were divorced in 1940, after which he married the Hon. Daisy Yoskyl Consuelo Pearson, daughter of the 2nd Viscount Cowdray, (whose mother was a Spencer-Churchill) in 1944.

Alexander Gibb was great-uncle to the current Lady Delamere. Lord Delamere later informed me that Alistair Gibb had bright-red hair, therefore half the Happy Valley children of the time were born with red hair. 'They all swapped men on a Sunday,' he said, 'the women staying at home and the men moving wives.' Lady Delamere laughed it off with, 'Oh well . . .' The Rooken-Smith brothers, former neighbours, told me later that John Gillett had managed Gibb's farm. Alistair Gibb himself, when he was around, generously supported the fledgling Ol Kalou polo club (Joss had been a great polo player, initiating the game on a rough field at Slains in the 1920s), becoming chairman. Ironically he was killed in a polo accident in 1955 in Britain.

The imposing house was visible from some distance away while we approached it down a long, straight drive. As we grew closer I could see that this stone building with its steep shingle roof still looked reasonably intact by Happy Valley standards. The Aberdares reared up close behind, with some caves over to the left, about halfway up, where the Mau Mau had once hidden, and where before that, according to Solomon, the Happy Valley-ites had gone to wine and dine around splendid fires, their gourmet meals carried up the steep paths by a fleet of obedient servants.

The spring that had once risen in the Aberdares and gushed down to supply water to the house had dried up, Solomon said. However, in spite of this former supply of fresh mountain spring water, he added, he'd been told by a former employee of Gibb's that this English gentleman insisted on bringing in bottled water. I looked at the cleft in the mountain wall behind us, imagining it once long ago, misty from the spray of the waterfalls tumbling down. Now the ravine was dry and the vegetation sparse.

We parked in front, on the lower terrace of what once would have been a vast green lawn, sloping towards dams and a long view. An old cabbage tree grew in front of the house, but otherwise there was little garden left. 'Colobus love this tree,' said Solomon. Unlike the cluster of eucalyptus trees behind the house, which, he complained, suck up valuable water and prevent the growth of indigenous plants.

We walked around the house, past semi-circular steps at the back door and the walled-in staff quarters to one side. We counted five chimneys. There were swarms of bees in the roof. I followed Solomon through an open side door, unable to shake off the feeling I was trespassing, down a long dark passage with locked doors at regular intervals. There was a pile of charcoal at the far end of the corridor. Chicken feathers were scattered around; either there'd been a cock fight, it appeared, or a chicken had been slaughtered in here. An old flip-flop lay halfway along the corridor, as if shed by some ghostly figure while running from something. Yet the whole place seemed extraordinarily empty, even of atmosphere. It somehow felt as though it had been built, but barely lived in.

Back in the bright sunshine, we walked around to the front door, facing west and looking out towards the distant blue ridge that was the far side of the Rift Valley. There was a sign on the door: 'Assistant Chief's Office'. Another haven of apathy, it seemed.

A neighbour had wandered over by now and he told us the old house was part of a secondary school. It was term time and the quiet behind the sealed doors was remarkable. Had the pupils taken vows of silence? Seemingly in answer to my puzzled thoughts, the headmaster himself appeared from behind a wall, introducing himself as Ngugi.

'Is this really a school?' I couldn't help asking.

'Yes, but it is not in use yet,' he told us. 'There is no money to renovate it, but if we can find money we will probably use it as dormitories for the girls.' He looked at me hopefully, but I couldn't see that it needed any renovations, just a good sweeping and scrubbing which wouldn't cost anything. He was unable to help us with any enticing titbits on the house's past, but stressed we were welcome to visit again any time, and bring friends, presumably rich ones who might help with the required funding.

Continuing along the road, passing the cleft in the Aberdares which had once been the waterfall above Slains and the desecrated forest that lay above Rayetta, we reached the ridges of Kipipiri, rising to our right. On its northern foothills, a small knoll showed us the position of Alice de Janzé's former farm, which back in the 1920s and 30s would have spread over Kipipiri's north-facing, forested shoulders. Now these were untidily adorned with a mishmash of metal roofs, garish in the sunlight. We were entering the top end of the steep-walled Wanjohi valley.

Nowadays Wanjohi town, the noisy new addition to the valley, nestles between these northernmost slopes of Kipipiri and the long, protective wall of the Aberdares. This green enclave, trapped in by mountains on two sides, is the only true valley, although of course none of the original scarlet women of unscrupulous morals ever actually lived in it. As I wondered what colour would be ascribed to men of similar morality, the shadows of the enclosing mountains fell on us. It was early, but the valley had already lost its sun. Solomon wound up his window while I shivered and reached for my sweater. We drove into Wanjohi town with its scruffy stone shops, butcheries smelling of last week's slaughter, piles of second-hand clothes for sale along the roadsides and vegetables stacked on makeshift stick racks in open kiosks. The only sign of wealth was a Catholic church with a metal steeple and a fairly modest (for the Catholics) stained-glass window.

'It was built when I was in standard two,' announced Solomon, following my gaze. 'I was ten and it was 1971.' Solomon had told me he was born in 1959, so he was evidently getting his sums wrong. 'See those big trees over there?' He pointed over to the right – far more excitedly now. 'That was my school and those are the trees I planted at the same time they made this church. Now my trees are taller than the church!'

It was remarkable how Solomon could talk about his childhood and youth with any enthusiasm. Things had improved marginally by the time he reached his twenties; his mother, though now ailing, had mellowed towards her youngest son, while always warning him to keep his head down. But after she died, Solomon was left at the mercy of his brothers, whose contempt for him had not waned over the years. During one of his many foot safaris through the wider Happy Valley area, Solomon had met Esther. Once she'd agreed to be his wife, he took her home, but his brothers opposed the match, refusing to accept her into the family fold, not least because she was uncircumcised.

Solomon and Esther built themselves a small hut on the edge of his family land where they constantly had to watch their backs. Esther gave birth to their first two children, both daughters, and cultivated a small corner of the plot to grow their food, while Solomon found temporary work in the tea estates of the Nandi Hills in western Kenya. Many people in Kenya leave their rural homes and families to find work in towns or on large farms, sending money home. Now Solomon was able to send Esther the bulk of his monthly wages, pitiful as these were, so at least she had a little spare cash for luxuries like tea and sugar, or in case one of the children fell sick.

Solomon was fired from his job after he'd reported the illegal charcoal burning that daily destroyed the nearby forest. He was lucky to find another job and even luckier when his constant cries about the destruction of the forest were heard by an expatriate manager. The man listened to Solomon, took him under his wing, promoted him and created a new job for him, starting tree nurseries with the aim to replant the area's decimated forests that had once surrounded the tea plantations. Solomon was ecstatic to be embarking on an environmental career at last, as well as now having a little more money to send home.

But his luck ran out. Tribal clashes hit the area, accompanied by violent killing, looting and burning. Solomon's expatriate friend returned to the UK. Solomon tried to continue his tree-planting work, but without his friend's support he soon discovered that no more money was forthcoming for 'unimportant' conservation projects. It was then that Solomon received the cruel news that his hut had been burnt down and his wife and children chased away from their home.

Solomon pointed out where his old home had been, on the lower foothills of Kipipiri, above Alice's former farm. We drove on, passing the Wanjohi River, which runs through the town, its pristine waters sullied by a jumble of plastic litter. Off to the left was the road that went up to Delap's, first crossing the river. We drove along it, as Solomon wanted to show me 'a historic house'. Immediately after the bridge, on the right, a stark brick ruin, stripped naked of roof, windows and doors, stood in the middle of an untidy field of green grass behind a broken fence. Once it must have been an imposing double-storey home and, going by the hand-drawn map, it would have been on Charles Gordon's Ketai Farm.

'Any idea whose it was?' I asked Solomon as we gazed at the ruin.

'It was the house of somebody called Davis.' Solomon had only known it in the early 1960s. 'Then later my mother took her pyrethrum there. Then it was the office of the settlement board. Now it has been grabbed!'

We drove back into Wanjohi, turning left, then left again to

Wanjohi hospital. Solomon's friend Suzanne, a Canadian volunteer studying AIDS, was temporarily staying there. 'Suzanne likes colobus monkeys very much,' Solomon enthused, 'and she helps me.' Suzanne was currently away, but had said we could stay in her house. 'It is a nice house,' Solomon smiled. 'It even has a toilet that can flush!' The relatively new hospital lay between two rivers, one of which was dry. Green grass, soiled with litter, surrounded the ample, mostly empty staff housing. White arum lilies stood stiffly to attention in a line along one side of the hospital. We walked past the long, open corridors stretching between the empty wards. A smell of eucalyptus and pine wafted across from the trees lining the river banks, but there was no whiff of disinfectant, chloroform or even hospital food. Through a window I could see an empty bed with a curtain rail around it, but no curtain. Apart from a poster about a World Bank project on sexually transmitted infections, there was no sign of life – or even death.

Somewhere underneath all this, Solomon said, lay the foundations of the former house of a white farmer the locals had called *Murefu*, meaning tall. One old man we spoke to said that 'Ceaserone' had lived here: was this Lyduska's Count Cesaroni? The 1954 map (which misspelt or simply missed out altogether some names of people and farms, but presumably once helped British troops work out what was where during Mau Mau) marked the dwelling beside the Wanjohi River as 'Turner' – next door to 'Case'.

I asked around exhaustively but nobody had heard of any Turner living in the Wanjohi valley. Finally Bubbles Delap unexpectedly came up with the answer. 'Oh yes, the Turners left for England,' she said, 'so we leased their farm – it was called Flau Farm.' (She spelt it out, in case I'd spelt it wrong, which I had.) 'It was right on the river – we used to swim there. Once I remember a buffalo swimming down it! We grew daffodils there . . .'

Another of Solomon's colobus-loving friends was introduced as Mama John, using the name of her eldest son. This is common in Kenya – I have grown used to being called Mama Michael. Mama John lived next door to Suzanne in another of several hospital staff houses – built on what was once presumably part of the Turners' and then the

Delaps' garden. Judging by the older, hand-drawn map we were on land that would once have been Charles Gordon's before the second wave of post-Second World War settlers arrived to try their luck on smaller farms, sized down from those of the original soldier-settler scheme.

Mama John's husband was a doctor, employed by the government, but he'd gone to work elsewhere as the hospital was devoid of equipment, including drugs. John himself, her eldest son of about three, was aptly dressed for the cold in a woolly hat and anorak. He jumped on to my lap with a beaming smile and said: 'Kendal!'

'Kendal was the volunteer from America who was here some time ago,' explained Solomon, 'and to us all white people look much the same!'

'We all liked Kendal,' said Mama John from the kitchen.

'Why are there no medicines at this hospital?' I asked Mama John when she came back with steaming tin mugs of sweet, stewed tea.

She shrugged.

'But what do people do when they are sick?' I persisted.

'Finding medicines is *bahati* [luck],' she replied. 'People just have to go to the private clinics. That is where my husband has gone to work.'

The doctor came back later. He explained that a Catholic missionary organisation had built the hospital, but then left it up to the government. 'But how can we work here when the government gives no money or equipment?' he asked.

John was showing me the exercise book in his school bag. Somebody had written the alphabet in capitals, and he had scribbled his own designs below each letter.

'Kendal,' he repeated happily.

The doctor told me that Kendal and her husband, both VSOs, had been deported for upsetting some political bigwig who was illegally selling endangered hardwood from the 'protected' forest. Such stories are so common in Kenya one's mind tends to gloss over the details.

Our hot water (for washing, Mama John explained) was heating outside on a *jiko*, a small charcoal-heated cooker, and meanwhile we were served delicious yellow omelettes made from eggs laid by the friendly chickens who kept wandering into the kitchen. Mama John's house was luxurious compared with most of Happy Valley's rural homes; its stone walls encased several rooms, albeit very small ones. The cramped living room managed to squeeze in a bed, two sofas, two low tables with crocheted covers in a loud pink, a very modern, shiny dresser and a sewing machine. The walls sported a glitzy clock, all gold paint and roses, and several out-of-date calendars with very European scenes – tulips and windmills, New Forest ponies and the Alps.

Outside, the grass was flecked with gum leaves and plastic litter. 'Case planted these gum trees,' said Solomon, indicating the 100-feet-high giants, quietly shedding their aromatic leaves around us. 'I remember a big dam here when I was a boy. There were so many birds then.'

Damp darkness descended like a heavy blanket, cold air blowing down from the Aberdares, catching us unawares. It was time to bed down in Suzanne's house, where there were light switches but no electricity. 'Once there was a generator, but it was stolen,' said Mama John, producing a candle. A few dim lights issued from one hospital window – 'the maternity wing,' she said. I consoled myself with the thought that as most Kenyan women are so practised at having (and delivering) babies, presumably the lack of light and doctors was not a problem.

The lights of Wanjohi town were on now, the evening star suspended above as if poised to guide the wise men. Voices floated up, and somewhere in the town a dog yelped. Exhausted from the long day on rough roads we slept well, grateful for a proper toilet and even a shower – with cold running water. I opted for washing in the hot water Mama John had heated in a *sufuria*.

Mama John brewed us more sweet tea the next morning. I took mine outside, drinking in the bracing air and wondering if Idina had stood on this same spot when she first arrived in Africa, a young bride for the second time, her two young sons back in England. How had she felt, beneath that initial giddy exhilaration of being in a beautiful, untouched valley in Kenya's highlands?

10

The First and the Cursed

After many farewells and John's disappointed face to see us, like Kendal, leave so soon, we drove on past a track on the left where Solomon pointed at the newly built house lurking behind a high kei-apple hedge: 'That used to be the home of W.H. Case. Now only the old chimney is left.' In Kenya people tend to have signs on their gates, usually with their initials and surname, which would explain why Solomon remembered the name and initials from his childhood days. There was something faintly disconcerting about the place. 'It is cursed,' said Solomon after we had passed. 'All the family there have died, and the ones who are left, they are mad!'

'Mad?' I asked.

'Yesss! See there?' Solomon pointed at a shadowy figure on the road ahead, who dived into a hedge and vanished.

Debbie Case, who lived in Naivasha and did tireless charity work in the area, was the granddaughter of William Case, who originally came from Australia. Excited to have first-hand information on another settler, I spoke to Debbie, who'd endured a difficult life and was to die prematurely of cancer. She explained that William and his wife, Elizabeth, had three children: two boys, one of them Debbie's father, and their sister Noey.

'Noel?' I asked, thinking of several books on Happy Valley which mentioned Noel Case.

'Not Noel,' Debbie insisted. 'Noey – the writers got it wrong.'

Vi Case, Debbie's aunt, had died fairly recently in Australia. They'd lived on the Malewa River, nearer Ol Kalou. Vi Case had probably been the last person alive who might have known Count Cesaroni and the Turners – she might even have remembered Charles Gordon.

'I remember the station was called *stationi ya sanduku* [Kiswahili for 'the station of the suitcase'],' Debbie told me. No railway had ever ventured into Happy Valley, so presumably she meant one of the stations on the now defunct Gilgil–Thomson's Falls line, which was begun at the end of 1928 and completed in 1930, making life marginally easier for settlers who, up until then, had to haul ox wagons through deep, glue-like mud which would regularly engulf the only road.

Former neighbours confirmed that the Case family hadn't been remotely interested in the parties of the Happy Valley set, although Noey had got to know Alice de Janzé well. When her parents were building their house in the late 1920s, Noey had ventured up the hill to look around Alice's farm. It was available for rent while Alice was in exile. The Cases took it on, Noey tending the garden and house, then staying on as housekeeper when Alice returned in 1933.

Still in search of Buxton, we drove deeper into the valley. With Alice's farm now up on our right, Solomon directed me left down a track until we came to a wooden house on the right, just beside the track. 'This was the house of Mr Shaht!' said Solomon. 'The manager of Major Bogosta.'

Karihe, one of the old men we'd spoken to in the *hoteli* above Alice's house, had remembered Buxton's manager. 'We called him Kanyinya. He trained horses. Everyone in Happy Valley took their horses there, until he left in 1939. He had cows too,' Karihe added with considerably more enthusiasm, 'and his other name was Mr Shaht.'

It was a small, modest, rectangular house: cedar off-cut walls, capped by a tin roof. There were no windows, only wooden shutters that looked as if they had not been opened for a long time, giving the impression the house was sleeping soundly. An elderly man in a torn shirt came out, taking off his hat to reveal white hair. He was delighted at our interest in his house. 'I was born here,' he told us in Kiswahili, 'I became the gardener for Mr Shaht. He was a very good man. I live in here now and I look after the garden. I built this new kitchen here after Kanyinya left.' He pointed to the outdoor kitchen, standing like a modern shrine to those old, colonial outdoor kitchens, where the *memsahibs* taught astonished Kikuyu 'boys' the intricacies of soufflés and brandy snaps. Today's affair was a basic kitchen, open on one side with a charcoal *jiko*, a low stool for the person cooking to sit on and a washing line stretching from its corner post to a tree. Tea and maize meal with a garnish of vegetables were probably the forte of this kitchen.

The old gardener pointed down the rough track. 'Major Buxton's house is just down there. It is even older and made with mud. I was told it was the first house built around here. But Major Buxton lived only half the year here, the rest of the time he lived in England.'

A little boy in flip-flops several sizes too big followed us around shyly as we looked at the garden, where surprisingly there was a profusion of red and yellow daisies, dahlias, a tangle of roses and even a productive orchard, with tree tomatoes and apples rising triumphantly above the maize. 'I planted these flowers and trees, so I will always look after them,' the old man said proudly, his eyes suddenly clouding. Then he brightened again: 'You will come inside for tea,' he said.

'We just had . . .' I began, but Solomon gave me a look. Nobody is allowed to refuse tea, let alone be in any sort of hurry, in rural Kenya, so we trooped into the dark house, ducking under the broken guttering, along a wooden passage, through a panelled room and into a dark sitting room with a red-brick fireplace. We met the old gardener's wife, then another younger wife – although I didn't establish whose – and a gaggle of youngsters who could have been children or grandchildren.

The young wife said in English, 'Wherever you go you must take breakfast!' and we were ushered into a small dark room and invited to sit on a new, imitation-leather, high-backed seat. The old gardener, wise to the ways of Europeans, forced open the shutter. The house, one eye suddenly open wide, was filled with a shaft of light down which specks of golden dust danced. We were looking on to the sunlit side of the Aberdares, so close you could see the cap of moorland above the feathery forests of bamboo, clinging to the steep upper slopes. The young wife chattered away, enjoying practising her English on us. 'My sister is married to a *mzungu*,' she explained. 'Myself, I am a nursery school teacher at Passenga. You know the place?'

All the old gardener's children lived here, he explained happily. The grown-up ones had their own wooden huts, erected in the field outside. There was a wonderful sense of security about it all, and a contentment seldom found in our own scattered, fragmented families. But the old wooden house was letting itself go, as if it was too old to care any longer. The planks of the floor were blackened by the *jiko* in the middle of the room. The smoke-darkened ceiling was pitted with vacant, black holes.

The old gardener talked about a Mr Griffin, who had also lived here. His memories came and went, suddenly melting away like the dew on the grass outside.

After we had been generously fed with *uji*, delicious maize meal porridge, and augmented by more tea, we thanked our kind hosts. 'It was a blessing to have you,' they assured us.

'Tell Mrs Shaht,' said the old man suddenly, 'that I still care for the garden every day.' He sighed and went quiet.

His grandchildren giggled behind their hands, but I shook his hand and said, 'Of course I will.' At that stage it was a rash promise, as I had no idea where the Shahts, actually the Charts, were.

Through Janie Begg's sister, Sheila, I was able to contact Jean Konschell, née Chart, in Zimbabwe. Jean wrote back promptly, delighted to hear the garden they'd enjoyed from 1930 for almost two decades was still blooming. She recalled her happy childhood 'in that beautiful valley, playing polo and fishing in rivers that were teeming with trout'. Solomon had already pointed out to me the old polo ground, still a flat open space, as if commemorating those galloping steeds.

Jean related how her father, Fred Nye-Chart, had been five when his family was one of those paid by the British government to come up from South Africa prior to the First World War. Fred's mother had been the eldest of nine Aggett children, some of whose descendants still live in Kenya today. Fred had later become farm manager for Colonel Buxton and his partner Sir Alexander Gibb. After the Buxtons returned to England, Fred had been made a partner in Satima Farm. The Charts had then moved from the small wooden house to the Buxtons' bigger, Tudor-style house.

'My father was known as *Bwana Siagi* [Kiswahili for 'Mr Butter'],' Jean wrote, 'because he made butter which had to go by ox wagon, taking two days, to Ol Kalou. The wagon then returned with supplies and the mail.' As well as the dairy herd, the Charts kept Arab horses. 'As children we didn't have prams, but were led on a horse, strapped in a basket saddle. Our father often rode in a horse and buggy. Later on we had an old Ford which was occasionally cranked up to take us to boarding school in Nakuru. But horses were our main recreation and transport. My sister, brother and I used to ride to the Millers' house next door . . . a beautiful home and garden and a lovely Norland Nanny named Marjory Thompson.'

She continued, 'Dad was not allowed to join up for the war as he was needed on the land, running all the surrounding farms for those who did join up. I remember my mother growing vegetables in that beautiful black soil and packing them into *kikapus* to go to Nairobi. That was her war effort.' Like all the other families in the colony, the Charts anxiously listened to every radio broadcast for news of family back in England.

Later on Fred Chart had several heart attacks and eventually had to move to a lower altitude near Lake Elmenteita, where he farmed – not far from my current home, near the southern end of Lord Delamere's Soysambu. The 5th Baron Delamere remembered him, relating how once, when invited up for lunch, Fred had given him some grass to plant which was supposedly good for feeding cattle. 'He'd bought it from what was then Southern Rhodesia and the grass is now all over the country,' said Lord Delamere, adding that Chart had the grass's scientific name wrong.

'Fred Chart was *kali*,' Janie Begg told me, using that wonderful Kiswahili word that emphasises the sharpness of a knife, the potency of a curry or the fierceness of a dog – or a *bwana* or *memsahib*.

Another lady who can be *kali*, Janie's sister Sheila Begg, wrote from South Africa. She remembered staying with the Charts in the manager's house in 1936. Margery Chart had home-schooled Sheila and her own two eldest children. As British schools were few and far between, most farmers' wives taught their children until they were ready to go to these boarding schools – although the unluckier ones were sometimes packed off at only five years of age. Sheila returned to stay with her childhood friend Jean in about 1944, she thought. By now the Charts had moved into the main Buxton house. They slept upstairs – the first time Sheila had been in a two-storey house: 'It had a beautiful, well-kept garden with a stream running through it and a water mill for electricity. Fred Chart was a very hard-working, go-ahead fellow and a colourful character.' She added: 'One of the Buxton brothers was keen on bowls so had built the long, enclosed veranda, the whole length of the house, for indoor bowls. The Buxton brothers also built Gilgil Club and the present Gilgil River Lodge. To me the Buxton family is far more interesting than Alice de Janzé. The Buxtons did something constructive for the country.'

After the Charts left in 1947 Satima was managed by John McLoughlin, who later went on to manage Ndabibi, the farm by Lake Naivasha that Diana, by then Lady Delamere, had inherited from her third husband Gilbert Colville. McLoughlin and his wife Hilda finally retired at Soysambu, where Diana ruled the sizeable roost. However, after Hilda had died of an asthma attack, John – unable to bear the loneliness – shot himself on the front steps of Jolai House, only a few miles from where I would make my home thirty years later.

Heading on to the Buxtons' house, we inched down a road where huge boulders alternated with deep ruts. It was evident that nobody drove, or even cycled down here – there was a much better footpath off to our left. The hardy Land Rover bounced along in a crescendo of rattles, until we were beside a lovely old house with chipped white plaster clinging to mud-brick walls: similar building materials to Slains, but this English-style home was double storey, with eaves and attic windows set prettily in its steep, mossy, shingle roof.

'It is very old,' said Solomon, 'it was built by Major Bogosta at the same time as Ramsden's house. Ramsden's house is a very big house and very interesting, but it is difficult to go there.'

I didn't pursue the matter of Ramsden's house. We could hear rivers on both sides, gurgling and swishing, bringing a constant supply of fresh mountain water to the verdant garden. A man sat in a low wooden chair on the sunny lawn, washing his face in a bowl. When we walked over to introduce ourselves, he turned out to be Solomon's old teacher, now elderly and smelling of alcohol. I later asked Solomon if he'd liked his teacher, but he shrugged. In most of rural Kenya you put up with any sort of teacher – you're lucky if you have one. He didn't ask us what we were doing wandering into his garden unannounced, just welcomed us with friendly interest.

'Yes, there are two rivers. There is a furrow here too,' he said, when I asked about the rivers. Golden-winged sunbirds flitted among the plants that grew along the closer river and across the other side there was a pair of noisy trumpeter hornbills, alerting me with strident braying calls. Behind the flourishing fruit trees that lined the river, the Aberdares ascended dramatically into a baby-blue sky. What a fabulous site for a house – and the surroundings were as I would imagine the garden of Eden to be.

The retired teacher was relaxed about us wandering around, although we were not invited inside the house. 'The garage has been demolished,' he explained. 'This room . . .' he indicated the long, low wooden bowling room tacked along one side of the house '. . . maybe for their animals?'

Geoffrey Buxton was the grandson of Sir Thomas Fowell Buxton – an MP known as 'the Liberator', who carried on William Wilberforce's great work after Wilberforce died, securing the Act in the House of Commons for the total abolition of the slave trade in the British Dominions. Sir Thomas died in 1845.

Geoffrey was born in England and educated at Eton. There he became good friends with Toby Finch Hatton, older brother of Denys, who himself was a great friend of Geoffrey's younger brother Guy: they were at Eton together and Denys spent many holidays with the

Buxtons. In 1906, Geoffrey Buxton, rather than going to university, left home to forge his future in British East Africa. Errol Trzebinski in her biography of Finch Hatton, *Silence Will Speak* (1977), says that the tall, dark, handsome Geoffrey's enthusiasm and confidence in East Africa inspired many friends and relatives to go there too, including Denys. When Denys subsequently met and fell in love with Baroness Karen Blixen, she also became a good friend of Geoffrey Buxton's. In 1920 Karen wrote home, enclosing some photos of Buxton's home in Wanjohi: 'You can see the sort of landscape it is up there, it is like an old painting or tapestry,' says a letter published in *Isak Dinesen: Letters from Africa 1914–1931* (1982).

I longed to see inside the Buxton house, but the teacher had returned to the business of shaving, so we left.

Solomon seemed dazed this morning. His sentences had all been half-finished: 'Oh what a lovely . . . It is a beautiful . . .'

'Are you feeling all right?' I asked him.

'I had a very bad dream last night,' he said, shaking his head. 'Very, very bad. I will write it for you. I dreamed that Jean came to me and told me that my son had died.'

By then Solomon and Esther had four children – two sons had followed their daughters. He was referring to Jean O'Meara, a middle-aged lady artist who had been a staunch supporter of Solomon's. She'd taught him to make paper out of various indigenous shrubs, sedges and elephant dung, as well as baskets for his tree seedlings out of dried maize stalks. When she died of pneumonia on 12 January 2000, a month before our first trip to Happy Valley, Solomon had been devastated. He planted a memorial forest for Jean at his home. His neighbours, who called Solomon *Karuru* (Kikuyu for 'bitter', or 'unpleasant tasting'), shook their heads at his madness. Now that year's drought was taking its toll on his trees.

This was before the days of mobile phones. It was mid-morning, and I asked Solomon if he would like to go straight home.

He shook his head slowly. 'We go back after this – we see one more house. The house of Mary Miller.'

11

House of Terror

The first I'd heard of 'Miss Miller', as they'd called her, was when we'd been talking to the *wazee* about Alice de Janzé. One of the elders, Karihe, had known her since he was a boy, when he'd lived on the Case farm. She was deaf, he said, and from 1941 he'd looked after her Jersey cows. She'd left after independence.

Solomon directed me, first backtracking towards Wanjohi town, then turning right towards the Aberdares. The house was a mile or so up another bad road. I had an uneasy feeling about the place before I even spotted it. As we rounded the bend I could see part of a house: a chimney, a slice of roof and a half-smashed wall. Invisible, ice-cold tentacles seemed to reach out from it. I glanced at Solomon who was sitting forwards in his seat, his expression anxious. 'This is a very bad place,' he said. 'Did I tell you about the oaths?'

Not a soul was around. I couldn't even see a bird, nor hear one sing. When we reluctantly emerged from the car, the air temperature seemed to drop further. There were the vague lines of terraces at the front and an old pink rambling rose had collapsed on to a broken wall. We walked behind the old house, over the remains of some steps. Like Satima House, it was made of brick, plastered with a muddy looking substance.

'Cow dung,' Solomon said.

The remnants of a shingle roof clung to splintered roof beams. Any remaining window panes had been broken, leaving jagged holes, their distorted star shapes looking inwards into ominous darkness. I kept my distance, disturbed by a sudden feeling that a sharp object had been thrust through from the inside and that the unseen person, or even creature, clutching the weapon was waiting there. The silence was beginning to unnerve me too and I had a moment of terror when I found that Solomon, who I thought had been right beside me, had vanished.

I recalled the part in Solomon's memoir about the oath-taking ceremonies he was forced to attend in 1969. They were created as an expression of Kikuyu solidarity. 'My mother and other people were talking in secret,' he wrote. 'There was to be a tea prepared by president Jomo Kenyatta and all the Kikuyu community must go and drink that tea. If anyone refuses he will be killed.'

A gang of masked men had come into Solomon's school, brandishing sticks, machetes and clubs. The children were told to follow them. Solomon's instincts made him question this, for which he was thrashed with a stick and tied to another boy. Thus they were marched to Mary Miller's empty house. On arrival Solomon was beaten again, stripped naked and made to join a long line. When it finally came to their turn, the group of children were sent inside the house where a man in a white robe presided over the ceremonies. Solomon remembers passing beneath a banana leaf arch, being shown a bloody knife and told the meaning of the colours of the Kenyan flag: black for the people, red for the bloodshed while fighting the white men, green for the country. They were made to chant: 'This is our soil and we shall not sell to other people and we shall not be ruled by other people, we shall forgive our enemies, but we shall not give our people twice to the hyenas. We shall shed blood for this country!' After swearing this oath, Solomon writes, 'We were given a piece of soft meat to eat, and a piece of banana and sugarcane as the sign that we had sworn. Ashes mixed with something was rubbed on our faces and we were warned not to talk.'

Elspeth Huxley's anthology *Nine Faces of Kenya* explains the power of oath-taking, which was an integral part of Kikuyu society. Donald Barnett and Karaji Njama in *Mau Mau From Within* (1966) describe a Mau Mau oath-taking ceremony, not dissimilar to the one Solomon

attended after Mau Mau was over: armed men in a hut, a banana
arch, the removal of any European clothes or trappings and then the
initiation. Seven people had a band of goatskin put on their right wrist,
then were bound together with the intestines of a goat and sprayed with
beer and millet. Their fingers were pricked and their blood smeared on
to the heart and lungs of a billy goat, before they were marked with
blood from a gourd, made to lick one another's blood and finally to
swear their oath, passing through the arch seven times. They vowed
not to reveal the secret and to die if they violated any rules of the oath.
Facing Mount Kenya, holding a ball of soil and encircled by intestines,
they swore again while pricking the eye of a goat seven times with a
kei-apple horn. A cross of blood and oil was made on their foreheads
to end the ceremony, the necessary warnings issued.

Whether it was the oath-taking that had given Mary Miller's house its
brooding atmosphere of ill omen I could not tell, but I felt gripped by
unfounded panic, deepening when I couldn't see Solomon. My heart
pounding, I ran back towards my car. 'Solomon!' I shouted.

'Madam?' he said, suddenly behind me. (He was nervous enough to
call me Madam instead of Juliet, as if he'd just run into Mary Miller and
was confusing us.) 'I do not like this place. I think we shall leave quickly.'

The next day Solomon rang to tell me that Caleb, his youngest son,
aged twelve, had died at ten the previous morning – the exact time we
had been at the Miller house.

The burial was two days later. Solomon had put up signs, but some had
been taken by wind or ill-wishers. After turning off the old Wanjohi
road running into Happy Valley from Captain, the roads were almost
non-existent – and Solomon had always confused his left and right,
even when he wasn't consumed by grief.

Lost in the middle of dry, desolate country, I stopped beside the
only person on the road. She had been badly stung by bees and her
lips were swollen. She had wrapped a *leso* around her head. 'I know
Solomon's house!' She climbed into the Land Rover. 'There are bad
people around here,' she said suddenly. 'Solomon is in danger.'

It was a fair distance from the main road – probably two hours' walk. Solomon and Esther's small compound was surrounded by a tidy fence and filled with Solomon's trees, those which hadn't died in the drought. There was a modest, mud-walled house and a smaller, wooden one next to it, into which I was ushered by a relative. Solomon wore his usual cap, with white trousers and a baggy white shirt. 'I thank you for coming,' he said, his voice cracking.

His wife, Esther, looked thinner and older. We'd only met once, not long before, when I'd taken my children to visit; their access road had put me off going regularly. She grasped my hand, tears pouring down her cheeks. She wore a white sweatshirt and white headscarf over a brown skirt and gumboots. Their two teenage daughters, Naomi and Julia, sat quietly, their heads also covered, both wearing white. The youngest boy, Adam, was sobbing.

It was time to move outside, under some shade netting and canvas that usually protected the young trees. Somebody had arranged seats. 'Please sit with the family,' said Esther, still holding my hand.

People were arriving, filling the seats, the garden, even sitting on my Land Rover – the only car. Caleb's classmates, relatives and elders congregated in the compound. Women carried sleeping babies on their backs. Esther seemed carried along on a wave of grief, her eyes misty, as if seeing nothing.

First of all a group of children stood and sang a haunting Kikuyu song – and yet its words (which I did not understand) felt uplifting, as if they were singing of somewhere better than this. I was the only white person there, but my mother and some of the other women artists had sent cards and letters, which I was asked to read out. Someone translated my words into Kikuyu. All the other speeches were in Kikuyu. A man stood up and read briefly in English from the Bible, from the book of Revelation. Then he apologised to me for being rude, but he would read the rest in Kikuyu – which he did for an hour. The only word I understood was 'Jerusalem'.

Babies cried, children sat still as statues, people came and went, and a relentless dry wind blew through the compound, dusting us all and passing over the lifeless body of Caleb, open to view in his wooden coffin. A toddler paused beside it and briefly touched him.

Finally a man took photographs of the family standing together – without their youngest member. It had become blisteringly hot by the time the coffin was closed up and lowered into the hole. I stood inhaling dust and pepper tree scent, shedding tears for a boy I had not known, wrenched into grief from watching Solomon and Esther's pain. We all threw in a handful of earth, as is customary.

I sat with them for a while and shared their tea and *irio*, then left them to their private sorrow. I gave a lift to two pretty girls from Naomi's class, two silent women, and a very chatty man who said he did research 'like Charles Darwin'. I barely noticed the bumps on the roads, painfully aware of the absence of my own two children, who were with their father and his new wife. Our recent, unpleasant divorce felt all the more raw. Life suddenly seemed too short for all this acrimony.

Later Solomon wrote down his strange experience: just before Caleb's funeral, Solomon had been in bed, half awake, when he saw Caleb sitting on the bed. His writing spiked with sorrow, Solomon relates how Caleb told him not to worry: he was in a place with no hunger or pain and with all his ancestors. He'd tried to talk to his mother and brother, but they couldn't see him. Just after he died, Caleb said, he watched his family and friends crying around his coffin. Solomon concluded: 'I understand those who died just change . . . they are still surviving, but they just crossed the barriers of nature.'

The next time I saw Solomon he told me he believed Caleb had been poisoned. 'I have many enemies,' he said. 'They want to do this terrible thing to us to frighten me. But I will not let them do this.' I maintained a shocked silence, not sure how to take this, feeling we should not go on any safaris to Happy Valley for a while.

I asked a couple of the old *memsahibs* of Happy Valley about Mary Miller. Bubbles Delap called her 'the merry widow'. Her third husband had been a jockey, Bubbles said, 'although she had lots of boyfriends and I never knew which was which. She rather fancied Bill.'

Mary Miller was 'completely mad' according to another *memsahib*. 'She had lived off lorry-loads of Champagne and booze before shooting herself.'

'Oh yes! She was very depraved,' said another old-timer, lips pursed. She married David Leslie-Melville after his wife died; she was the governess, 'very much beneath him', sniffed yet another, adding that Mary then became stepmother to David's children, Gillian and Jock.

The truth is somewhat different. Mary Miller wasn't the governess, but was the real mother of Leslie-Melville's children. According to the online peerage, Capt. Hon. David William Leslie-Melville was born, one of six, in 1892. His parents were the Hon. Emma Selina Portman – daughter of Lord Portman, a British Liberal MP – and Ronald Ruthven Leslie-Melville, 13th Earl of Leven. David married his first wife in 1914, was decorated and awarded an MBE in 1919, divorced in 1928 and in 1929 married Eleanor Mary Barrell Abrahall, daughter of Arthur John Abrahall. David and Mary had two children – Gillian Mary, born in 1930, and John David (better known as Jock), born in 1933. David died in 1938, aged forty-six. Eight months later Mary married Capt. Arthur Miller, who died in 1942, while on active service. Mary lived until 1974.

Jock Leslie-Melville married a Baltimore girl, Betty, becoming her third husband. She would have slotted into Happy Valley (had it still existed) as she fitted into Kenya, like a hand into a glove perfectly designed for it; as a profile in her hometown *Baltimore Sun* put it, she had 'scampered across two continents like the heroine of a picaresque novel, leaving a glittering wake of crazy and glamorous stories'. Now saving giraffes in Kenya became Betty's new *raison d'être*. After Jock's death in 1984, Betty returned to the USA and remarried. She once remarked to journalist Peter Marren: 'I have one philosophy. You are only sorry for what you don't do, so try everything on for size and wear what fits.'

Betty Leslie-Melville's son from another marriage, Rick Anderson, later ran Betty's giraffe centre on the outskirts of Nairobi with Bryony, his wife. Bryony was able to fill me in with some additional information on Mary Miller. Apparently Mary had been married by proxy in 1919 to a farmer in Uganda. Travelling out on the ship to Mombasa to join him, she'd met the handsome cavalry officer David

Leslie-Melville, who was returning to Kenya to farm. They became lovers. On reaching Mombasa, Mary travelled by train, then ox cart to join her husband in Uganda. Soon after her arrival, she headed for the Wanjohi valley – with two donkeys – in search of David. Mary went down with malaria during this epic journey and was given a heavy dose of quinine by some missionaries; it saved her life, but she was always hard of hearing as a result. Mary and David had three children, but one died of leukaemia. David himself died of peritonitis, Bryony said, while Mary's third husband, Arthur Miller, died in a riding accident crossing a river.

'I remember meeting Mary and was quite intimidated by her very blue, blue eyes and obvious strength,' Bryony wrote in an email. 'Mary was one of those really tough women that did so much for Kenya's development.' According to Bryony, Mary was too busy to be part of the Happy Valley scene, remaining on the periphery of the parties, although she once talked to her daughter-in-law, Betty, about 'pick-a-dick' parties. Mary supposedly didn't do drugs, although latterly she probably overdosed on what Jock called her 'morphine cocktails', but she had the genuine excuse of being in terrible pain before she died of cancer.

I'd also heard it said that Betty had inevitably asked her mother-in-law the million-dollar question: who shot Lord Erroll? Mary had been in no doubt. It was her neighbour, Alice de Trafford, of course!

12

The Bones of Alice

I t was over a year after our meeting with the *wazee* at Kiambogo that Solomon discovered another *mzee* living near the school who had known Alice. And so we drove the long road back to Happy Valley School, now renamed 'Satima Primary' by a new headmaster. We left the car beside the dry stream, on the disused road that had once been Alice's drive, walking across a green field spotted with cow-pats to meet Danson Mwaura, who lived in a small wooden house. We could hear the distant shouts of the schoolchildren.

Mwaura turned out to be Alice's former herdsman. He showed us a tattered newspaper article with some stained pictures of Clouds, and Alice holding her lion cub on her lap defensively, like a shield, but couldn't remember who'd sent them to him.

'But I will show you something better,' he said.

It was early evening now and the schoolchildren were heading home, the last lingering groups laughing their way up the track. We walked across the broken bridge, past Alice's old manager's house, pausing at the foundations of her own home. 'It was a big house,' Mwaura explained, showing us around as proudly as if it were still there in all its 1930s splendour. 'There were plants climbing up the walls and the roof, here beautiful flowers and there so many fruit trees. These ones were the flower beds for decoration and this was the swimming pool . . .' (Further questioning revealed that he actually meant an ornamental garden pond, fed by a furrow from the river.)

'Here the bedroom where she had a photograph by her bed, here the kitchen.' We walked over the crumbling stones that lay in barely discernible lines, stepping like ghosts through spaces where walls had once been. One of Alice's former neighbours had told me the rooms were partitioned but had no ceilings, creating some interesting sound effects when people paired off at parties . . .

It was cold, in spite of the slanting rays of sun, and the chilling atmosphere was disconcerting. Solomon kept looking over his shoulder as if someone was following him. We stood on short, green grass with clumps of pink thistles, in a space that had once been the courtyard. 'Over there,' continued Mwaura, 'were pig sties – but they were destroyed and their materials used for some of these classrooms. That was the house for her clerk.' He pointed at the wooden house. 'The big house also looked like this – with wooden walls and a roof of wooden tiles. Alice's house was a school for some time, but then they pulled it down to increase the playing fields. And then new classrooms were built. That was about 1987.'

We walked past a classroom which had some of Alice's old window frames and doors slotted in amongst its more modern materials, until we reached a grassy bank where we sat with the old man above the river, looking towards the enormous hulk of the Aberdares, indigo in the failing light. The neglected fires of charcoal burners breathed misty smoke that writhed around shadowed ridges and valleys like claws of doom.

Mwaura pointed: 'Here Alice and her dog Minnie are buried. The dog was very small.' The unmarked grave, unrecognisable as such, was roughly halfway between the football goal posts and the school pit-latrines. 'Myself, I dug the hole for the dog too, beside the hole for *Wacheke* – in 1941 when she killed herself.' For effect he dramatically re-enacted the drama. His cracked yellow teeth flashed as he pointed an imaginary gun at his chest, made an explosive noise and fell back on to the grass. Three Hadada ibis, their dark wings splashed with glowing green, had been pecking about near us, but they suddenly took off, uttering the hoarse shriek that gives them their name. There was a gust of cold wind and that disturbing atmosphere I always felt around Alice's old home deepened into something almost sinister.

'This football field was once covered in trees,' said Mwaura, heaving himself upright again.

Some children had appeared in the golden light of early evening and were playing football with a bundle of plastic bags and feathers, tied up with string, apparently oblivious to any strange vibes. 'They are the school team,' explained Mwaura.

As we sat watching the sunset, the footballers suddenly decided that watching us was more fun. Their noise and cheeky shouts were becoming irritating, but they ignored Solomon's remonstrations. 'These children are not good!' he complained. 'They are influenced by the bad spirits in this place.'

'Did Alice live here all alone?' I asked the old man.

'*Wacheke* had a clerk,' said Mwaura, 'but one day she got angry and sent her clerk to Nakuru. She told the staff to keep out of the house and she wrote a letter then poisoned her dog and herself. But she didn't die and at two in the afternoon her clerk came back and called for help. Three people came – one I remember was a woman from the Charts' house, but it was not Mr Chart's wife. They gave *Wacheke* first aid. She was taken to hospital – to Nakuru and then King George, but after six months she was back. When she died the next time they put her in a cedar coffin and many mourners came. They lit a fire.'

I looked at the ragged skyline: gums, pines and a few cedar trees pointed heavenwards. The light was dimming and Mwaura's eyes seemed misty. 'She kept very private in her house,' he said when I asked about Alice's drinking and drug-taking tendencies. 'She was very nice. Her husband was a tall pilot but he went to Uganda, and crashed and died.' No, he didn't know his name and she never had another husband, nor did she have any children.

Only parts of Mwaura's story agreed with what I'd read. He was an old man and perhaps his memory wasn't always accurate. Suddenly he said proudly, '*Wacheke* came from the royal family – she had crowns on her cups and cloths.' After Alice's death, he added, there was another lady who lived here for about five years. 'We called her *Nyakaroki* because she woke early and made everyone work hard. Then Sterling came.'

I'd made a mental note and when I returned the next time I brought the children a football. They crowded around us again, potentially terrifying my visitor from England, until I repelled them with a severe lecture about manners – then produced the football. They fell back slightly with a variety of shamefaced grins and less respectful grimaces. All eyes were on the football, which was kicked into action as soon as we left.

'Mwaura has died,' Solomon told me as we walked around the side of the wooden house. We were welcomed into the headmaster's office. My eyes were drawn to an old picture of the school amongst the clutter – packets of aspirin, piles of papers, a pot of paint, an out-of-date desk calendar – on the shelf above his desk. The photograph was taken in 1966, a group of pupils in the foreground, in front of Alice's original house. The headmaster obligingly stood on his chair to reach the photograph. Something indefinable which seeped out of it made me inexplicably depressed. It looked dark in every sense of the word.

After signing the visitors' book, which rural Kenyan schools usually produce to ensure they have your address in order to invite you to the next fundraising event, I peeped into a classroom where children were squashed on to an odd assortment of stools and benches, sharing desks and pencils. The lady teacher, a former pupil herself, told the pupils to stand up and greet their visitor, then came outside to chat, while the pupils swivelled round, stood and even peered through the windows to get a better look at us. She remembered Alice's old house: it had been U-shaped and rather dark, but it had served its purpose as a useful building, big enough back then to contain the whole school.

'Nowadays it's all harder because there are many problems,' the teacher explained. 'There is a shortage of government teachers. We are paid very little – less than eight thousand shillings [around £65] a month. There is a shortage of funds. The parents must pay for books and uniforms, as well as activity fees, a district education board levy, cost sharing levy, evaluation tests, exam registration fees and development funds.'

'What if they can't afford it?' I asked.

'We try to assist a few of the children, mainly ones who are orphans,' she told me, 'but there are too many children. Half of them attend in the morning and the other half in the afternoon, because we do not have space for them all at once.'

After sitting their Kenya Certificate of Primary Education (if their parents can afford the examination fees) at about fourteen years of age (although some are as old as eighteen by the end of their primary career), these kids, however bright, have little hope of going to secondary school. 'Secondary will cost eight thousand shillings a term or more, so they must just stay at home and do nothing,' the teacher said.

Kiswahili, English, maths, science, GHCR (geography, history, civics and religious education) are compulsory subjects, she explained, warming up to my interest, while music, art and craft, and business education are extra. But there are no pianos or flutes or art materials and the majority of parents cannot afford such luxuries anyway, so any talent in those fields will remain dormant in these children – along with so many other youngsters all over Happy Valley, and indeed Kenya and Africa. Meanwhile, African MPs and their cronies blithely send their kids to vastly expensive British public schools and to universities in the States.

A few months later I received a letter from the head teacher of Happy Valley School, or Satima Primary as it now was, inviting me to a fundraising event. 'Please attend and participate,' said the green invitation card that also listed all the expected guests of honour and old pupils of renown. An accompanying letter said: 'I would like to assure you that the stakeholders of Satima Primary school are very happy with you people.'

'You must not give them money,' warned Solomon. 'If you want to give them something, it is better to take pencils or other useful equipment.'

*

I had a surprise call from a friend of a friend, asking if I could take a lady from France up to Happy Valley – she was related to somebody up there who'd died back in the 1940s. I invited her to visit, delighted when she turned out to be Alice de Janzé's granddaughter: Angelique was a charming, elegant woman and I could see in her fine and suddenly familiar features, traces of the Alice I had studied in the photographs. We got on instantly, sipping our tea in between the excitement of a disgruntled buffalo appearing on the nearby track.

After Angelique had returned to Paris she wrote to me with a few snippets about the grandmother she'd never known. Formally, aptly too perhaps, she called her Alice:

> According to my mother, Alice was mad about animals, part of her attraction for Kenya . . . I suppose. In Paris she kept a monkey . . . to the delight of my mother and my aunt. He played lots of tricks and one day he was locked up in the bathroom where he decided to turn on all the taps full tilt and pulled the chain of the loo so that the water ran over down through the floors! He also liked to pour the water out of the vase on the grand piano carefully into the neck of a guest sitting conveniently below.

According to Angelique, Alice also had 'small alligators in aquariums'. I wondered if these unfortunate creatures had actually been crocodiles, taken from some Kenyan lake or river to a Parisian life of incarceration. There's something disturbing about anybody wanting a pet that could snap your hand off.

Angelique's aunt, Alice's other daughter, had got on better with her mother, according to Angelique, having a similar affinity with animals. Both girls only saw their beautiful, elusive mother occasionally on her annual visits to Paris to stock her glamorous wardrobe – and briefly kiss her rapidly growing daughters. Angelique told me the story of when her mother, Alice's elder daughter Nolwen, had written to Alice proudly to say she had got into Vassar College in America, but when Alice had called her a 'blue stocking' she'd changed her mind and gone to a more avant-garde, less academic college – which she'd always regretted. Nolwen had apparently talked very little about Alice, although she'd once admitted that her mother must have suffered from the loss of her own mother at the age of four. Alice's mother had died of pneumonia after being turned out by her drunken husband on a winter night. Angelique wrote: 'He felt guilty for the rest of his life which was not going to be beneficial for Alice.'

Meanwhile, Solomon had suddenly announced that he had found Alice's 'real grave', which was 'somewhere else'. This is not surprising in Africa, where supposed truths suddenly disintegrate before your ears and eyes. Angelique visited again, this time while I was away, and accompanied Solomon to visit her grandmother's latest grave site. Afterwards she left Solomon with enough money to erect a gravestone and to arrange subsequent payments to the school for the upkeep of the small garden he would plant around her grave. All of this Solomon did with great enthusiasm, visiting me regularly with updates so I could email the latest to Angelique back in Paris.

'But,' I questioned warily, 'how do we know it is Alice's grave this time?'

'Because,' said Solomon, suddenly lowering his voice to a conspiratorial whisper, 'the people who I hired for digging to make the grave nice, they were digging too deep and they found Harris. I saw the bones!'

13

Monkey Man and More Mischief

During our early meanderings into the area, Solomon had said he would take me to 'Patricia Bowles' house'. She wasn't someone I knew anything about, although I'd remembered her mentioned in *White Mischief*. 'She was a friend of Harris,' Solomon said, 'her farm was called *Munungu* because Patricia Bowles, she planted very many *mununga* trees.' These attractive forest trees are indigenous, and thus Patricia had incurred Solomon's admiration. My tree book actually spells the Kikuyu name 'mungnga', unlike Solomon, who gave me the spelling that eases pronunciation.

Mununga was between Clouds and Alice's home: 10 miles from Clouds and just under 5 miles from Alice's – although it would have been much faster cross-country on a cantering horse, than jolting about in my Land Rover in first gear.

The name had lived on. We'd passed 'Mununga Girls' Secondary School' with that excited feeling of 'getting warmer' like in hide and seek. Some of the classrooms, although not old themselves, had very old *mabate* (corrugated iron sheeting) on the roofs, faded red, as if it had been stripped from older farm buildings.

Just up the road, a couple of mossy fence posts, a few stone barns with chipped and dirty white walls, and fading red tin roofs, and a defunct cattle dip, indicated an old farm. We were there at last.

'Some say the house it has gone,' said Solomon. 'But there is an old wooden house inside the mission just here, so maybe that can be the house of Patricia Bowles!'

We ventured into the walled, gated compound of a large Catholic secondary school where Patricia's house, we hoped, might be lurking somewhere among the glut of new buildings. Smartly dressed schoolgirls stared at us curiously as they said 'Good morning' and hurried past to lessons. A friendly administrator sat inside a bottle-green office – she had never heard of Patricia Bowles, nor had the deputy principal, Sister Theresa. But we were welcomed and taken on a guided tour of the whole place. 'There is one old building down here,' Sister Theresa finally said, leading us down a path that ran alongside a furrow, towards a grove of leafy *mununga* trees. 'I think it was once a house for some white people.'

We walked past washing hanging on fences and I caught a glimpse of a chimney and a faded roof, then suddenly we were standing by an old house, built of cedar off-cuts. This old house was probably very similar to Alice's. It wasn't unlike her manager's house.

'This is our St Peter's polytechnic for girls,' explained Sister Theresa.

Past the trunks of the old, gnarled *mununga* trees we could see patches of new cultivation and funnels of smoke as farmers and charcoal burners continued eating their way up into the Kipipiri forest. Behind us the view stretched across the plateau into the Rift Valley, ending in the pale blue line of the Mau escarpment. These old settlers had certainly picked prime sites to build their homes: isolated in those days and probably lonely – but beautiful.

An old rose bush straggled over one corner of the house, and there was a row of drooping moonflowers, a member of the deadly nightshade family, their poisonous trumpet-like blooms glowing white in the shady gloom cast by the *mununga* trees.

We walked through the old house over creaking floorboards, opening heavy doors with beautiful brass handles, looking at wood-panelled rooms with fireplaces. Water had leaked into the back of the corner fireplace of what must have been the sitting room. The kitchen was separate, situated at the back. The master and guest bedrooms were now dormitories, crowded with bunk beds. It was swept and impeccably tidy: there were no posters or pictures, no hints of the young women who slept and studied here.

In a large, long room that might once have been an indoor veranda or children's playroom, rows of girls in neat black ties and immaculate blazers were seated in front of old-fashioned treadle sewing machines. They stood up as we came in. Sister Theresa made a hand signal to the two girls nearest the door, and they hastily went out, returning with chairs for us. Then the girls sang us a song ('of welcome', explained Sister Theresa) and recited a poem, before sitting down again, looking at me expectantly. Sensing it was now my turn, with nothing poetic or musical in my mind, I made a rather fumbling speech of thanks, explaining that we were here to look at the old house that was now their college, that I wanted to write about it. Solomon did far better, rising confidently to talk conservation. He pointed out that the house looked down towards Lake Ol Bolossat, an important wetland in dire need of protection, emphasising the appeal of its hippos and bird life, explaining how it must be preserved for future generations and that it could bring in an income if managed properly. The girls listened politely but they were watching me, taking in my windswept, dust-laced hair, scruffy shorts and T-shirt and old flip-flops. I usually dressed in my hardiest, most comfortable attire for these arduous expeditions. I probably looked as if I was about to start begging from the nuns.

'Who knows what is a colobus monkey?' Solomon asked. He was talking about Kipipiri forest now.

Nobody moved.

Solomon said the name in Kikuyu.

Then most of them nodded.

'Who has seen one?' asked Solomon.

A few hands went up.

'When I was a child there were so many colobus monkeys,' Solomon said sadly after we'd left. We were driving past a dam, choked up with weed: a few sacred ibis, a brown hammerkop and a pair of duck pottered across the spongy surface. Solomon clicked in exasperation: 'And look how they have neglected this dam!' I had a sudden flashback to my own angry tears as a teenager, when I'd visited my grandparents' former farm in the late 1970s, hoping to relive happy childhood memories. The farm had been reduced to barren, treeless waste, with no sign of the lovely old house, nor even the many varieties of fruit trees.

Thanks to my frequent visits to Happy Valley with Solomon, I was inevitably becoming involved in his life and work, which are inextricably intertwined. His life, back in the days the family still lived on Alice de Trafford's former farm, continued to haunt me.

Naturally Solomon had been forced to leave his childhood home in Happy Valley after the mindlessly cruel burning of his and Esther's simple home that destroyed their few possessions. As soon as Solomon had heard the grim news from Esther, he'd rushed home. It would have been challenging for Esther to contact Solomon – she'd have had to get to the nearest town to make a phone call or send a telegram. But bad news tends to travel at high speed and Solomon knew about the loss of his home very soon after it had happened.

Moving must have been a relief in some ways – but it didn't mean his life would get easier. Thus he'd bought some land from another of his brothers, closer to Captain, moving Esther and the children there, building a new home from scratch and settling down to his conservation work again. Money was paid to his brother, but title deeds were not forthcoming. Solomon shrugged this off without giving the matter too much thought; he knew such things take time and carried on regardless. But the police quickly discovered his whereabouts and, once again, Solomon was being watched and harassed, as if he were a political dissident or convicted criminal. His new neighbours kept their distance – he was obviously a troublemaker and they weren't prepared to be associated with him.

Solomon's ordeals with the authorities ended abruptly, bizarrely, when he met two artists, one of whom had first brought him to my house. He'd heard about these 'tree ladies' and found his way to their home. Astrid von Kalckstein, who initially seemed another glowering *memsahib*, listened to Solomon's story on the back step, invited him in to talk more – and has ever since remained his friend and supporter.

Then he met Astrid's friend, Jean O'Meara, who also became involved with Solomon's conservation projects.

It puzzled me that two intrepid but harmless and elderly white lady artists, both slightly eccentric albeit ardent conservationists, who pottered about painting watercolours of the scenery and collecting shrubs to make homemade paper, could 'protect' Solomon. But he felt safer, he was gaining credibility, and maybe his enemies and the authorities imagined Astrid and Jean had powerful connections. Or perhaps they simply shied away from two ordinary people who were fearless in their honesty and integrity. After Jean's death, just before I met Solomon in early 2000, Astrid continued to support Solomon's projects. Then, after Caleb's death, I had become involved too. By the end of 2000, having failed to drum up interest in his life story, I was to find myself supporting his causes instead.

I leafed through a file Solomon lent me, containing stacks of letters and many old newspaper cuttings that he'd kept – a jumbled summary of his remarkable career. There was the letter to the *Nation* newspaper in February 1998 from my mother, appealing for help with Solomon's efforts to save a dozen colobus monkeys: he was getting no joy from the Kenya Wildlife Service (KWS), even when he was up against two 'foreigners' buying the skins. There was a volley of concerned responses from groups and individuals, most of whom wanted 'funding', supposedly to help Solomon, but no financial assistance was forthcoming, apart from an advocate in western Kenya who sent a cheque to contribute towards buying Solomon a bicycle so he could get around faster. The same newspaper's 'Cutting Edge' column commented: 'Why is it that whenever we see a reader's letter headlined *Save Our Forests* or *Protect Our Monkeys* . . . we just know it's going to be signed by a *mzungu*?'

Back in 1996, Solomon had first appealed to the KWS for help after sixteen of Happy Valley's monkeys had been killed. He was told to feed the monkeys to keep them together for possible capture and translocation, but no assistance was forthcoming and nothing else was heard from them for over a year. It's not as if Solomon has the money to buy endless bunches of bananas for monkeys – even now he has to quickly find somebody to buy a stack of his homemade paper just to find the cash to get his youngest child, a toddler, to hospital.

Finally the translocation happened – albeit slowly and after fighting through the tangle of red tape that accompanies the required scientific research and co-ordination of such a project. From the initial site visit in mid-1998 it took a year and four months to move four groups of colobus, some of them to the acacia forest beside Lake Elementeita on Soysambu, assisted by an NGO called Wakuluzu Friends of Colobus Trust, to whom Solomon was very grateful. But many of the monkeys had been killed during the long wait. There was also another matter that left him embattled: he felt that a handsomely paid project researcher had turned her back on the fact that a cage left behind after the translocation was now being used as a trap.

For a while the *Nation* ran regular articles on Solomon, praising the saving of Kipipiri's endangered colobus 'spearheaded by Solomon Gitau'. They published an article pointing fingers at the two foreign men, with a Dubai-registered vehicle, who were buying skins for between 300 and 500 shillings, as well as criticising KWS for their total lack of help. They quoted Solomon, saying how concerned he was about the twenty monkeys killed in only two months and asking why KWS were totally incapable of fighting the poachers.

The many letters Solomon keeps in a plastic bag are a mixed collection: some are from people wishing to help, others from farmers asking him to remove colobus from their farms. There's a circular letter, written by Astrid, telling the horror story of a female colobus monkey in a trap, unable to feed her baby, which starved to death; Astrid wrote this in the hope of getting funds to help Solomon, but an initial trickle of money soon stopped. There are endless pleas from Solomon to KWS, with notably few replies. One handwritten letter, by Sylvia from Sagana, wanted the names of the foreigners who bought the colobus skins because she could offer them leopard skins and rhino horn!

By 1999, after the first successful translocation, an increasing number of local Kikuyu landowners were demanding financial recompense for damage the monkeys had done to their crops. They were in agreement with Solomon that the surviving monkeys should be moved, even if some of them were motivated by the prospect of a back-hander from any wealthy NGO they were hoping would become involved. But no funding was forthcoming. In early 2000 Solomon wrote a circular, which Astrid and Jean circulated among their friends. Solomon wrote passionately: 'I term myself spokesman for the colobus monkeys for they cannot speak for themselves.' He outlined the threats to these beautiful monkeys and begged people to help them.

To try and raise enough money, a group of local artists and conservationists began meeting in Gilgil to discuss a sponsored cycle through the Malewa Valley, which runs from the Aberdares through the edge of Happy Valley to Lake Naivasha, also aiming to raise awareness among the young Kikuyu who lived in the area, teaching them more about conservation. There were only two black Kenyan members in the group: one was Solomon, who usually had grim reports at the meetings – three more dead colobus, another mother and baby who'd been stoned to death, snares, poisoned maize, even fires lit under trees to get rid of these 'pests'. As he frequently pointed out, translocation was only a short-term solution. The bigger picture was about steady forest encroachment. His reports to the district officer and area chief had fallen on deaf ears.

In between all his activities and trips into Happy Valley, Solomon also rescued and looked after snared monkeys, a tree duck with a broken leg and even a baby bongo which had lain next to its dead mother for three days. The latter is Kenya's rarest antelope, still found deep in the Aberdares and a few other forests, but barely ever seen. Legally, Solomon was required to hand any wild creatures over to KWS, but by now his faith in the organisation had dwindled after too many occasions when he sought their assistance and failed to get any support.

Solomon continued to monitor those creatures that survived and tried to motivate others into protecting them. In the late 1990s he had formed the Good Children Society, teaching youngsters – as Jean taught him – to make biodegradable bags out of dried maize stalks in which to grow tree seedlings. If cared for properly these could either be sold, or simply planted out for the good of the environment. Solomon encouraged his Good Children to clear up roadside rubbish, teaching by example, while also making homemade paper using a variety of plants, including maize husks, grass, papyrus and reeds. Overall, he preached respect for all wild creatures. The chameleon, for example, is often killed for bringing 'bad luck', or at best feared. Solomon taught his Good Children that a chameleon doesn't bite, but in fact eats the flies that spread diseases. He proudly informed me that, at one primary school, he had twenty Good Children – out of 645 – the latter an incredible figure when you looked at the limited classroom space.

Throughout all this, Solomon was dealing with another family tragedy. Since Caleb's death, his beloved wife and soulmate, Esther, had never been well. Like Solomon's supportive friend, the late Jean O'Meara, Esther had a weak chest and was prone to bouts of pneumonia. Just over a year after losing her son, she was admitted to Nyahururu Hospital, where she later died.

Solomon, wracked by grief, had to deal with a substantial bill at the hospital – which he couldn't possibly pay – and the hospital refused to release Esther's body before the bill had been settled. As a result of such policies, there are bodies stuck indefinitely in hospital mortuaries all over Kenya.

Esther's family, albeit in a financial position to help Solomon, refused – they had never condoned the marriage anyway. Meanwhile, Solomon's European friends passed around the hat to enable him to bury his wife. His Kikuyu neighbours jeered at him: 'We shall see his environment come and educate his children,' said one. Another sneered: 'He will get married to colobus monkeys and get them to make his hats.' They were referring to Esther's small but lucrative cottage industry: she had collected waste plastic bags and crocheted them into attractive hats, mats and baskets. Astrid had sold these at Women's League and other functions to help Esther and Solomon pay the children's school fees.

Solomon ignored his neighbours' remarks. He hand-wrote the latest chapters of his story in a new exercise book. *The Black Days* told his heartbroken story of Esther's death. This book is dedicated 'to the children born in this country, who will grow up and ask where have all the trees and animals gone?'

Esther's burial was attended by a large crowd of Kikuyu well-wishers and friends, and a few family members, as well as some of Solomon and Esther's European friends. Solomon used the occasion to move forward with his usual indomitable spirit, opening an educational conservation centre in her memory: The Esther Wairumu Memorial Conservation and Field Study Centre. People listened quietly as Solomon talked in broken English about how deeply Esther had loved animals and the environment, how she had worked alongside him tirelessly, as well as involving herself in other voluntary work, including starting the Rural Women's Crusade to empower other women to assist in various ways. These included feeding and clothing children whose mothers were alcoholics or drug addicts. Esther had also bottle-fed various wild orphans brought home by Solomon. Throughout the ceremony the plump brindled dog called Hippo wandered through the gathering. Solomon's Good Children from his 'Kindness Clubs' sang songs they'd made up, including a touching one called 'Mother Esther'. Some of the children read out poems. The occasion was a moving and generous celebration of a life well lived.

We planted trees in Esther's memory. As I scooped up the rough dry earth with my hands and patted it around a sapling African olive, an iridescent blue starling alighted on a nearby bush, regarding me with its yellow beady eye as if contemplating my work. I stood up and sighed. In rural Kenya the elderly tend to be revered, looked after by their extended families, imparting wisdom and wonderful stories to their grandchildren and great-grandchildren. Esther would never grow old, nor would she see her children's children.

A shadow passed over us, making me glance up. A large eagle was circling overhead, dark against the blue sky. The starling flew away.

14

Tales of Torture and Many Cups of Tea

Solomon has remarkable courage when it comes to picking himself up and carrying on with life. Our explorations of Happy Valley continued, although our missions diverged: while I hoped to find out more about Ramsden, and his reportedly large and interesting house, Solomon had a broader agenda. On our next safari, we took the road from Captain, turning right after a short distance on to the 'shortcut' to Clouds, which probably took longer because it was so rough. We passed a gloomy stone house on a ridge, stark naked to the winds, all its trees and hedges slashed into spindly stumps. The sign at the bottom of the drive said 'Ihiga Primary School'.

'That was David's house,' Solomon said. As I took a photograph a blast of wind blew from behind, whipping my back before obscuring the road up to the house, engulfing the dry trees and the exposed house in a cloud of dust.

'The spirits are saying no,' Solomon muttered.

A little further up the dusty road we stopped to talk to a man on a bicycle who Solomon vaguely knew. I suspected that Solomon also wanted to be seen in a Land Rover, especially one driven by a white woman. There remains a myth in Happy Valley, indeed in most of rural Kenya, that white people bring money with them – vast amounts of it. This in spite of the fact that today's moneyed crowd, mainly black politicians, own all the glitzy palatial dwellings, surrounded by security gates and electric fences and are watched vigilantly by minimally paid guards. Sometimes there are even walls topped with slices of broken glass, in case anyone wishes to shred their hands and feet trying out that particular route in to steal whatever it is the wealthy Kikuyu bigwigs are protecting so fiercely.

The cyclist had such vast, brown, triangular and protruding teeth he couldn't close his mouth. He was the adult education officer, well enough respected to order a random passer-by to take over his bicycle so he could get a lift with us. We crossed the S-bend of the Kimuru River, known as *daraja tatu*, literally meaning 'three bridges'. Back in the 1920s someone had worked out that the easiest way to cross the ravine was actually twice — at its narrowest places, which were on the bends. So originally two smaller bridges were built out of vast logs to convey the settlers and their belongings up to Kipipiri and on to Happy Valley from Gilgil. These old bridges were still navigable on foot, but now a newer concrete one had been added (in 1972, Solomon said). The map actually labelled the Kimuru River as the Olokoronyo. Solomon explained that this was a Maasai name, another reminder that the Maasai had been here first — the Kikuyu came later, with the white settlers. This and many other rivers that rise in the Aberdares and Kipipiri flow into the main rivers, the Wanjohi joining the Malewa, which feeds Lake Naivasha. Flying over the whole area once, I could see that it was cut by many steep gorges, a few of which still provided forested refuge for colobus monkeys. But the sacks of charcoal on the backs of bicycles and the roofs of *matatus* tell the story of the fate of these trees and warn of their future.

Further along the road our passenger alighted at another old house, now Malewa Primary School. It was the house of Columbus, Solomon said, and the area had also kept the name of Columbus.

Survey maps made in 1947 by the RAF marked this area as Colobus Farm, with two houses belonging to Ori and Vetri. The map marked 'David's' house as belonging to Davies.

A teacher came out and introduced himself. He told me he was writing a book on the Mau Mau. 'It's called *Kimathi*,' he said. Could I find him a publisher? His face had been badly scarred and damaged in some past accident. In Kenya there are an unnerving number of road accidents, but also many small children are burnt by fires in the centre of the hut, as Solomon himself had been. Solomon's earliest memories go back to when he was just a toddler; he vividly recalls the excruciating pain he felt when his unsympathetic brothers rubbed car grease into his burns. If this teacher had been burnt, it looked as if somebody had tried to repair the damage with a pitchfork. Plastic surgery isn't an option in rural hospitals: if it were, how many could afford it anyway?

We were joined by a lady with a bad squint and an elderly man with his leg amputated at the knee. I was beginning to wonder if this was actually a nursing home, until I realised I was playing Pied Piper to hundreds of staring children who had silently streamed out of a classroom behind us. The mad-eyed woman introduced herself as the English teacher, requesting that I give the children a lesson in English – there and then in the barren playing field behind the school, where Solomon, the education officer, the teacher-writer, the one-legged man and now she and several hundred children stood watching me expectantly. Her English was so poor that I decided I could at least let her pupils hear some mother-tongue English spoken, so I told them about being a writer, that my job was not high earning, but that I'd followed my dreams. My words were punctuated by frequent cries of 'Yes!' One brave little girl had managed to get close enough behind me to stroke my hair, so strangely pale and smooth to her.

'I would like to read your book!' said one bright-eyed boy in his very best English.

We bumped on past several dried-up dams. One, fed by a seasonal stream, had a puddle of water and a pair of coots dabbling about in it.

'These used to provide water for cows and many wild animals too,' lamented Solomon. 'They were made by Gordon, and this is his house.'

'Gordon?' I queried, wondering if he was an in-law of Lady Idina Gordon, as she was when she first came to Kenya . . .

I followed him to a solitary stone tower, three storeys high – evidently built for fortified protection during Mau Mau, but now badly cracked. (Bubbles Delap later told me it had been very similar to the fortifications built at Rayetta.) Only one wing of the actual house remained: dusty, grey stone and surrounded by rubbish. Its austere, featureless windows and doors looked very 1950s – purpose built with minimal funds.

Today's owner of the tower and slice of house, Silas Karoga, had a few scrawny chickens and one skinny old cow who looked as if she wouldn't even make good biltong. The wind picked up the dust and blew it through the corridors of dead maize. Silas's very large, hungry-looking family had spilled out from the bottom of the tower where they evidently lived, crammed in. The wooden stairs in the tower had rotted so there was no upper section now, and the house, what was left of it, was for the chickens and cow. The children were dressed in rags, but their smiles were broad, even before we gave them sweets.

We drove on to the small, tin-shack town of Machinery, where we stopped at an earth-floored shack called the Destination Café. The lady owner, introduced to me as Mama Maina, who helped Solomon with his colobus projects, offered us *ugali* (maize meal) and *sukuma wiki* (an accompaniment of a green, leafy vegetable, although the name actually means 'push the week' – referring to the plant's ability to go on pushing out leaves against all the odds, feeding the five thousand).

Six young men were already tucking into the feast and Solomon joined them, sitting on the rickety bench beneath a crudely illustrated poster that proclaimed 'I was crying that I didn't have shoes. But I thanked God when I met a person without legs. JESUS IS REAL', it concluded. From an unseen radio an American voice was crooning: 'We gotta stop hurting each other,' only she pronounced it 'herding'.

I had been suffering from a bad stomach and it caused great mirth when I declined food. I sat on a stool beside a wall painting of flamingos and braved some extremely sweet tea in a mug with a snowman on it, not without apprehension, for there were no flushing toilets up here, only pit-latrines that require you to squat and aim with precision. A brindled cockerel joined me in the café, defecating under the table while giving my shoe a sideways look. Through the plastic ribbons that fluttered from the doorway I could see sheep picking their way across the litter-strewn patch of bright-green grass. A gaggle of barefoot kids wandered past, stopping and giggling at the doorway when they saw me. Suddenly they scattered and ran as three older men came in. Dressed in threadbare jackets and felt hats, they greeted me in Kiswahili and proceeded to hold an animated conversation in Kikuyu, which, when you listen without understanding, seems a language crafted almost entirely out of vowels. They sat in a corner and Mama Maina served them mugs of tea. The young men appeared to have left without paying for anything, and I wondered whether our hostess ran the Destination Café on endless credit, or whether all these people were relatives and had to have freebies. Perhaps Mama Maina simply was not a good businesswoman, because when we left she refused to take any payment, ignoring my protestations while loading up the back of my Land Rover with fruit, and insisting we sat down again and had one more mug of tea. 'You are a visitor here,' she said firmly, 'and you are very welcome.'

Defeated, humbled by her generosity, having given up getting anywhere else soon, I sat down again and watched the world go by. A woman was sitting just outside the door knitting something at great speed in violently orange, synthetic wool. Beside her grazed a sheep in need of a haircut.

Solomon always seems to know everybody. He kept rushing outside to glean more colobus news or ask about a tree nursery. The walls beside me were decorated with newspaper cuttings on subjects ranging from salvation to malaria, offering reading material to accompany the tea. While reading all about how Nice and Lovely products could care for my skin and hair I wondered why this place was called Machinery, because there wasn't any sign of anything remotely mechanical.

We made a diversion to Clouds with some outgrown clothes from my children for the Nuthu grandchildren. Gilgil Club to Clouds, via Captain and *daraja tatu* with the old bridges, was just under 33 miles, and had taken ten minutes short of two hours if I deducted the stops. We then turned back towards Wanjohi and Alice's house, stopping just before Mununga at a primary school where Solomon wanted to see some of his Good Children.

As we left the school we nearly fell over the scruffy, barefoot pupil who waited to see the head, standing wretchedly under the sign telling us: 'Dedication is the answer'. The child looked as if he had not eaten for days, nor had anyone washed or mended his clothes for months. His eyes were fixed on the broken cement floor, his hunched, resigned posture suggesting he was probably in for a caning. I could only hope he wasn't being punished for his appearance.

Solomon wanted to show me 'Hall's house', so he guided me back to the sprawling town of Miharati, lying between Machinery and Mununga Farm, just below Gordon's. Like Machinery, Miharati has rapidly expanded from farmland to a noisy, grubby, busy town – all in less than fifty years. At the edge of Miharati an old wooden house stood starkly at the edge of a narrow ravine, its roof long gone. 'That was Hall's first house,' Solomon told me. He took me deeper into the town to Hall's second home – another European-style house: grey stone with a red-tiled roof, surrounded by an overgrown hedge. There were rows of agapanthus lilies lining the drive. Kipipiri rose behind, the Aberdares behind that stretching on towards the peaks of the Kinangop, mottled with afternoon light. The building was now a police station.

We drove on through Miharati, up a dusty, uneven street, to find some more tea in a nearby 'hotel'. Red, silver and gold Christmas decorations cast surreal patterns on the walls as they danced in a light breeze and we drank our tea out of mugs decorated with teddy bears in red vests catching fish. We were served cold, leathery *mandazi*, the Kenyan equivalent of a doughnut, but flatter and usually triangular. They are delicious when fresh, but these were definitely yesterday's leftovers. The only other customer nodded and returned to his newspaper, but the kids outside kept peeping in at the door. When I waved they ran, exploding into fits of giggles. Then they'd come back again, creeping, daring each other, as if this was a game of grandmother's footsteps. A visiting football team came in, the young men sitting down and staring at me as if I was a freak. The children outside fled and the man with the newspaper ignored us all.

Solomon was sitting beneath a handmade sign with a crudely drawn picture of a man on a bed outside a hut. 'He who relies on his relatives dies poor' was the cautionary message.

'That police station is the place where I was first locked up,' Solomon told me. 'The police, they beat me very badly and after that I became afraid to even sleep at my own house because they were always coming after me . . .'

In the politically repressed one-party state of the late 1970s, the majority of people were at the mercy of greedy politicians, already accelerating flat out along the freeways of corruption, dragging mistrust and suspicion in their wake. No surprise, then, that Solomon was accused of having political motivations: his conservation activities were banned and he was threatened repeatedly until he was forced to move away. He'd found a job in western Kenya – but lost it after complaining about the company's use of child labour. Back home once again, it wasn't long before Solomon was arrested for his alleged anti-government stance and locked up for a week without food.

Solomon, naively perhaps, continued to set up conservation clubs, whose members he encouraged to form football teams. It was his solution to keeping unemployed young people like himself busy and motivated – with a competitive edge. But Solomon was further hounded by the local authorities and the police. Under such circumstances, if you've got any sense you answer as expected or risk further beatings, but Solomon refused to lie and say that yes, he was politically motivated. So he was kept at Miharati police station for no reason. After being brutally beaten, he was finally let out and warned that next time he would be killed. The message was clear: don't mess with us any more, and keep your head down . . .

Worried and upset, Solomon took a *matatu* to Nairobi to visit Professor Wangari Maathai, coordinator of the Green Belt Movement, the woman who later won the Nobel Peace Prize for her efforts in conservation. Maathai rang the local district commissioner, gave Solomon money for his bus fare home and assured him of his safety.

But soon afterwards Solomon ventured far up into the forests of Kipipiri to investigate fires left burning by charcoal burners. Here he stumbled upon an illegal marijuana plantation and somebody saw him. This latest 'interference' put a price on his head, for Solomon had overstepped the mark – right on to the toes of political bigwigs who happened to be profiting from the venture. Now, it seemed, he was being watched.

One clear day, after the long rains had carpeted Happy Valley with lush, green grass and wild flowers, Solomon had been slogging away to clear an old dam to provide water for his tree nurseries. In need of a break, he went to the local town, Ol Kalou, to meet up with friends. As soon as he'd got off the *matatu* and walked down a street, two policemen in plain clothes materialised at his elbow, pointing a pistol at his head and ordering him to go with them. In the words of his autobiography:

> They took me to the iron hut near the DO's office where there were many policemen waiting for me. They asked me questions and told me to say yes, but I said no. Then I was beaten and they caught me by my private parts of my body, and burned my hand with cigarettes. Then they took me to the Ol Kalou district mortuary. They switched the lights on so that I could see the bodies of the dead people. Then they took away all my clothes and chained me to the body of a dead girl. Near my feet there were many bodies lying there. They told me to play sex with that body of a dead girl . . . Then the policemen switched off the light and said: 'OK enjoy yourself Solomon.' I stayed there three hours, then they came back and said: 'Now Solomon, are you enjoying yourself with your lover?'

The football team listened with a weary sort of resignation as Solomon's story chilled my bone marrow.

'People asked me why I wasn't giving up,' he said, 'they were asking me did I want to be killed?' A few members of the football team sitting in the *hoteli* with us nodded knowingly.

Although I'd read Solomon's story in his book, it felt more immediate listening to him now, so close to one of the offending police stations.

Eventually the football team left, but I didn't even see them go. I noticed out of the corner of my eye that a man wielding a 6-foot pole had come in and sat down opposite us. He wore a hat made out of some animal skin and his suit, worn out at the knees and elbows, was decorated with many safety pins. He was too young to be a war hero from the Mau Mau era. He didn't seem too interested in us, or in anything for that matter except for his sizeable stick.

'It is OK, he is mad,' said Solomon reassuringly, seeing that I was trying not to flinch every time the stick was raised and examined.

The picture opposite me was of a chimpanzee dressed in a suit, tucking into a plate of frankfurters. My head was spinning with Solomon's alarming stories of brutal torture and I had half an eye on the 6-foot stick. I felt a little crazy myself.

The madman followed us out and stood in the middle of the road, staring at nothing in particular as we drove away.

We stopped outside the Quickserve Duka, flanked by Ebenezer Tailoring and Popular Café. Solomon had spotted a kindred spirit. 'He is a colobus man,' he threw back at me as he leapt from the car. After all, these sojourns into Happy Valley were also colobus-counting trips. Solomon always had places to go and people to see.

I peeled and ate an imported South African orange that I had found in the mess of my car, looking through a dusty windscreen at a world I couldn't fathom: a jumble of potholes, litter, goats, chickens and loitering people. A lady stopped to talk to me, her eyes shifting all over the inside of my car, unnerving me. 'I own a bar,' she told me, then added: 'also I am a public health officer.'

Her eyes fastened on my orange, so I gave her the other half and she walked off, munching happily, tossing the peel into the road.

Our final stop that day was the simple mud-walled, earth-floored home of an old man called Njoroge, who together with Solomon had arranged for a handful of Kikuyu elders to come and dredge up some memories. Njoroge's elderly wife brought in firewood to make tea as we sat down to listen. Njoroge didn't know his age, but thought he had been born in 'about 1927'. Many Kenyans, especially older ones like

Njoroge, would never have celebrated a birthday in their entire lives. They couldn't when they didn't know the day or month, let alone the year. Njoroge had worked for 'a *bwana* called Barker', helping with the chickens and ducks. He remembered 'another *bwana* called Dowson' arriving at the same time. 'After that,' he confirmed, 'the white people left and the big hay barns were used to store government machinery when the land was being allocated to the Kikuyu people.' This would have been when Kenya gained independence.

Muthoki, older and equally vague about his age, was born in 'about 1920', he thought. He worked for several white *bwanas* and *memsahibs* as gardener, builder and *fundi* (which roughly translates as an odd-job man, or jack of all trades). 'Dowson,' he said, 'drove very fast.' His memories went back further, to when Ramsden – who they called *Kimondo* – lived there. 'He had a very beautiful house, made of mud and bricks. It had a beautiful courtyard and many ponds, and short, green grass where no cows were allowed to graze.' He remembered being a young boy, in awe of the rich, powerful white man. '*Kimondo* was very tall and very rich!' he said. The local name *Kimondo* had apparently been coined because Ramsden always carried a bag full of nails, and other bits and pieces that might come in useful. It literally means 'the one carrying a goatskin bag'.

I had now read a bit about Sir John Ramsden, a friend and neighbour of Joss and Idina, as well as Alice – and then again of Idina, when she'd later lived at Clouds. A wealthy owner of vast tracts of land, he'd been a contemporary of the 3rd Baron Delamere.

I also remembered that a pilot friend, who'd flown over Happy Valley and the surrounding area in a light aircraft, had talked excitedly about one very well-preserved house on the side of Kipipiri, with grand, well-clipped topiary. 'It must be Clouds,' he'd said.

'Clouds doesn't have any hedges,' I'd replied. 'What colour is the roof?'

'Red.'

'Then it's not Clouds.'

'It is called Aberdare House,' Solomon had told me. 'It is a very beautiful house.'

'It belongs to a political bigwig,' somebody else had said. 'You'll never get in there!'

There were all sorts of stories about the current ownership of the hedged-in house. It belonged to the President. It belonged to a powerful minister. It belonged to the chief of the CID . . .

'Moi was hiding here when people were saying that he had died,' Solomon later told me. He was referring to Kenyatta's successor, the dictatorial President Moi who reigned supreme until 2002; supposed to be dying of throat cancer decades ago, at the time of writing he still looked good. 'Nobody was supposed to know, but we all knew.'

I asked the old men about it. 'It was the house of Lord Ramsden, before Dowson,' Muthoki nodded. 'He was the father of Lord Erroll.'

Njoroge disputed this: 'No, *Kimondo* was father of Idina . . .'

'Yes!' Solomon agreed, less interested in the offspring than ownership, 'it was the house of Ramsden! It is near to Clouds House!'

Njuguna, who had no teeth or hair, was very deaf and almost blind. He seemed the oldest of them all. Nobody had any idea when he had been born, but he actually remembered Idina, as well as *Kimondo*. 'Idina didn't have one husband all the time,' he said, 'but she was never on her own.' This made Solomon laugh. Njuguna laughed too, adding: 'But we were always in the kitchen, cooking them big meals – sometimes as many as fifty of them all ate together there.' Solomon asked if he ever witnessed any wild parties, probably hoping to get a lurid description of an orgy, but Njuguna shook his head: 'No, we didn't know their business.'

A young woman – another wife, or perhaps a daughter or even a granddaughter, served us tea, eyes shyly averted while she laid out the steaming tin cups, then silently left on bare feet.

The old men sipped their tea while joking about the food the white people had liked, suddenly remembering English words for alien things like 'ham', 'roast' and 'something called pudding'.

'There was a vegetable-like cabbage eaten cold and uncooked – with carrots,' said Njuguna and they all laughed.

'They called the sauce DRESSING!' chuckled another of the old men.

The Erroll murder had passed them by, but when Mau Mau started, Njuguna and Muthoki had been arrested and moved to Fort Hall, where they remained until 1957. Njoroge had joined his fellow freedom fighters in the forest. He'd already learnt a lot about white men and about fighting in Burma, he said, when they were fighting the white man's war there.

It was time to go home. As always, part of me wanted to linger in Happy Valley. The slanting rays of mid-afternoon sun accentuated the red berry-like blooms thrusting above the spiky aloe plants, warmed the golden grasses and breathed features into the indigo mountains jutting into a pale sky. The rains had been good and the roads were awful. As those clouds, which had inspired Idina to name her home, rolled in from the Rift Valley, the sky turned stone grey and the colours began to fade. Suddenly the black, pregnant sky cast a premature and foreboding darkness over us and the first huge drops began to hit the windscreen. And thus the heavens opened, pounding us with equatorial rain. At which point we got a puncture. Solomon and I struggled with my brand new hi-lift jack, which stubbornly refused to go up or down, or do anything it was supposed to do. I cursed the rain, which was making our hands, the ground and the jack increasingly slippery, but as I later discovered, it wasn't only the elements: they had actually overdone the paint job on the jack, preventing the teeth from gripping. No amount of dry weather or expertise would have made any difference.

All we could do was retire, shivering, to the car and wait. We watched the rain move across the plateau, and the sun suddenly came out again, sparkling and dancing through the fields like a joker. We were on a road nobody ever drove along, judging by the state of it, so there wasn't much hope of anybody else coming to our rescue – and even if they did, would they have a jack strong enough to lift a heavy Land Rover? Various passers-by gathered and began to offer advice. One old man, less interested in the jack, asked me if I'd known the Barkers.

'Well . . . kind of,' I said. 'I have heard of them. Did you know them?'

'I was their cook,' he replied.

Somebody had come back with a spade and somebody else had a machete. Between them they were digging a hole under my punctured wheel. Now the rain had subsided, we were able to sit on the damp grass. The old cook told me how during Mau Mau, the freedom fighters had spied on Ramsden's former home, Kipipiri House, from a tall cedar tree. 'They could see the white men, and they knew when they went away and when they came back. But the *bwanas* did not know they were there, watching from that tree!' We sat on the bank, the Barkers' old cook and I, looking out at the lovely mountains, united in our separate thoughts inspired by the vision of the unseen spies in the tree.

About half an hour later, having dug deep enough under the front wheel to remove and change it, we were on our way again. Then my rear wheel suddenly started making a gruesome grinding sound, which I tried to ignore.

'Oh!' said Solomon ominously, leaning out of the window to listen, 'maybe we get these bad devils from Happy Valley.'

Oddly enough, when we reached Captain, with its roadside glisten of plastic bag litter, and I turned towards home, the noise stopped.

15

The House with the Golden Door

After the old men's talk of Ramsden, I was determined to visit his Happy Valley home, Kipipiri House, supposedly the best preserved in the whole area.

So Solomon and I drove towards Clouds once again, crossing a deep gorge on a steep, winding road, where a few remaining indigenous trees, their lower branches chopped away, stood naked and exposed. A little farther on Solomon told me to turn left, bluffing his way through the gate of the large flower farm, although the guard was already opening it when he saw a white woman driving, my skin colour and sex rendering me doubly harmless. Kipipiri reared up behind, its higher slopes still darkly forested, as we drove between military rows of plastic greenhouses.

'My friend Peter is a manager working here,' said Solomon. 'You can try to ask if we can see the Ramsden house . . .'

The handsome young Dutchman leaned in at my car window and shook our hands. He seemed amenable, but I quickly realised he was only an employee of the wealthy Kenyan landowner. Behind him stood a massive and impenetrable cypress hedge. He must have thought I was one of those people who constantly glance over your shoulder during conversation, hoping to spot someone more interesting. In truth I was trying to find a chink in the hedge, glimpse the house lurking among its splendid topiary, so near and yet so far. But the hedge was as concealing as a midnight blackout on a foggy night.

Solomon and I used all our powers of persuasion, to no avail. 'You are welcome to my house anytime,' Peter said consolingly, indicating the newly built manager's house by the road, 'but I cannot let you visit the big house – I do not have the authority.'

'OK,' said Solomon, 'so now we must go up to the place I know we can turn the car around.'

Peter melted back into the greenhouses, while we drove up to Solomon's turning place, which he indicated with a triumphant: 'Now you can see!' A wooden side gate in the hedge opened out into a view of the expansive gardens, contained by vast hedges that swept grandly up to the side of the house itself. A long, low bungalow, it was black and white, mock-Tudor style, its red-tiled roof dusted with moss. Taking in the stretch of emerald lawn, the elegant line of smoothly clipped hedge and some shapely exotic trees, I suddenly thought I saw a face looking at us from one of the windows of the house.

'We will just go quickly into the garden,' whispered Solomon, clutching my arm. 'There is nobody there.'

It didn't take any more to persuade me to switch off the engine, jump out of the car and stand excitedly beside the low gate. A watchman appeared from behind a hedge, wearing a trench coat and carrying a club. As he hurried towards us I thought, Well, that's the end of that idea, but to our surprise he was friendly. '*Karibu!*' he beamed, which is Kiswahili for 'close', and also means 'welcome', so we climbed over the gate.

'Is the owner here?' I asked.

'No,' he said. 'Nobody is here.'

I decided not to mention the face at the window. 'May we see the garden?'

'Of course.' Intrigued at our interest, he accompanied us around the beautifully kept gardens, smooth green lawns descending in terraces to ponds and water gardens, ornamental trees, clipped shrubs and hedges 30 feet high, entwining the enchanted gardens in protective green arms. There were two sculpted lions keeping stony watch over the front door. The imposing side door was a light, golden polished wood, carved with floral designs and a family crest which also incorporated a lion.

I tentatively approached the beautiful door, followed by the intrigued watchman. 'Do you come from America?' he asked. 'Sweden?'

Solomon suddenly said to me in a dramatic stage whisper, 'We must leave quickly – there is *that* woman at the window.'

'Who . . .?' I began.

But Solomon was already striding back to the car.

'But you are welcome to come back,' said the watchman sadly, opening the gate for us to save our stepping over.

'Who was that woman, then?' I asked as we drove away hastily.

Solomon was in a reverie.

'Solomon?' I said.

He looked up. 'But it is a beautiful house,' he said sadly, adding secretively, 'I have been in long ago, but now there is a mad Kikuyu woman inside, with a *panga!*'

We drove on to Clouds, a few more miles up the road, passing a small, neat homestead surrounded by hedges clipped into triangular and ball shapes, as unusual in this sort of area as Father Christmas would be.

'The *mzee* who lives there now, he is one of Ramsden's old gardeners,' said Solomon, explaining away my bafflement as if I'd somehow passed it on telepathically.

After we left Clouds and drove back to Machinery, passing Kipipiri House again, in my mind I could still see the face at the window, and yet I was sure it had been a pale, ghostly one: a vision from the past.

I was excited by the house – after all it was the first totally intact old house with a well-kept garden we'd seen in Happy Valley.

Sir John Frecheville Ramsden, as he was correctly called, had made his fortune from the rubber estates in Malaya. He then bought vast estates in Kenya: Kipipiri Estate up by Happy Valley, and Waterloo flanking the shores of Lake Naivasha, now called Marula and still a prosperous farm, today owned by Italians. Kipipiri Estate once flanked the whole western side of Kipipiri mountain, its northern reaches bordering Alice's farm, with Clouds and the area of the white highlands called North Kinangop to the south. Once he'd secured the corridor for his sheep, his land stretched all the way to the acacia-lined shores of Lake Naivasha. Not much over a decade earlier, before the First World War, Lord Delamere had been refused his application for 100,000 acres of land stretching from the Aberdares to the Rift Valley on the grounds that it was intermittent grazing land for the Maasai. Delamere had already had a previous application for Laikipia land (in between the Aberdares and Mount Kenya) turned down because it was too far from the railway. In the end, says Elspeth Huxley in *White Man's Country*, Volume 1 (1930), he had to settle for unoccupied land at Njoro, before he managed to buy Soysambu. But after the war the picture changed dramatically. The Maasai and anyone else would have to make way for the new soldier-settlers – even the likes of Lady Idina Gordon, and including the more respectable Sir John Ramsden.

One of Ramsden's neighbours in Naivasha was Delamere, the other Ewart Grogan, who had impregnated Bubbles Delap's mother. Grogan owned Longonot Farm and was also developing estates at Taveta near the Tanzanian border, in the domed shadow of the high, snowy peaks of Mount Kilimanjaro; here he built a palatial dwelling – some called it a folly – on a small hill, where it stood deserted and reputedly haunted for many decades until somebody converted it into a lodge. It was largely thanks to Ewart Grogan that Happy Valley's rivers were stocked with trout: he originally imported 40,000 of the fish to Kenya in 1906.

According to Edward Plaice in *Lost Lion of The Empire: The Life of Cape to Cairo Grogan* (2001), at the end of 1938 Grogan needed more funds, so he enticed two big spenders, Ramsden and Maurice Egerton (4th Baron of Tatton and a farmer from Njoro in the Rift Valley), to join him in partnership. Elspeth Huxley states in *White Man's Country* Volume 2 (1935) that in 1925, Colonists Ltd, a land agency in southern Tanzania, was formed with £6,000 provided mainly by Ramsden, Egerton and Delamere. Ramsden had certainly been one of the big shots. Tim Hutchinson's *Kenya Up-Country Directory* mentions him as being at Kipipiri Estate in 1926, and also records that he was President of Gilgil Club from 1926 to 1933.

Errol Trzebinski refers to Ramsden's 70,000-acre estate stretching down from Kipipiri. She adds that a builder from Norfolk had built the house and that 'Chops' Ramsden, as he was known to friends, also built Slains before Idina and Joss's arrival. Ramsden, had he been around, probably would have had plenty to say on Joss's murder. Latterly I'd been hearing more about Mau Mau and those more recent killings, but the question of who murdered Joss continued to needle at me.

It was a few months later when Solomon summoned me for an interview. 'I have found a very, very old man. He is more than a hundred and ten years old! He built Ramsden's house!' he shouted excitedly through a crackling phone line.

We drove for miles across high, open plateau country along the Kiambaga Ridge, running between Gilgil and Wanjohi, until finally we came to the simple homestead. A white-haired, white-bearded man met us – he certainly looked a century old – and introduced himself as Amos. I assumed that Amos was the old man we were to talk to, but Amos said, 'My father is ready to welcome you.' He added that he'd only been born around 1930 himself, but his father had been born in the 1880s, which would make him as old as Broughton and Colville, and even older than Idina, had they still been alive!

We followed Amos along a pathway to a round mud hut with a conical grass roof: the traditional way of building, avoiding corners for bad spirits to hide in. Around to the far side, an ancient man, bent over his stick, stood in the doorway like a cracked dusty statue. Amos said something in Kikuyu and the old man held out his hand. It felt like dry, worn leather and I was almost afraid it would come away in mine.

As the old man used his stick to find his way to the low stool and eased himself on to it, I realised he was blind. His eyes were milky white but bright, while his nails were like long, twisted extensions of his bent fingers. His bare feet were as crooked and dry as old tree roots. As he sat warming himself in the sun like an old tortoise, leaning forwards over his knees because he could not straighten his back, he suddenly seemed to come alive. He welcomed us in Kikuyu, which

Amos obligingly translated into Kiswahili for my benefit, and told us that although they never came here now, he remembered the arrival of the very first white people in these parts.

I gazed at the old man. In these back-of-beyond places, a man who has had a hard life can look old in his sixties: was this *mzee* really born in the 1880s? As if sensing my scepticism, Amos explained that they could determine the old man's approximate age by his circumcision age set and what he had done before this, even though they had no idea exactly how old he was.

The old man talked slowly, his voice husky and bubbling with phlegm, which he frequently spat out on one side of the stool. He remembered being a young boy and the excitement amongst his people when those first white men had passed by. Later came the first farmers, he said, then the First World War, when he went with the white men to fight in Taita and then Tanzania. Much later, after the next war, which he also fought in, although by then he was old, Mau Mau began. But by then he was too old to do more than watch and wait.

'But I did,' added Amos, 'I fought against the white men.'

The old man had gone to Maasailand to get circumcised after the First World War, by which time he had already built Kipipiri House. 'So that's why he brought his bride very late,' explained his son, referring to the old custom of paying cattle or other valuable assets to his future wife's family. 'So he was old when he had his children.'

'How many children does he have?' Solomon asked.

This stalled the old man, and eventually after counting with the help of his gnarled fingers and his son, the verdict was only four sons and two daughters. 'But I have fifteen children,' said Amos proudly. He turned aside and blew his nose into the grass, using his hand to apply pressure to one nostril while clearing the other.

'So he built Ramsden's house?' I prompted, not wanting to go off on a tangent.

The old man nodded, his misty eyes shining as he talked about his skills in bricklaying and carpentry. He was chief builder, he added. After that, he'd also built the Gilgil Golf Club and the house that became Pembroke House Preparatory School. But he'd still divided his time between Gilgil and Wanjohi, as he was also, by then, building Alice de Janzé's house.

'I built *Wacheke*'s house with timber, but it had stone floors – she was there living in a tent, alone . . .' he said, using the same name for Alice as the Kiambogo elders. On one occasion when he'd returned to Gilgil to put in the windows and finish the roof at the club, somebody had done a shabby job in his absence: 'The roof fell down and killed three builders . . .' Amos translated matter-of-factly.

I asked him to tell us more about building Ramsden's house.

'It was a very big house and we had to get it exactly right,' he explained, 'but *Kimondo* was not living there.' Ramsden, who was busy in Naivasha, had moved in after they finished, the old man continued, but even then he had divided his time between his Kipipiri and Naivasha farms. He gave a sudden, toothless grin: 'He was a very good man. Those first white men, they were very good, but the later ones, the Boers from South Africa, they were very bad. They beat their workers.'

Tea arrived, stewed in a tin kettle. We took our steaming tin mugs, their handles almost too hot to grip, and moved our stools from the increasing glare of the sun into the shadow cast by the hut. The old man stayed to soak up more warmth, still talking while his son translated: '*Kimondo*'s house, it was a very expensive house. The people were afraid of it. They said the door was made of gold.' He couldn't remember exactly when it was built, but his son said he thought it was in the early 1920s.

'I was not so young then, although it was before my circumcision,' confirmed the *mzee*. 'So I had not yet taken my first wife. *Kimondo*, he had a wife, but I never saw any children.

'We built the house of earth and stone and timber, with a tiled roof,' he continued. 'It was very cold there – and dangerous: we saw many lions, elephants and hyena in the surrounding forest. *Kimondo* used to come to check on our work, but he would stay for no more than three days before going back to Naivasha.'

I listened to the rasping intonation of the old man, his son's low voice quietly filling the gaps with Kiswahili translations. I could imagine him sitting on this stool in the evening sun, entertaining his great-grandchildren – he must have many – with stories, as is the custom.

There was a pause and I felt that perhaps we should leave: the old man must be tired. But suddenly he rapped his stick in the dust and laughed: 'The white men had too much land. All the land was Delamere's and Ramsden's!' The *mzee* looked out with sightless eyes towards an empty blue sky where a tawny eagle circled. 'If you rode on horseback from one end of the white man's farm to the other, the horse would drop down from exhaustion.'

'We must find a way to go inside this house of *Kimondo*,' said Solomon thoughtfully as we laboured back along rough, dusty roads.

16

From Caves to Grandeur

Soon after this, when passing through the Nairobi suburb of Karen, I bumped into Janie Begg. I told her about the old man.

'My father,' she said unexpectedly, 'was Ramsden's sheep manager. He also looked after Cartwright's sheep. His brother was another sheep *fundi*, back in Scotland.' The insertion of Swahili words into everyday conversation is common in Kenya.

I looked at her in surprise, but she was off on another subject. 'Did I tell you I have Idina's chair?' I accepted her invitation to coffee back at her small rented cottage, part of a converted stable block in Karen, where she showed me a very high-backed, wooden, carved dining chair. 'Probably a set of twelve, a reproduction they say,' she went on, as I sat gingerly in the chair imagining the conversations that must have gone on around it in its murky past. Idina had left it to James Bird, better known as Jimmy, who Janie described as Idina's 'last boyfriend'. How curious to leave someone only one chair, I thought as Janie said accusingly that he had gone to South Africa, leaving it behind for Lily Begg to look after, but he never returned nor had he ever contacted the Beggs again. 'I remember Jimmy Bird,' said Janie darkly. 'He drank like a fish!'

I closed my eyes once more, imagining Idina sitting in this chair, quaffing excellent wine. I wondered about her thoughts the last time she sat here, many loves and losses down the line . . .

Janie was saying something about a cave along the Kimuru River on Ramsden's farm. 'My father used to take the sheep up to the high pastures,' she said between heavy drags on her cigarette, 'so we all went – we lived in the cave!'

I blinked a bit, but she said. 'I was very small, but my sister remembers it well.'

At Janie's bidding her sister, Sheila, wrote to me from South Africa:

> My memory goes back to the age of four when we lived in the cave and I only have one distinct memory of it. I was squatting down on my haunches looking towards the entrance as Mum was cooking our lunch in a saucepan over three stones. At my back was the Kimuru River with a hazardous precipice at the edge. As I was so small it probably was not as steep and hazardous as I thought.

Janie was psyched up to find the cave, so we headed to Happy Valley again with an excited Solomon, taking the road from Captain to Machinery, stopping at *daraja tatu*.

Somewhere near here, on this river that Janie, like Solomon, called the Kimuru, was the cave.

We asked an old man, digging his field beside the road, about caves.

'Eeeeh,' he said, 'there are some old Mau Mau caves up the hill.' He laid down his *jembe* and joined Solomon, Janie and me as we scrambled up a steep, winding path, lined with spiky green aloe plants and ash-blonde tufts of dry grass. The old man, delighted at Janie's fluent Kikuyu, said, 'I remember that once, a long time ago, some white people were living in one cave!' But he wasn't sure exactly which cave.

Janie had her pendulum in her pocket – she was confident it would tell her. We looked at a couple of caves, including a very spacious one that would easily have housed a family, but Janie's pendulum apparently said 'no'.

Some way upstream we came upon a horizontal slit in the hillside at ground level. 'We need to go into this one,' said Janie. I looked at her in disbelief but she was already worming her way in on her hands and knees, followed by Solomon. The old man crawled in too, so I followed, muttering to myself that this really wasn't a proper cave. Janie's voice drifted out from the tunnel, sounding even more gravelly than usual: 'It seems to have got very silted up!'

When we all got inside we could sit up – just. Solomon, the tallest, had to bow his head.

Janie's pendulum went wild. 'Yes!' she said delightedly. 'This is it!'

I eyed Solomon sceptically in the gloom, but the pendulum was very much his thing and he said, 'Ah, yes, it is very good!' The old man added admiringly in Kiswahili that Janie was indeed a *muganga* (witch doctor).

Brushing off the earth, our mission accomplished, we headed back to Gilgil, Janie regaling us with stories from the 1940s and 50s, pleasantly distracting us from the tedium of the rough road. Moving Ramsden's sheep between his estates at Kipipiri and Naivasha had required veterinary certificates. But this became an inconvenience, so Ramsden bought the corridor as well.

'That's quite a distance to walk the sheep,' I said.

But Janie, whose father had done it many times, shrugged: 'Not really.'

I still longed to get into Kipipiri House. I thought about it often and even dreamed I was there, a step ahead of the mad woman, looking out through the windows on to green lawns and huge hedges . . .

I asked Janie about it.

'Yes, I remember Kipipiri House well – it was beautiful,' she replied, 'Chops Ramsden got an architect from Norfolk to design it.'

I explained that we hadn't been able to get in.

'Oh?' said Janie. 'I can get you in there!'

I had been wondering if she was going to conjure up Ramsden's ghost with her pendulum or work some other alarming spell, but she said in matter-of-fact tones, 'I used to teach a very nice lad who is a friend of Kanyoto – the owner. I'll get in touch with him. Nobody lives there anyway – it's only very occasionally used.'

Janie duly found her ex-pupil, a charming, soft-spoken young

Left to right: The Hon. Josslyn Hay, Major Roberts, Jos Grant, Lady Idina Hay,
Cockie Birkbeck, Princess Philippe de Bourbon, Nellie Grant; in front of Slains, 1924.
© Illustrated London News Ltd/Mary Evans

Clouds, Lady Idina's third
home in Happy Valley, 1930s.
Courtesy of Lyduska Piotto

Lady Idina Gordon and the
Hon. Josslyn Hay in Italy, soon after
their engagement, September 1923.
© Illustrated London News Ltd/Mary Evans

Gilbert and Diana Colville at the Djinn Palace, Oserian, late 1940s.
Courtesy of Janie Begg

David Begg and Jimmy Bird, 1946.
Courtesy of Janie Begg

Lady Colville's Gilgil Hotel, 1928.
Courtesy of Janie Begg

Sir Jock and Diana Broughton's house, Karen, in 2010. *Author's collection*

Delap's stone house at Rayetta Farm, early 1950s. *Courtesy of Maureen Delap*

Bill Delap, circa late 1940s.
Courtesy of Maureen Delap

Delap's first wooden house at
Rayetta in 2000. *Author's collection*

House at Slains in the 1940s with Aberdare forest behind. *Courtesy of Lyduska Piotto*

Lyduska Hornik at Slains farm, circa 1946. *Courtesy of Lyduska Piotto*

Solomon on the windowsill at Slains, 2000. *Author's collection*

Juliet on the top step at Slains, 2011. *Nigel Pavitt*

The old dairy at Slains, 2011. *Nigel Pavitt*

Giuliana Moretti at Slains, in the late 1950s. *Courtesy of Dianella Moretti-Proske*

Alice de Janzé's first wooden house in 2011.
Nigel Pavitt

Alice de Janzé in court, December 1927
© *Bettmann/CORBIS*

The old man who built Sir John Ramsden's and Alice de Janzé's houses, in 2001.
Author's collection

The old Wanjohi road with the Aberdares to the left, and the foothills of Kipip to the right.
Author's collection

Danson Mwaura, who buried Alice, showing her grave site in 2001.
Author's collection

Sir John Ramsden's Kipipri house, 2011. *Author's collection*

Facing West from Kipipiri House, 1930's
Courtesy of Tobina Cole

Left to right (adults): Derek Fisher, Katinka Ramsden (John wife), 'Chops' Ramsden, John Ramsden (son of Chops) at Kipipiri, 1936.
Courtesy of Tobina Cole

Tobina Cole and Diana Hay, October 1932.
Courtesy of Tobina Cole

Giles Cartwright and dog Flora in front of Kipipri House, circa 1930. *Courtesy of Tobina Cole*

Facing West from Kipipiri House, 2011. *Author's collection*

Geoffrey Buxton's Satima House taken from the back, 2011. *Author's collection*

Geoffrey Buxton's Satima House taken from the front, 2011. *Nigel Pavitt*

The sweeping view towards Fergusson's house from Morgan-Grenville's former garden, 2011. *Nigel Pavitt*

An artist's impression of Morgan-Grenville's former house, in the 1940s.
Courtesy of Richard Morgan-Grenville

Solomon in Morgan-Grenville's garden,
beside the river that ran beneath the house,
2011. *Veronica Finch*

No money for repairs, but time to smile. *Nigel Pavitt*

The Leslie-Melville/Miller house at Airdrie Farm, 2001. *Author's collection*

...tai Farm, initially Charles Gordon's, and old house, recently renovated, with Aberdares in background, 2011. *Nigel Pavitt*

Elizabeth Nuthu at Clouds, 2011.
Veronica Finch

Idina in the courtyard at Clouds, late 1940s.
Courtesy of Lyduska Piotto

Tap above Idina's famous bath at Clouds, 2011. *Nigel Pavitt*

Sketch by Sophie Walbeoffe, of Idina in drawing room at Clouds, 2011. *Author's coll*

Mzee Nuthu and grandchildren in front of gate houses at Clouds, 2000.
Author's collection

A Nuthu grandson in the courtyard at Clouds.
Author's collection

Mau Mau veterans at Kipipiri, 2012.
Author's collection

Solomon and
fires on the
Aberdares, 200[
Author's collection

Juliet and Gra[
Nuthu in front
of Clouds, with
Kipipiri behind[
2011. *Nigel Pavit*

'The Great Road
of China' 2011.
Author's collection

Kikuyu man called Peter Mutua. We all met up at Gilgil Club and embarked on another long day's safari to Happy Valley. Along the road Solomon pointed out people and places of interest for Peter's benefit. 'That's Beth Mugo's house' – referring to a well-known Kenyan politician – '. . . that man running along the road, that's the athlete John Kagwe . . . there used to be colobus in that valley . . .'

It was 50 miles from Gilgil to Kipipiri House – quite a distance to carry materials from the nearest railway station. Ramsden, as club chairman, certainly had to travel far to attend meetings and events there.

Peter, the Dutchman, had left the estate. Whoever had replaced him didn't spot us as we sneaked past the greenhouses and up the road that allowed us the tantalising glimpse of green lawn, coiffured hedges and the lovely old house. We drove on round to the back gate, the official entrance to the house, where we were stopped by a one-eyed watchman. This was not the friendly guardian of our last visit and I wondered if we'd instigated his being fired. Meanwhile, his replacement glared at us with hostility.

'May we park inside?' asked Solomon. We were near the house now – I could have sprinted over and touched its old walls.

The watchman stood firm and eyed us suspiciously with his one eye. 'You may not enter!' he said.

Peter Mutua said something in Kikuyu but even he, with his politically useful connections, seemed doomed to failure.

Like a vision, a woman in a headscarf, anorak and long skirt suddenly materialised at his elbow, and I was reminded of a song my grandmother used to sing about the lady 'with her one eye in the pot and the other up the chimney'. The squinting woman also clutched a *panga* which she held at the ready. It all felt very *Jane Eyre* and I wondered if she was the mad, locked-up wife of some important person who perhaps used this place as a bolthole.

Peter had dug from his pockets an impressively expensive mobile phone – a new mast had recently been erected in the area – and made a call. After a few minutes the watchman spoke to whoever was on the line in rapid Kikuyu. Then he looked us all up and down, and opened

the gate, saying something to the mad woman before she raised her
panga any higher.

She looked at me murderously. 'Do you know Jesus?' she asked.

I nodded rather weakly. It seemed imprudent not to.

She looked at Janie, who said something soothing in Kikuyu. She
gave Solomon a crooked glare that was enough to put the forest behind
him on fire, then seemed to make up her mind. She led the way towards
the back door, glancing behind her to see if we were following.

Thus we were finally allowed into Kipipiri House, tiptoeing along
corridors that flanked an open courtyard, unable to believe our luck,
not daring to say too much in case the mad woman raised her *panga*
or the watchman cursed us. Most of the rooms were locked, but the
dining room was open. I silently admired wood-panelled walls and a
stone fireplace, although the modern furniture was too ostentatious for
my taste. Then Janie said, 'I wonder if this chandelier is original . . .'
Out came the pendulum and before it had time to tell us the age of
the chandelier, the mad woman took exception to such divinations
and began to shriek, which turned into some sort of fit, the occasional
religious utterance frothing forth. Janie, it was evident, was now being
seen as the devil in disguise. It was time to leave, which we did in haste.

Janie wanted to see Mary Miller's old house. I tried to dissuade her,
suggesting we go to Alice de Janzé's instead, which was also closer.
But Solomon needed to find somebody who knew about a group of
colobus in Wanjohi, and so we drove back around the northern end
of Kipipiri and into the valley, passing Wanjohi and turning left up
to Mary Miller's house once again. It seemed even more ruined than
before, as if something had eaten away another part of it. There was
less roof, less wall and fewer windows. The place still felt as if it were
shedding gloom into the surrounding atmosphere. Solomon wouldn't
get out of the car. I only walked to the fence. Janie's pendulum froze,
so she did not go much further.

'This place is horrible!' said Peter, who'd stayed behind me.

I remembered what had happened after we were here last time
and Solomon echoed my thoughts: 'This place can bring you very

bad luck.' Peter, a large and robust Kenyan who didn't get fazed by trivialities, had turned pale under his dark skin.

'We shan't take any bad luck home with us. Let's stop right here,' Janie said as I drove away faster than usual, crossing the bridge over the Wanjohi River, not far from the house. So I stopped and at Janie's bidding we all walked to the river's edge and 'cleansed' our faces, arms, necks, feet and hands in the icy water. The pendulum woke up and we all felt better.

A gaggle of small children who had emerged down a path from the other direction dropped their empty water vessels and ran like hares at this unlikely sight of two white women and two African men, who stood on the green grass amongst clumps of nettles and thistles and shook themselves vigorously in the midday sun like mad dogs.

17

Times of Change

Although, like Mary Miller, some settlers remained, Ramsden had left Kenya and Erroll's murder was old news when more new expatriates arrived in the colony after the Second World War. The newcomers built a flush of houses on smaller farms, subdivisions of vast estates like Ramsden's. This was a very different type of farmer: my grandparents, by then farming below Mount Kenya, the other side of the Aberdares, would have referred to them as 'respectable types'. These Happy Valley settlers became a close community by necessity, helping one another and working overtime to get their farms up and running. They planted wheat and kept cattle. A few kept sheep. The second year they planted pyrethrum, which thrived in the high altitude and brought these struggling, hard-working farmers some very welcome cash.

Elspeth Huxley perfectly sums it up with understated wit in *Forks and Hope*: 'The Wanjohi became a productive valley: still happy, on the whole, but on more bourgeois lines than in the days of its notoriety.'

Idina had left Happy Valley by then, and her light-headed lifestyle had departed with her.

A number of these ex-Happy Valley settlers are still around but their houses, purpose built after Happy Valley's heyday, haven't survived as well as some of the older ones. Indeed, they are often hard to find at all. I had imagined that these dwellings, built in the late 1940s and early 50s, wouldn't harbour stories as gripping as those of their predecessors, but I was wrong. These were interesting times, not least because of Kenya's new war of independence.

Mau Mau in Kenya has often been selectively reported, even misinterpreted, in history books, and it remains a popular modern trend to heap all blame and shame on the British side. The reality was far more complicated and I found fascinating reading in some of the lesser-known books on the subject – such as David Lovatt-Smith's *Kenya, The Kikuyu and Mau Mau* (2005) – which offer an interesting, albeit unfashionable, perspective on this portion of Kenyan history.

Three years after the end of the Second World War, in 1948, a Kikuyu oath-taking ceremony was held in protest at the imminent arrival of Britain's Duke of Gloucester, who was to award Nairobi city status. In 1951 the British government refused to increase the number of elected Africans on the colony's legislative council and Mau Mau began in earnest, with the state of emergency declared the following year. This was the same year that HRH Princess Elizabeth visited a treehouse hotel called Treetops, in the Aberdare forest, a prelude to the unfurling of a new chapter in British history.

Hunter Jim Corbett's last book, a beautifully illustrated booklet on Treetops, vividly describes that day, 5 February 1952: the forest with its pink-flowering Cape chestnut trees and view of the Aberdares. That same morning he'd had, by telegram, an invitation from Princess Elizabeth to accompany the royal party to Treetops. They had arrived at the Royal Lodge in Sagana two days earlier – and the previous day the Duke had played polo at Nyeri, on the far side of the Aberdares. Corbett, concerned about security, had missed the polo to ensure their safety. As it happened, the biggest threat turned out to be elephants, who uprooted four of the biggest trees – plus ladders built for people to scale the trees to escape the elephants and other dangerous animals.

Corbett, who'd shaved twice, apprehensively watched a herd of forty-seven jittery elephants with their small calves approach the salt lick – right below the tree in which the hotel was built. As the important guests approached, Princess Elizabeth, in front, remained completely calm. Luckily the wind was on the side of the royals and Corbett heaved several sighs of relief when all were up the ladder and safely in Treetops. He praises her courage, adding: 'A minute after climbing the ladder the Princess was sitting on the balcony and, with steady hands, was filming the elephants.' HRH was rewarded with excellent game viewing and, entranced, requested tea on the balcony.

As evening drew on, Corbett talked to the Princess about her father's illness, although she was confident he'd seemed much better when waving her off in London. After dinner the royal party returned to the balcony to watch nine rhinos and, at dawn, Princess Elizabeth was out on the balcony to do more filming, making notes on all the animals. Corbett marvelled that 'though she had spent so few hours in sleep the Princess had started that day with eyes sparkling and a face as fresh as a sunflower'. He noted that it was a 'radiantly happy princess' who returned to the Royal Lodge – only to receive the sad news that her father had just died. Corbett wrote the famous words in the Treetops register, noting that for the first time in world history a princess had ascended a tree and descended a queen, 'God bless her.'

Treetops was burned down by Mau Mau on 27 May 1954, as was Nyeri Polo Club, allegedly in protest at British anti-terrorist operations. Both places had the royal visit in common. Operation Blitz had run through the Aberdares in late 1953, resulting in the deaths of 125 Mau Mau, followed by the King's African Rifles' Operation Hammer and its shoot-on-sight policy.

Seventeen months before Treetops fell prey to arsonists, at dinner time during the evening of New Year's Day 1953, the brutal murder of an elderly white farmer and his young apprentice took place under cover of darkness – at their own dining table. It was almost thirteen years since Erroll's murder, and eight and a half since the end of the Second World War. The Africans who had fought foreign wars for the British in various parts of the world had, as in the First World War, seen the vulnerability of men – including white ones – and now they were embarking on their own battle to gain independence for their country.

When I'd talked to the Kiyuku elders about their memories of Alice de Janzé, the conversation had inevitably touched on Mau Mau. One-eyed Gichuki, who didn't seem to know anything about Alice, told us – after announcing with pride that he had eleven children – that he'd been an informant during Mau Mau, which had begun in earnest a decade after Alice's death. 'Eeeeh! I took tobacco and food into the forests – and the forests were very big in those days.' There were murmurs of assent. 'Once you took an oath, you must die if you break it,' he cried. More agreeing murmurs.

Major Mururi, who'd acquired his rank as a freedom fighter, warmed up to the subject. 'Eeeeeh! I was young and unmarried in those days,' he said. 'But I ordered the slaughtering of the white men's cattle!' Several others nodded conspiratorially.

'The *wazungu* made up the word Mau Mau,' Major Mururi continued disdainfully. 'Once there was a meeting of elders. African informers to the white men were listening outside with their ears to the walls so that they could tell the white men what was said. They heard nothing but mumbling: M-m-m-m-m-m! So when they were told this the *wazungu* invented the word Mau Mau.'

It was a good story and caused much hilarity, although Solomon commented in an aside that Mau Mau actually comes from *Uma Uma*, Kikuyu for 'Go! Go!', which of course could equally be corrupted by eavesdropping.

I then discovered that my daughter's school friend's grandmother, Elspeth Harte, née Dawson, had known the area after Ramsden left and during the Mau Mau era. Her sister had lived at Kipipiri, she said, putting me in touch with Belle Barker, who now lived in South Africa.

Belle wrote to me, filling in some of the history post-Ramsden. The company Block and Massada had bought Kipipiri Estates from Ramsden in 1950, then dividing up and selling the farms in the early 1950s, while the government offered generous terms to encourage new settlers. Belle's brother-in-law had carried out the survey of the twenty-three farms, after which Belle's (and Elspeth's) brother, Fergus Dawson, bought two blocks, including the one containing Ramsden's main Kipipiri House. The Dawsons lived there before selling both farms to Italians and renting Clouds in early 1954. Belle's husband, Peter Barker, also bought a farm. Another couple, Randall and Vi

Franklin, bought two blocks including the main manager's house, Manunga, where Belle said that Derek and Pat Fisher had lived.

'I believe Sir John Ramsden also built Clouds for Lady Idina,' Belle wrote, explaining she'd read about the Happy Valley crowd in the book she thought was called 'White Magic' but had never met Idina. Below the Barkers, Belle informed me, John and Didi Gordon bought a farm. She was an artist.

'Didi was Danish,' another elderly *memsahib* said. 'She was very pretty – and very flirty!' This threw more light on the Gordon who'd have built the tower we'd visited, near Machinery, but nobody seemed to know if John Gordon was any relation of Charles, Idina's second husband.

A 1956 RAF map charted all these houses and dwellings for the sake of identification for British troops brought out during the emergency. The Barkers' home is marked at 7,850 feet, below Kipipiri House, then Dawson's at 8,150 feet. Clouds is highest, at 8,200 feet. The majority of other names of the time are South African – Potgeiter, Van Rensburg, Nel, Kruger, Steyn, Pieters, Spooner.

'Our farm was called Mara,' Belle wrote, 'as that was what the Maasai called it, which means "shadows", or "black and white", as there were mounds on the land which gave this effect.' When the Barkers first arrived there had been nothing on their farm apart from a sentry box, from where a guard had kept watch over Ramsden's sheep, fending off wild animals. The Barkers started off living in a shed, building their stone house in 1956. Peter Barker was a former district officer, so farming was new to him. Luckily for him his neighbours were seasoned farmers: his brother-in-law Fergus Dawson and friend Randall Franklin. Belle wrote: 'None of us had very much capital so we all worked very hard indeed, in fact my brother had his tractors working all night to try to get in the maximum acreage the first year. One night the driver fell asleep and the tractor came to rest just at the edge of the steep gorge.'

When, after some more correspondence, we'd established the whereabouts of the Barkers' former home, I wrote back to explain to Belle that their old house had now been swallowed up by the untidy tin-shack village called Machinery. Belle replied: 'Maybe the village is called Machinery because we had two big wheat sheds on the farm and they may have been used later to house machinery.'

She enclosed a photograph of a painting of the Mara farmhouse done by Rowena Bush – an artist's impression with flowery surrounds and sunny fields stretching into far horizons. She also sent a cine film of the area taken in the 1950s, which my father managed to show on his old and temperamental projector. Between erratic jumps and behind surface scratches that leapt across the screen like hyperactive stick insects, the beauty of Mara Farm unfolded: golden fields of wheat stretched towards an indigo Kipipiri, its mantle of forest touching the edges of the expansive and productive farms. The farmhouse itself, a modest stone bungalow, was surrounded by beds of lovingly tended, colourful blends of exotic flowers, in front of which toddled blonde children. There were two large wheat stores just behind. Otherwise the horizons were devoid of any buildings. It was hard to believe that all this had disappeared under the flimsy shacks and exploding new population of Machinery.

Belle's accompanying letter praised the 'magnificent gardens' of all the houses in the area: she thought Ramsden's had been laid out by a professional landscape gardener from South Africa. 'The beautiful cedar forests came right down to the houses and they were full of colobus monkeys, elephants and buffalo. One night five elephants walked right through our wheat fields leaving a very neat path, but little damage, whereas the warthog did tremendous damage digging up the wheat.'

Once the Barkers had climbed to the top of Kipipiri mountain through magnificent cedar forest, Peter slashing a way through stinging nettles. I didn't like to tell Belle that now the forest does not even begin until halfway up the mountain and that the vegetation is thinning out daily, well-worn paths of charcoal burners and poachers like a growing spider's web networking new routes between remaining pockets of forest.

When Mau Mau began, Belle explained, all the Kikuyu were removed from the area by the British government. This was basically all the available labour, so farmers had to bring in other tribes to help. Meanwhile, many of the Kikuyu freedom fighters were hiding in the

Kipipiri forest – which stretched down to the edges of the farms. Most of the women and children were sent away to safer areas, while the men stayed together at Kipipiri House, going out on terrorist search patrols and trying to keep the farms running. Times were suddenly tense for the white settlers, the nights filled with terror as stories whipped round of grisly murders, of faithful servants taking Mau Mau oaths before opening doors to gangs of men who would murder their white employers.

My mother's neighbour, Maureen Barratt, who used to visit relations in the Wanjohi area, remembers Dawson's tower at Kipipiri House. 'It was more like a strong room than a tower,' she told me, then – visibly shuddering as she remembered sleepless nights – 'It was creepy up there in those days of Mau Mau.'

Belle explained that the freedom fighters, however, were more inclined to raid farms situated further from the mountains, making it harder to track them back into their forested hiding places in a vast area of impenetrable terrain, full of wild animals. 'When the women and children returned home, we still carried guns all the time and the army surrounded our houses with security fences as well as the labour lines,' she added.

According to Ian Parker in *The Last Colonial Regiment*, in 1953 the British 'C Coy' under Major John Klynsmith was based at Ol Kalou. In November they were at Dawson's farm, near a pencil slats factory, moving on to patrol Kipipiri and the Wanjohi valley.

Peter Hewitt, a police officer stationed in the area soon afterwards, wrote in his diary on 3 May 1954, published in 1999 as *Kenya Cowboy*: 'The weather is awful! Really Scottish in its misty, damp drizzle. Worst of all is the mud created. It all but isolates us; the roads are impassable.' A few days later he wrote about visiting the inspector at the 'Sattimer (sic) police post', also on the slopes of Kipipiri: 'His post is appalling; they all sleep in tents. Furthermore, like many others, he is at loggerheads with the local settlers – they like to dictate, he won't permit it. Had an awful ambush session tonight; poured with rain, scrambling and sliding in inky darkness.' In October he records that the Mau Mau made an abortive raid on Barker's, after which Hewitt and his men attempted to track the gang 'right over the stark and forbidding mass of Kipipiri' until they were defeated by rain, along with lack of food and blankets. Days later the Mau Mau stole twenty sacks of newly harvested wheat from a farmer just below Dawson's. On 4 November Hewitt watched the Lincoln Bombers targeting the Aberdare forest, 'which means that the terr's [terrorists] will flood this area in no time at all. Where do they come from? Why are we always several steps behind? Where do they vanish to? It is virtually their war, they dictate the terms.'

But in spite of troubling times, Belle Barker concluded her letter nostalgically: 'Before Peter died he said that the happiest days of his life were the ten years spent developing Mara.'

Belle also contacted Randall and Vi Franklin's daughter, Sheilah Simons, who wrote to me from South Africa: 'I understand that Sir John ceded the estate to his son to avoid death duties, and then the son was killed in Malaya by terrorists when his regiment was stationed there, and due to death duties Sir John had to sell his land at Kipi.' Sheilah had also been to the Catholic mission to revisit her childhood home. She wrote unemotionally that a huge church had risen up in what was once their horse paddock. Her father was called '*Mununga*' by the African staff and her mother '*Nycambati*', meaning 'the one whose voice shakes the rafters' – Vi could be, according to her daughter, 'quite peppery at times'.

Sheilah also mentioned another close neighbour, Michael Allman Hall, 'newly married and fresh from the UK'. He bought a farm bordering theirs and the Barkers', naming it Ndatura, place of the doves. Initially he built a cedar house on the edge of a small ravine, against local advice, right in the middle of the elephants' biannual migratory route. When the elephants inevitably arrived, puzzled by this obstacle in the middle of their ancient trail, they milled around it, drinking water from the rainwater tank and scratching their sizeable behinds, making the walls shudder. Sheilah related how Michael Hall sent his wife Dawn to the Franklins for help, while he stayed inside the house playing Beethoven on the grand piano.

Hall was set apart from the surrounding farmers by virtue of the fact he had capital and could afford a manager. At some stage he moved to the high, tea-growing hills of Kericho, where he had another farm. Meanwhile, Sheilah explained, a manager called Alan Gray ran Ndatura.

Coincidentally Alan Gray happens to live in South Africa, near his old friends – my aunt and uncle. Their bond is reinforced by the Kenya connection. It seems that this becomes a lifeline to many old colonials who left Kenya. 'They call us the "when-we's",' my uncle explained, 'because we all get together and start every sentence with "When we lived in Kenya . . ."' Through my aunt I established that Alan Gray had actually been manager for Dr Roy Thompson, who'd purchased the empty 2,000 acres abandoned by Hall. Gray set about developing the farm from scratch, stocking it with dairy cows and sheep. He planted pyrethrum on the poor soil, which had to be drained, gradually mechanising the farm. Cream was taken to Gilgil where it was transported on to the Nakuru creameries – it had to be kept fresh so it wasn't shaken into butter on the rough roads. Dried pyrethrum was also taken to Nakuru to be made into insecticides. The average rainfall, said Alan Gray, was about 45 inches a year, high by Kenyan standards. There wasn't much time for anything other than hard work.

A year after visiting Machinery, I was having tea with Annie Dunn, a Soysambu neighbour, who was relating a wild-sounding but not uncommon story for Kenya: while she was out on a walk, a very large python had wrapped itself around one of her spaniels. Unable to disentangle it, she and her son had carried the dog home, along with the tenacious python which endeavoured to bite them – so one of them had to hold its head, swathed in a sweatshirt. When they arrived home to more helping hands, the dog survived, but the python didn't! Annie's mother, Joan Heath, was visiting and she laughed off Annie's lack of fear, jokingly relating it to her 'hardy upbringing up at Kipipiri'.

'Kipipiri?' I cried, more interested in that than the snake.

'Yes,' Joan said, going on to explain how she and her late husband Peter had managed Hall's farm before moving to their own, which they bought from an Afrikaner called Davies. 'It was below Mara Farm on the road to Gilgil. We lived in a converted barn with pencil-slat parquet floors,' said Joan. 'We grew lovely peaches and plums, and elephants visited us and drank at the dam.'

As it happened, Solomon and I had visited an old house just below Machinery. There was the remains of an orchard and glimpses of a panoramic view through a straight line of tall, spindly cypress trees that once would have been a clipped hedge, their soft pine scent pervading the cabbage patch that had covered the terrace. We were invited in by the owner and sat chatting to him on a window seat. 'This was the house of a white man we called *Tuchora*,' he said, using the Kiswahili word for artist.

'Neither of us were artists,' said Joan when I told her about it and showed her the photograph, 'but that was our house!'

Delighted I had found another person who lived near Clouds in the 1950s, I questioned Joan without mercy. Luckily most of her generation enjoy reminiscing, although of course the human memory is not infallible. But somehow the variations and contradictions add to the intrigue of those bygone times.

'I visited Clouds in 1955. It had a water garden and there were even daffodils and bluebells,' Joan recalled. 'Idina had left such a lovely garden!' It felt refreshing to hear praise for Idina's creativity with plants, rather than disapproving judgements regarding her inventiveness from earlier decades. Joan also remembered Mununga when the Franklins had lived there: 'A lovely, cosy old house with a hedge of rambler roses.' She added how horrified she'd been to revisit Kipipiri House, after the last white settlers had left, to find that the walnut trees had been cut up into firewood, then stacked in a beautiful old pink bath.

It wasn't all drudgery. With a twinkle in her eye, Joan told me about a New Year party at the Hall house when she'd been dancing with Bubbles Delap until Bill had objected to his young wife having so much fun. He'd dragged Bubbles home and locked her in the tower, where, according to Joan, she whiled away the long hours painting imaginative pictures.

'That first police station where you were beaten up by police was once Hall's house?' I asked Solomon later.

'That one,' Solomon assented.

I suddenly had a flash vision of Michael Hall playing his grand piano. Nobody had actually concluded that story: had Beethoven sent the elephants running on their way or encouraged them to stay for another long drink at the tank?

18

Murder Beneath the Mountain

Looking back to my first trip with Solomon to Clouds, I realised how much my quest had changed and expanded. Inevitably, perhaps, I'd initially become riveted by the Happy Valley hype – drugs, sex, scandal and murder. It's a 'forbidden' world that horrifies, even repulses, and yet we can become caught in a compulsion to find out more. I know plenty of people in Kenya today who are overly dependent on alcohol, sex and drugs for their pleasure and even their 'survival'. My paternal grandmother was an alcoholic whose marriage and career were destroyed by her addiction; as a child I watched her blot out each day before we'd even got as far as breakfast. Perhaps this explains why I was attracted to research a part of Kenya of such tarnished repute.

But then Happy Valley's history takes a U-turn, with a new generation who remind me of my maternal grandparents: hard-working farmers with little money, often managing somebody else's farm, or struggling to save up enough to repay the purchase of their own. My grandparents, after decades of managing a farm, bought their own small one in 1958, just when my 21-year-old father proposed to my mother; they'd met in Nyeri, where she was teaching at a boarding school and he was posted during Mau Mau. And thus we move into the realms of living memory, my interest stimulated by my own family's stories about this new episode in the life of Happy Valley. Farmers like my grandparents struggled to keep their farms productive, while in the rest of the world friends and relations read with mounting alarm newspaper headlines that told of horrifying murders on Kenyan farms – and particularly those near the vast forests of the Aberdares where the terrorists were hiding. The murder of Charles Fergusson and Richard Bingley sent shock waves worldwide, but for their neighbours, it must have been thoroughly nerve-wracking.

Bubbles Delap told me about one night when she'd heard Mau Mau intruders. 'They were on the roof, breaking in that way. Bill, after a few whiskies, heard nothing, but I called my daughters into one room, then ran around the house slamming doors and shouting until they went away. Later we heard they had planned to kill us!' After that incident they'd built a fortified extension with an iron door and barred windows where they could sleep securely at night. 'I felt safe in that fort. We were all nervous at night of course. We used to see Fergusson and Bingley sometimes in Ol Kalou Club, but I never went to their house. That murder was terrible. At about nine at night, just after it had been discovered, all the neighbours came over to us; the men rushed out with guns and the women stayed at our house. I learned to use a gun after that.'

Caroline Hanbury Bateman lived closer to Fergusson and Bingley, making it clear that the 'Happy Valley lot', as she described them in denigrating tones, were worlds apart from those nearer Ol Kalou, the lifestyle of the former not remotely representative of the majority of settlers. After the murder on the evening of New Year's Day, her mother and stepfather, Joyce and Durban Cowen, rushed over to the tragic scene. Caroline, who was with them, was only ten, but her impressionable young mind absorbed two sharply contrasting moments, 'a thatched back porch with the outside light on and then carnage inside . . .'

I'd seen an old black and white pictorial record of Mau Mau, *A Collection of Photographs Recording Kenya's Battle Against Mau Mau.* Printed and published by The English Press Ltd, Nairobi, Kenya Colony, the price was three shillings and fifty cents. I looked through it with some trepidation. There was the most unflattering photograph of Jomo Kenyatta I had ever seen, followed by gruesome images including cows with their back legs broken and innards gouged out, captioned as 'bestiality'; sheep eyes impaled on kei-apple thorns captioned 'accessories of barbarism'; a hanged cat; an abducted Asian baby; and fires lit by arsonists. Most horrific were the pictures of human murders: bodies after nocturnal Mau Mau attacks, including the Lari massacre of 150 Kikuyu women and children whose husbands were loyal to the British; and of an African chief, who'd also been on the 'wrong' side. There was a photograph of the bedroom of a young British boy, Michael Ruck, murdered on a North Kinangop farm, not far from Clouds: blood-stained sheets beside a train set, a globe of the world and a teddy bear. A chamber pot had been placed underneath the bed, presumably a sensible precaution so the little boy didn't have to go outside. He'd never need to again.

Then came the photographs of the Fergusson and Bingley house after the murder. 'A young farmer, Mr Richard Bingley and an old settler of 30 years' standing, Mr C.H. Fergusson, were attacked at their Ol Kalou Farm as they sat down to dinner, and killed', read the caption. 'Neither Mr F nor Mr B had time to use their weapons and they were struck down as they sat at the table.' In the lounge were visible the ruffled carpet, books on the floor absorbing blood, pools of blood around the coffee table, and an ominously open door behind a blood-spotted chintz chair. The photos of the dining room gruesomely showed a soup plate on a round, polished table, swimming in blood, with a bloodied spoon and fork, blood all over the side plate and butter dish, soaking the crumbs of bread. Then there was a picture of their cook after he was arrested. Fergusson's house, I thought with some trepidation, must have a dark atmosphere considering what had happened between those walls. But nobody seemed to know where it was.

I happened to have an old, gold-framed mirror that needed fixing and a friend recommended Frank Daykin, 'the best antique restorer you could find in Nairobi'.

It turned out that Frank had read a couple of articles I'd written on the old Happy Valley houses. 'We lived up there once,' he said, 'closer to Ol Kalou, near Fergusson's house.'

That's how I ended up spending the best part of a morning with this slight, grey-haired man, captivated by the sparkle in his incredibly blue eyes, listening to his stories, as we sat among a treasure trove of broken furniture and dusty old clocks that all told different times. I sat on a three-legged chair beside a scratched walnut bridge table, making my notes.

Frank Daykin's father, he said, had worked for a man called Morgan-Grenville.

This rang a bell: Solomon had once told me, 'There was a man called Morgan who had a very big house that was high up the Aberdare Mountains. It even had a river underneath.' I had wondered a bit at this, but Frank now confirmed that yes, Robert Morgan-Grenville's house had indeed been perched on the steep sides of the north-western Aberdares at the top of a road that had mounted the precipice in a series of hairpin bends. 'It was a cedar house, with twenty-seven rooms, stuffed with antiques,' said Frank. 'It also had a magnificent garden with rhododendrons, willow trees and bridges arching over a river that flowed right under the drawing room. This was a special room, only used occasionally.'

Morgan-Grenville had two adjoining farms, one of which Frank's father had managed. The young Frank had run the workshops. 'Morgan-Grenville was a nice man — always had a cigar in mouth — like Churchill,' said Frank. 'He gave the impression of being stern, but we got on well.' As he elaborated further, I began to picture the man he described: tall and aristocratic looking, talking with a slow drawl, wearing a Stetson . . . a man of habit, doing his weekly shopping in Nakuru, driving over the Dundori ridge, then spending the night at the Rift Valley Club. Frank had also liked his wife Mabel: 'She sparked off my interest in antiques, took me with her to all the sales.' Cars were another of the young Frank's interests. 'Morgan-Grenville had a huge Buick Cadillac,' Frank added, 'then a Jaguar: he loved American cars.'

I suddenly remembered that Lyduska had also mentioned Morgan-Grenville. 'He was very rich. He was shy — quite weird,' she'd said, adding, 'His wife Maisie was very learned. A very good gardener.'

Frank didn't think Robert had another wife. It was more likely a confusion of names. He told me that Morgan-Grenville first arrived in Happy Valley in 1938 with his business partner, Archibald Fraser Allen – and the latter's wife, Mabel. After Fraser Allen's premature death, Mabel married Morgan-Grenville. It sounded suspiciously Happy Valley sort of stuff, but Frank assured me there were no affairs or murders – it had been death by accident.

Frank's father, Frank Joseph Daykin, had been a labourer in London, 'one of the last to lay cobbles in Fleet Street', Frank said. He'd left his first wife, running off with a barmaid called Elsie, Frank's mother. One day in 1954 Frank Joseph walked past South Africa House and paused. On impulse he walked in and asked for a job. Morgan-Grenville happened to be there too. Six weeks later the Daykin family were on a boat to Kenya.

Once they'd docked, the Daykins travelled by train to Gilgil, where they were met by an Austin lorry and a Mercedes pick-up, noted by nineteen-year old Frank and committed to memory. He was brimming with excitement at this wild adventure which had taken them across increasingly warm seas, into the hot and muggy but exotic port of Mombasa. Then there'd been the train ride across stunningly beautiful landscapes, replete with wild animals, pausing in Nairobi before finally descending into the dramatic Rift Valley. They passed Lake Naivasha and finally disembarked at Gilgil station. They then began climbing up out of the Rift Valley again, now driving on wet, slippery roads that stretched endlessly into a darkly mysterious African night. The rains had come, transforming the dust into perilously slippery mud known as 'black cotton', causing the vehicles to sashay and spin, sliding into ditches and thudding into the banks.

Frank's mother, very much an English city girl, was horrified. Then, when they eventually arrived at their new abode in the dark and the rain, Elsie Daykin discovered that the long-drop toilet *and* the kitchen were outside in the cold. She'd been one of twelve daughters and had produced five children herself in six years, so she was reasonably hardy, but arriving after such a long journey at this cold, bleak, primitive dwelling somewhere in Africa was totally overwhelming. Elsie burst into tears.

When the sun arrived the next morning, its warmth taking a long time to have any effect because it had to rise above the huge hulk of the Aberdares, the new arrivals must have looked out at the golden light spreading across the vast plateau, towards distant blue mountains at the other side of the Rift Valley and gasped. Perhaps Elsie Daykin was moved by such an expansive, beautiful view, or maybe she just wished she could hotfoot it back to London to find a few 'modern' conveniences – and friends to chat to. This place, in the shadow of a cold mountain, with nobody to gossip with except the boss's wife, must have felt like the world's end. It was even less comforting to have arrived when Mau Mau was in full swing: the British press had not made light of it, and one of the grisliest murders – that of a white farmer whom everybody described as 'a delightful old man' and his poor young student – had recently taken place a stone's throw away.

Home was now a cedar house, perched beside a gorge on a ridge running up the high Aberdares to the Morgan-Grenville house. Frank loved it all. At least there'd been an indoor bathroom – with a tin tub, he pointed out, and piped water. 'I wonder if the old Dover stove is still in the kitchen?' he mused.

A stone house was being built lower down the slope. As soon as this second house was ready, the Daykins moved there.

'Our first house was near the Malewa River: you crossed over a rickety bridge and then drove up a steep hill. The second house was down below, not on the river. Down to the right of the workshop,' Frank said, as if giving me directions to come to lunch.

Both homes had looked down on to vast, open plains stretching west, towards where this high country drops down in a series of steps into the Rift Valley.

Before I left Frank's workshop, we'd made a plan to drive up to the area, so he could find his old homes – and look for Fergusson's. I'd forgotten all about the mirror.

19

Finding Fergusson's

It was a cold, grey day with incessant drizzle when we headed up to the northernmost end of Happy Valley, somewhere I'd never ventured before. This was probably the sort of weather Frank's mother had arrived in half a century ago, although we had the advantage of daylight and nor had we come all the way from England.

Frank and his wife, Anne, had stayed at Gilgil Club the night before, along with Janie Begg, who was accompanying us. The rattles made by my Land Rover, when I arrived very early in the morning, were enough to convince everyone we should go in Frank's Pajero – thankfully, as it didn't leak. Solomon joined us at Captain, also delighted at a chance to explore Happy Valley's northern reaches.

We took the tarmac road to Ol Kalou, cursing the vicious, hidden speed bumps at every small village or school. Then we turned right on to the road that eventually takes you to Wanjohi town, passing Slains on the way. It was a bleak and flat high plateau – particularly unappealing in bad weather. Somewhere over to our left, surrounded by swampy country, was Lake Ol Bolossat.

According to Errol Trzebinski in *Kenya Pioneers*, in 1903 the East African Syndicate were given the lease of 500 square miles between Ol Kalou and Ol Bolossat. In 1916 it was surveyed and farms were up for sale: the first crop to be tried was flax, but in the early 1920s its price dropped, so flax was dropped too. By the end of the 1920s the Happy Valley crowd had moved in, not far to the south, where they were fast forging their reputation below those mauve and blue mountains, hidden by cloud this morning, but usually clearly visible from Ol Kalou. By the early 1930s Happy Valley's reputation was spilling down steadily, tarnishing and toxic, reaching Ol Kalou town, now home to six Europeans, a hundred Asians and three hundred Africans. Many more local farmers passed through regularly with livestock, wheat and pyrethrum to sell, while elephant, lion and hippo still wandered through at will.

Frank commented on former neighbours as we passed their old stamping grounds. Kruger, 'who had good parties'; asthmatic Spooner with a 'dolly-bird' wife; a farm manager called Davidson who was a first-class shot and was rumoured to have been a bodyguard for Al Capone; Trudy Vidor, an Austrian who grew roses and bred dogs . . .

Frank was confused by today's roads. 'I remember Kruger's house being on the left, not the right. About four miles past Kruger we forked left, then it's about eight miles to Morgan-Grenville, and only a mile and a half on to Fergusson and Bingley . . .' he said, sounding a little uncertain.

'. . . if anything is left of any of it,' Janie wondered aloud.

'It was very bad,' Solomon told us, 'because some of Morgan-Grenville's farm was just grabbed. It was never sold properly.'

Land-grabbing is a Kenyan grievance that has wormed its way into this century, with title deeds either not existing, or appearing in triplicate as many people lay claim to one piece of land. Even the British-driven million-acre scheme, it seems, had not been immune to such problems.

We'd come to a section of broken tarmac where deep holes were concealed by water, causing us to hit almost every one. The ditches, too, were waterlogged, running alongside the road like canals. The horizon was heavy with thick, dark cloud and there was still no sign of the Aberdares. After a wild goose chase, misled by Solomon down a muddy road to nowhere we wanted to go, we stopped at a misty village we'd already been through.

'It all looks completely different,' Frank complained.

We halted beside a *mzee* who stood impervious in the cold and rain. 'Where are we?' I asked in Kiswahili.

'This area is called Morgan,' he replied. We felt we must be getting warmer, metaphorically if not literally.

As if in response, a slice of the Aberdares suddenly revealed itself: a tantalising flank of moorland in the mist. It was much closer than we'd realised. Slains was somewhere off to the right, then.

After establishing where we were heading, the old man pointed back down the road we'd come from.

Back at the junction where we'd gone wrong, we picked up a rain-sodden young man called Wahome, who squeezed into the back with Solomon, Janie and me, apologising for making us wet. He said there were so many roads he'd be better to just show us the way; and yes, he knew the way to the old stone house Frank was looking for. His grandfather Noah Kamau, who had died in 2001 aged 103, had worked nearby – for a man called David Fraser Allen. As he talked about his grandfather's life, albeit before he himself had been born, he referred to those former times, astoundingly, as 'the old good days'. Perhaps his grandfather had too.

'Happy Valley was full of lions back then,' said Frank suddenly.

'So was Karen,' said Janie wryly.

This brought me back with a jolt to the murder of Lord Erroll, which I had shelved in my mind while going to so many other old houses. Indeed – it suddenly occurred to me, why would Broughton, or Diana, or anyone else, walk a mile in the dark through Karen, back from the quarry where the body of Joss lay curled up in the footwell of a hired Buick?

Wahome directed us left, past the Step Hotel, on to a very stony road that slowed us down further. He was thrilled at Janie's mastery of the Kikuyu tongue. Meanwhile we drew nearer – we hoped – to our goal. Solomon remained silent, casting suspicious glances into the grey surroundings.

'Morgan-Grenville's house was up there – over eight thousand feet,' Frank explained, looking at the bulk of mist in front of us. 'He used to grade the rocky road.' He shrugged at the road we were rattling along. 'Maybe this was our access road, but it seems different – it was more than fifty years ago.'

'It must have been miserable up there in the cold season,' I commented.

'September was the worst,' Frank replied. 'The thin ice on the puddles was like fine glass – it crinkled as you drove though, then slowly the sun would rise over the Aberdares, reach our houses – and thaw us out.'

We passed a place where a shallow stream spilt over the road. Frank suddenly brightened as he exclaimed, 'This is the river that passed beneath Morgan-Grenville's old house, supplying water to all of us.' His recognition of something at last on this lonely, misty road was a relief to us all.

'But it only runs when it is very wet like now,' Wahome told us. 'Otherwise it is always dry.'

Frank raised his eyebrows. 'It never used to dry up. I remember walking upstream with a sieve to clear Morgan-Grenville's blocked drains. I used to fish in his garden too.'

We crossed the bridge over the Malewa, then passed the old workshops, now disused.

Frank suddenly cried out: 'There it is! There's our old house!'

Veiled in grey drizzle, the grey-stone house sheltered like a tramp beneath a threadbare shingle roof, the many holes patched up with flattened-out tin cans. We walked around, chilled by the persistent rain. An overgrown muddle of salvia, nasturtiums and daisies were struggling valiantly to break through a mantle of litter. At the front of the house, beds of healthy carrots, beans and potatoes seemed better cared for. A group of young men gathered around: white faces were evidently a rare sight here. When they discovered that Frank was revisiting his old home, they became fixated, following his every move and hanging on every word he said. An elderly Kikuyu *mama* let us into the house, almost reverently, welcoming Frank back into his home as if she had somehow expected him.

We went from room to room as Frank retraced his footsteps of many decades ago. As he stood in one dark room, a pale and ghostly figure against the smoke-blackened walls, he whispered: 'This was my bedroom!'

I had grown used to the dim light by now and I suddenly realised that his blue eyes were bright with tears, his cheeks wet. I stepped back outside, not wanting to intrude.

The Daykins' first, cedar home, where Frank's mother had broken down in despair upon their arrival, was higher up the hill. It no longer existed, according to Wahome, but he could show us where it had once been. Damp and shivering, we climbed back into the relative warmth of the car and headed towards the site. This weather, Frank said, reminded him of arriving, that very wet night, decades ago . . . the type of adventure a young man craved. He'd found it impossible to fathom his mother's exhausted sobs.

The road climbed in a series of slippery bends before Wahome told us to stop on a shelf of green land. Frank got out and looked around, then said quietly, 'Yes. This is it.' There were still pink and white lilies springing from the verdant profusion of Kikuyu grass, mingling among stinging nettles. The trumpet-like blooms grew in a circle, as if by magic, giving the impression that their exotic, stiff beauty could protect the scattered stones that Frank identified as the veranda floor.

'Here was the sitting room,' Frank said, standing beside a clump of blue agapanthus that had taken the liberty of spreading themselves into the space that once might have held a sofa. Behind him the long view stretched out into the grey distance. At the back, the former kitchen was another pile of stones, beside which a few guava trees had survived. The outside bathroom was now deep in nettles, concealing the deep pit which had been the long drop. Going outside on cold, wet nights cannot have helped Elsie's rheumatoid arthritis and pleurisy. Frank told us that Dr Anne Spoerry, of Flying Doctor fame, had looked after his mother. Dr Spoerry had lived nearby, before moving to Subukia. 'She was a nice old bird,' said Frank.

Solomon had discovered a shallower series of pits. 'The trout ponds,' said Frank. He now stood on a flat area with periwinkle and amaryllis carpeting the spot where his parents had once slept. 'Their bedroom looked out on flower beds and tall hollyhocks.' Frank's blue eyes were bright as he gazed out of the imaginary window on to a view that was familiar – but changed. 'There were so many more indigenous trees than there are now,' he said softly, averting his eyes from the crowd of staring people who had arrived, most of them in bare feet and ragged sweaters. Just about everyone wore woollen hats or balaclavas. A few of the older men wore gumboots. Solomon quickly commandeered a *panga* from an old man, and went off to dig up some plants. The children stared at us as if we were aliens, giggling at anything we said or did.

'Where do you go to school?' asked Anne, who is a dedicated learning support teacher.

The replies were in their best broken English, as they pointed down the slope. 'In the river,' said one; 'There down,' added another.

Frank retreated into quiet thought as we left his old home and headed north along the base of the mountains to look for Fergusson's house. The rain persisted as we passed a seasonal waterfall, a trickle of water threading down the jagged cliff. The blanket of cloud had lifted – only very slightly – so we could see the lower slopes of the Aberdare Mountains now, but their hidden heights had a giddy air of mystery as they vanished into sodden, grey skies. An uneven patchwork of *shambas* clung on to bare foothills. 'That was once wheat, with fields terraced by my brother,' Frank suddenly said.

'But there are no trees anywhere here – it is very bad!' Solomon shook his head sadly.

Somewhere to our right was the old road that had wound up the Aberdares to Morgan-Grenville's. 'But it is too bad for the vehicle,' said Wahome, 'we would have to walk.' Nothing at all was left of Morgan-Grenville's home, he added, not even a stone. Nobody wanted to walk anywhere in the rain, although I longed to see if any rhododendrons still survived – I've never seen one in Africa.

'What happened to the Morgan-Grenvilles?' I asked.

'They retired at Blue Lagoon,' Frank said, referring to the northern-most beach at Watamu, a couple of hours' drive north of Mombasa. 'They'd always had a house there, opposite the rock shaped like a turtle. When they moved there permanently they had to increase the size of the house to fit in all their antique treasures.' Frank was living in Nairobi by then, but Robert Morgan-Grenville still brought his car over 300 miles to Nairobi for Frank to service.

The electric fence, built to protect the Aberdare National Park from human encroachment, was only half a dozen kilometres away from here, according to Solomon. To our left we passed a wealthy and well-kept homestead, with neat fences, a small stone house and a flourishing patch of maize and beans. 'It belongs to Morgan-Grenville's old cook,' Wahome said.

A little further along the road, also on the left, was another neglected colonial relic. 'That's Fraser Allen's old house,' said Frank.

We parked by the road and walked in, inhaling the eucalyptus smell in the soggy air. The rain had finally stopped, but persistent mud clung to our shoes, making them as heavy as wooden clogs. The rusting remains of an ancient car crouched in front of the cedar off-cut walls and tin roof of the house, like a fossilised watchdog. '1950s Ford Escort,' said Frank, looking at it with interest.

The house looked small and poky, with tiny windows: if I'd lived in this bleak, damp place, letting in the light would have been a priority, but of course you had to get the glass panes up here on these terrible roads. We walked along an old hedge, now a row of tall cypress trees, into the orchard. Attached to a fence post was an old, defunct grinding mill, still bearing its inscription of origin: 'R Hunts and Co, Earl's Colne, England.' Behind an oleander hedge, the upper reaches of the Aberdares were finally emerging as the clouds lifted and dispersed, blowing smoke-like into patches of blue sky. A *mzee* came from the fields to meet us, unfazed by the host of white strangers tramping in – it seemed no big deal. He had been Kruger's carpenter. 'I can show you the tomb of the white man who lived here,' he said, adding: 'It is on my land now.'

'That will be Archibald Fraser Allen's grave. He died in 1942,' said Frank. We followed the old Kikuyu landowner through muddy, turned earth, where he'd been digging up potatoes and beans. We waded through more clay-like mud, our shoes becoming bigger and clumsier with each step. Small children had suddenly emerged around us, their mud-stained skins and tattered clothes blending into the muddy terrain as if they were spirited from the soil. The smallest ones, presumably the old man's grandchildren, had never seen a white face: they screamed and ran at the startling sight.

After we'd picked our way through another field of carrots and chickweed, we halted by a patch of brambles, protectively entwined around whatever was underneath. Wahome explained the concealment: 'We Kikuyu keep the headstone covered up so as not to be haunted.'

The grave had that peaceful feel, exclusively reserved for the resting places of the dead. The remains of Fraser Allen certainly had a lovely view of Lake Ol Bolossat, I noted, following Solomon's gaze as he stared out distractedly across the cabbage field towards the lake.

'A soft granite,' Frank said, pushing aside the thorns and fingering the smashed pieces of the old headstone. A jumble of inscribed letters was discernible: *42 . . . D . . . In . . . Har.*

'Why is it broken?' I wondered aloud.

There was no reply.

As we left Fraser Allen's grave, Frank explained, 'He was killed under a tractor which caught fire when he was lighting a fag.'

Janie Begg shuddered. 'Oh yes – that was a horrible accident. I thought it was in a harvester.'

The Daykins had, of course, arrived well after the tragic event, by which time Mabel Fraser Allen had become Mabel Morgan-Grenville.

We headed on towards Lake Ol Bolossat, and Frank began to talk about Charles Fergusson and Richard Bingley. 'They were murdered at the very beginning of 1953,' he said, 'just before my family arrived.' The news can hardly have helped lift Elsie's already dampened spirits. Then she learned that she and her husband would have to be armed and that there was an electric barbed-wire fence around her new house, powered by a generator that worked all night, its noisy rattle masking more sinister sounds that might be out there. Added to this was the constant Kenya Police Reserve presence. Special enclosures, called *bomas* in Kenya, were built to protect the cattle, though Elsie didn't get one of the towers built by some settlers to protect their women and children. The Black Watch were based on the Kruger farm, Frank told me, and every evening one person from Morgan-Grenville's farms had to go out with either the Black Watch or the King's African Rifles to check the labour lines in the areas. 'One guy with a beard, who we called "Harpic Round the Bend", used to bring bodies in a truck for us to identify,' Frank said. Presumably for Elsie the outdoor kitchen and latrine quickly paled into insignificance beside such grisly occurrences. However, apart from cattle being let out of their fields at night, there had not been much Mau Mau trouble on the Morgan-Grenville farm.

'This was Fergusson's house,' said Frank suddenly, stopping before I'd even noticed the nondescript grey-stone building with a red-tiled roof. It was small and built in the typically conservative style of the 1950s, very obviously as a bachelor dwelling, making little effort to be attractive, even if the imagination tried to visualise its better days. The only saving grace was a panoramic view of Lake Ol Bolossat. The French windows and front steps faced on to this view – which, I thought, would be beautiful at sunset on a better day. I thought of the elderly Fergusson, whisky in hand, looking at this same view on that fateful New Year's Day, savouring those moments which he could not know were his last.

The house had its back to the Aberdares, like other old settler houses between here and Wanjohi. I can see why they wouldn't want to face such a big bulk of mountain – too diminishing.

The sun was now dancing in and out from behind clouds, allowing patches of blue sky to give us occasional windows of warmth, but there was still a predominant chill to the air.

'This place makes me feel bad,' complained Solomon.

'It was deserted for years after the murder,' said Frank, 'but it looks like it's used now.'

The grass was neatly cut and there was a spartan garden: arum lilies, daisies and periwinkle. But perhaps with no *memsahib* to plant trees to yield succulent peaches or delicious-scented gardenia blooms, nor to lovingly tend beds with phlox and narcissus, it had always been dull.

Anne had discovered a sign: 'Kirima Dispensary, Ministry of Health, open Mon to Fri 8–5.' This was Saturday, so the house was all locked up and there was nobody around to let us in – if indeed we wanted to enter, which Solomon didn't. I was actually surprised to find the place devoid of atmosphere, as if any ghosts had departed in peace despite the violence of their end. Perhaps the dedicated work and prayers of those running the clinic had cleansed the place.

I wondered about that fatal night, what had gone through the minds of the older farmer and his young friend before they were hacked to death with machetes. Had they seen their cook, who'd apparently let the Mau Mau in? My mother remembers Bingley: 'Such a nice young man.' According to one Kipipiri resident of the time, he'd had rheumatic fever when he was young. She remembered going to his twenty-first birthday party, not long before he was murdered.

'The cook threw soup in his face before they chopped him up,' another elderly *memsahib* added gruesomely.

Had the two men been victims of a random attack, or an easy target – or did somebody have a vendetta against one of them?

Two new tin porches had been added on to the house, looking out to the unruffled surface of the lake which mirrored a brightening sky. We climbed the porch steps and pressed our faces against the window: I could see the living room, a new wall slicing through the middle of the room, cutting the unused fireplace in half. Then we walked around to the back door to the kitchen, and looking through the window could see this was now a laboratory, newly painted blue and white. 'This door is where the cook let the freedom fighters in – he'd been forced to take the oath,' said Frank.

We turned away. 'Behind the house it was all forest,' Frank said, gazing at the naked foothills. Solomon clucked angrily. Now the lower slopes were an example of poor farming: without terraces to contain it, the soil was surging down in the powerful sweep of every rainstorm. A rocky cliff stood like a scar on the naked hill. 'That used to be a waterfall,' Frank said, watching the goats and sheep clawing their way up the steep sides like multicoloured ticks.

Solomon was chatting now to Wahome, who was surprised to hear that the lake had 300 species of birds, although he knew about the resident hippo. 'It is such an important lake,' said Solomon. 'I would very much like to start an indigenous tree-planting project in this area!'

There wasn't the usual gathering crowd of spectators, just one woman who told us the doctor was on leave, assuming that was the reason for our being here.

'We are just looking at the old house,' Solomon explained.

She gave us a puzzled glance, before walking on.

Solomon wanted to see somebody about his idea for a new tree nursery at Ol Bolossat, so we stopped in Ol Kalou on the way back, opposite a shop building with its date – 1946 – carved into the stone above its entrance. Further along the street an old house had been awkwardly absorbed into the new town. Now Hunter's Butchery, its disintegrating shingle roof and dirty walls clung together as if in sorrowful respect of the fact it had once been somebody's beloved home. An angora goat wandered past its entrance, seeming somehow as unlikely as seeing a Thompson's gazelle in London. A *matatu* emblazoned with the name 'The Morgan' blared past us, kicking up dust into our windscreen. Presumably it was in a hurry to get to the place we'd just left.

Frank and Anne wanted to stop at the old St Peter's church in Ol Kalou. Its history is told in *They Made it Their Home* (1962): during the Second World War, Morgan-Grenville had given land, money had been raised locally, and the church and the vicarage beside it were built. The women of Ol Kalou, many of whom kept the new and large-scale wheat farms going, had a place to congregate and pray for the safe return of their men.

St Peter's graveyard was bursting with stiff arum lilies and red-hot pokers, shooting up above a riot of brightly coloured geraniums and dahlias that crawled over the mounds and depressions of unmarked graves, concealing old stones with missing plaques. Some dated back to the war. These few names didn't include any of the old Happy Valley lot: even if they'd wanted to be buried here in the nearest church to their old homes, they were probably too wicked – and suicide cases like Alice wouldn't have been allowed a Christian burial anyway.

The old, square church tower with its corner buttresses and short nave had a tacked-on extension of a rear nave and porch, its unimaginative windows smacking of 1950s taste. As the caretaker told me that nowadays over 400 people attended Sunday services, I looked along the rows of old wooden pews with crosses carved into their sides, lining an aisle where spots of sunlight stole through the holes in the roof, playing on the old brown carpet like elusive gold coins. There was a pump-action Stevenson organ which still worked, and in the vestry an old wooden font with a tarnished bowl, some old books and a register of services dating back to only 1963. Behind the wooden altar rails, a brass plaque on the chair commemorated 'A.H. Fraser Allen (died 1942)'.

As we left there was a loud peal of thunder from over Ol Bolossat way.

A few weeks later, I was drinking freshly ground coffee on Frank and Anne's Kitengela veranda, looking over Nairobi National Park towards the distant high-rise buildings of the city, dwarfed by distance. Pekinese dogs squirmed round Anne as she said, 'I think it's amazing how pleased they were to see Frank in view of the history!' I thought about this on the long road home to Soysambu. Over a mere half a dozen years I'd explored Slains, with its secrets and stories going back to the 1920s, then, at Fergusson's former home, flitted between dark memories from three decades later. And now Elsie Daykin's former garden was rambling unrestrained over the slopes above it all. Perhaps I'd glimpsed and understood the meaning of rapid change. Maybe I'd even gained deeper insights into times of war. I'd certainly realised one thing: if Lord Erroll – or indeed Mr Fergusson – had been murdered during times of peace it would have been an entirely different story. Or perhaps in both cases there would have been no murder.

III

Politics, Bullets and Broken Hearts

20

The Bolter's Love, Loss and Pain

The years had passed relentlessly since *Mzee* Nuthu's death in 2002. As I became embroiled in various other concerns, looking at foreign boarding schools for my children, then agonising over the unpalatable idea of sending them away to South Africa or the UK, my visits to Happy Valley had become few and far between. I realised with a pang of guilt that I hadn't even visited *Mzee*'s grave at Clouds when Idina's great-granddaughter, Frances Osborne, contacted me from England, wanting to visit Happy Valley as she was researching a book about her notorious great-grandmother: Frances's grandfather was one of Idina's two sons from her first marriage to Euan Wallace. Idina had, not surprisingly, abandoned both sons when she ran off to Kenya with Joss. The Happy Valley-ites didn't tend to keep kids around them – they can't have fitted in with the lifestyle. One simply doesn't imagine the elegant Idina with milk stains on her blouse and lumps of baby food in her hair, fondly reading about the Flopsy Bunnies.

Frances was on a quest to dig out the truth about Happy Valley. 'Were those Clouds parties really so debauched?' she asked me. What did I think?

Well, actually I imagined Idina's parties were fairly shocking at the time, but are probably pretty bland compared with what goes on at parties nowadays.

Naturally a visit to Clouds was essential. Now that mobile phone networks had reached the area we could contact Peter before we came.

The Nuthu family were delighted, as well as curious about meeting Idina's great-granddaughter – especially Paul, who'd inherited his father's copy of *White Mischief*.

After a warm welcome and a tour of the house, Solomon, Frances and I walked with the Nuthu family to the old dams. They were overgrown, but clumps of arum lilies still stood stiffly to attention beside their still waters. Solomon was ecstatic to see evidence that colobus monkeys had been raiding the crops and launched into a lecture on why we should be protecting 'our brothers', although I sensed his audience weren't convinced. Frances might have been more monkey friendly, but the speech was in Kiswahili, so it didn't have a stirring effect on her either.

We visited the old man's new gravestone and I felt a deep sadness that I had not said goodbye, nor been there at his burial. I'd never known his first name was Norman. I'd always known him as simply 'Mzee'. I also learnt that he was born in 1932, when Idina was married to her fourth husband, Haldeman, and living at their relatively new home, Clouds. That same year in Nairobi, the Carter Land Commission was appointed to inquire into the question of Kenyan native land grievances. Further away, Oswald Mosley was setting up his British Union of Fascists.

Mzee Nuthu had died aged only seventy. 'You were the pillar of our strength,' read the inscription. 'Those who live good lives find peace and rest in death.' I wondered what Idina's inscription was: apparently she'd been buried at English Point in Mombasa in 1955.

Frances Osborne's book, *The Bolter*, came out in 2008. I read it as soon as I could get my hands on a copy, and discovered that Idina's brother, Buck, had flown to Kenya for her burial. There he lay a headstone revealing only the date of her death, but inscribed: 'In loving memory of a warm, generous and courageous person.' After Frances's visit I had gone down with brucellosis, tick fever and two types of amoeba – all at once. 'Probably as a result of spending time eating and drinking in strange places when you're in Happy Valley,' said a friend. Meanwhile, no publishers wanted a book on Happy Valley, or not one that involved a Kikuyu conservationist who had wacky dreams. I even tried, albeit briefly, to turn my back on Happy Valley, but failed.

But Idina continued to puzzle me. I know, having supported someone close to me through rehab, that those who tend towards excessive lifestyles are often the most complicated, loving and intelligent people, many of whom have become lost on their search for life's meaning.

And now — at last — Idina's life, not such a bed of roses after all, became clearer. By now I had read a variety of books with a range of ideas about Idina, but Frances's highly readable and comprehensive biography painted a vivid and more sympathetic portrait of her: after an unhappy childhood in a broken home, Idina's young heart had been broken by her first husband. Not that she wasn't culpable too — she'd liked the good life and committing adultery came easily — but overall Frances's Idina comes across as a likeable character. She was born Lady Idina Sackville in England in 1893, a couple of years before the birth of the East Africa Protectorate or the Uganda railway. It was the same year that missionary Stewart Watt arrived in Machakos with his family — having walked almost 300 miles through predator-infested, hostile bush to spread the Christian word. This was a world that was changing rapidly, and the changes were nowhere more dramatic than in this new and faraway continent that would eventually seduce Idina away from her home country and family.

The silver spoon in Idina's mouth did not compensate for the agonies of a broken home: her father, the 8th Earl de la Warr, Gilbert Sackville, had married her mother Muriel Brassey for her money, in return for the title of countess. When Muriel had her second daughter, Avice, Gilbert left his family in the Manor House in Bexhill-on-Sea, and ran off with a can-can dancer.

Lady Idina married Euan Wallace in 1913, but six years and two sons later, they were divorced. The war was over, caps were being thrown in the air, and Idina married Charles Gordon, joining him on the ship to Kenya, and leaving behind her two small sons, David and Gerald (known as Gee). In those days plenty of virgin brides arrived in Mombasa, were met by their betrothed, married quickly and respectably in Mombasa Cathedral and then were packed on to the train to impossibly remote places where they somehow managed to create comfortable homes. Idina's arrival, as always seductively clad in an expensive designer outfit, would have raised a few eyebrows. More tongues must have waggled at her introduction to Nairobi society in Muthaiga Club.

Meanwhile, at Nairobi's Theatre Royal, over 2,000 soldier-settler applicants held their breath while revolving drums paused for names and numbers to be drawn. The number indicated the order in which the applicant could choose his farm from the government's list, which didn't often describe the land accurately. But Charles and Idina Gordon were in luck: his prize in the land lottery was 3,000 acres in the coveted Wanjohi valley.

Pith helmets and spine pads were not for the glamorous Lady Idina Gordon, but nevertheless her lifestyle quickly plummeted from beautiful socialite, flitting between Paris and London, to pioneering wife on a remote farm, living rough, and surrounded by wild animals and African labourers, none of whom would have appreciated her expensive fashion sense. Having probably married Gordon on the rebound from Wallace, the man her great-granddaughter believes was her true love, Idina soon found she had also lost her two sons by running off to Kenya into a doomed marriage. She was thrilled by Kenya, but bored by Gordon, who accused her of being a nymphomaniac, probably because she was not faithful, possibly, too, because she was just using him – or sex – to escape her unhappiness.

She kept herself in touch with designer trends by wafting back to Europe on a regular basis, a habit that would continue almost until she died. On one of her jaunts 'home' the following year, she visited Wallace, possibly to renew old passions, but instead found he was getting remarried while making it clear that Idina's sons now had a 'new' mother. Not the type of girl to wait around in sorrowful celibacy, Lady Idina returned to Kenya and Gordon, distracting herself from her broken heart with endless safaris. Ten months later, realising her second marriage was truly over, 25-year-old Idina returned to London in mid-1921.

After a handful of years billowing through Europe's party circuit, Idina was back in Kenya again, wreathed in scandal and on the arm of the handsome future Earl of Erroll. Accounts vary as to whether she bought, leased, or inherited as a divorce settlement the 2,000 acres where she built Slains. Frances Osborne settles the matter, quoting from a letter Joss wrote to his mother, explaining that they leased the farm for fifteen shillings an acre over a period of ten years. But Idina was not destined to become a countess. Early on in their liberal marriage, Joss had already met the woman who would have that title conferred on her, beautiful, auburn-haired Mary, then married to Cyril Ramsey-Hill. He began flirting with her while Idina was in hospital having his daughter, Diana, nicknamed Dinan. Joss then hopped between the beds of Idina, Mary and Alice de Janzé, until 1928 when he finally ran off with Mary.

As Idina returned to England with Dinan, their dream home, Slains, up for sale, a politically inclined gentleman called Johnston Kamau (better known as Jomo Kenyatta) went to London to promote the Kikuyu case concerning his people's rights – especially concerning land, now that foreign farmers were settling in the highlands. Oblivious to such potential threats, Mary managed to get sole possession of the Djinn Palace, her grieved ex-husband's exotic home on the verdant shores of freshwater Lake Naivasha. Joss was quick to marry her and return to the good life.

Idina must have been hiding her emotions well at this point. She'd had her heart broken by Wallace, then Joss, having been denied the right to mother her two young sons. All she had left was her daughter. The 'easy' way to deal with such painful feelings would have been to anaesthetise them with drugs and alcohol – while finding another husband to ensure one wasn't alone with too much time to think about things. Idina and Dinan returned to Kenya in 1930 with Idina's fourth husband, Donald Haldeman. She bought a new farm and built Clouds, which was to become headquarters of the next episode of *Carry on Happy Valley*.

By 1934 Idina was ready to leave another husband. Haldeman was a jealous, controlling man – neither of which trait would have made life with her easy. Nellie Grant wrote to Elspeth Huxley in 1934 from their Njoro farm, as recorded in *Nellie: Letters from Africa*: 'Have just agreed to go . . . to Clouds tomorrow for one night only, as Dina wants moral support in facing Donald. Anyway we shall get some garden loot even if Donald does shoot us all.' Perhaps, if he liked shooting, Donald was responsible for the heads that I'd found vanished from those plaques on the walls surrounding the courtyard on my first visit to Clouds. Nellie liked to visit Clouds, according to Huxley in *Out in the Midday Sun*, 'to swap plants, the Wanjohi being a splendid gardening region, and must have been unlucky, for she never struck an orgy; though she did once find one of the visitors, Alice de Janzé, asleep on the floor at four in the afternoon'.

Even if Haldeman threatened to shoot any man who touched his wife, he evidently had respect for his superiors. Elspeth Huxley also quotes from Daphne Moore's diaries, in which she describes Gladys Delamere's party at Muthaiga Club on New Year's Eve 1932. The Haldemans were among the guests, and Idina met and danced with Byrne, the new governor: 'The whole club held their sides to see Kenya's most notorious vamp clasped in the arms of the King's representative who was apparently making the most of it.'

Idina managed to escape to England in March 1934, taking Dinan and leaving the little girl there at school, although I cannot help wondering if Idina later regretted that decision. Meanwhile she returned to Kenya in July with her new boyfriend, Chris Langlands, a pilot. But he didn't last either and by 1939 Idina was on her fifth husband, Vincent Soltau. According to Frances Osborne, Idina was a kind stepmother to Soltau's two children. The same year, Hitler invaded Poland and Mary, Countess of Erroll, died from the excesses of her lifestyle, alone, her arms covered in abscesses from injections of heroin and morphine.

The early 1940s were difficult years. Soltau, whom Idina nicknamed 'Lynx', had been posted to Cairo, and it seems he never returned permanently. Loneliness must have been a new and terrifying prospect for Idina, who until now had successfully managed to avoid her own company. She would doubtless have continued to throw wild parties at Clouds, and there would have been no shortage of willing young men who needed to let off steam whenever home from war duties. But drink and drugs ravage the mind and body over time, and this couldn't go on for ever. Idina was almost fifty and the menopause would be looming.

Then Joss was murdered. At the news, a devastated Idina drove from Happy Valley to his Muthaiga home on the outskirts of Nairobi, where she failed to find the valuable family pearls that she was determined should be inherited by his daughter. (Maddeningly, the Erroll pearls had last been seen round the lovely throat of Diana Broughton.) Dinan was left to read the news of her father's death in the headlines of the English newspapers. The same year Euan Wallace died in England of stomach cancer, and Alice de Trafford, Idina's old friend and Happy Valley neighbour since the early days, committed suicide.

Even if the parties did go on, they could not mask what must have been considerable emotional pain for Idina: she'd finally 'met' the sons she had with Euan Wallace, both brought up by a stepmother. David she'd met up with in London in 1934, and Gee – finally – in 1943 at Muthaiga Club. While Idina had been dancing with Gee, clasped in his young, handsome arms, somebody had commented to him that she was old enough to be his mother, only to be told she *was* his mother! Idina adored her grown-up boys, making frequent efforts to see them or stay in touch, but she was grasping at borrowed time. The war would take both their young lives.

After losing David and Gee, this time for ever, Idina was – according to friends – drinking too much, presumably to drown her sorrow. Her pain spills from the stark words, quoted in *The Bolter*, that she managed to write to Pru, David's young widow and mother of his children: 'What are words when one has lost all one loves – thank God you have the children . . .'

The pain was not only emotional: Idina had mounting health problems. By early 1945, she had been through some sort of a nervous breakdown and was suffering from neuritis, or inflammation of the nerves, and had been medically advised to move down to the coast. Thus the ageing high priestess of a decadent and dying era finally left her beloved Happy Valley to live at Mtwapa on the Kenya coast, accompanied by her loyal lover James Bird (known facetiously as James VI), the man she never married and the only one she never left.

Bird, the man whose chair was later to be abandoned to Janie Begg's mother, was, according to Janie, a former sailor – complete with tattoos. He managed Idina's farm, and evidently her too.

Gee's wife committed suicide and Idina never met her grandchildren. During this time, her estranged daughter, Dinan, seemed in no hurry to meet this absent mother of dubious repute. Correctly named Diana, Countess of Erroll, she had been at school in England since the age of eight, hadn't set eyes on her mother for as many years and was now twenty and engaged. Idina was not invited to her wedding. Nor did she agree to see her mother in 1948, when her son Merlin was born. Idina thus returned home to Kenya nursing the pain of what must have felt like yet another loss. It turned out to be cancer of the womb, as if Idina's body was responding to long-suppressed agonies. And now it was time for the final twist of the knife.

Two years later, Idina returned to England again and this time managed a reconciliation with her daughter. Determined not to lose touch again, Idina planned to save money to bring Dinan and her husband out to Kenya, but Mau Mau began in 1951, its violent killings aborting Idina's dream of planning a Kenyan safari with them. Idina didn't even live to see the end of Mau Mau.

'Poor Dina had had a desperate cancer for a long time', wrote Nellie Grant to her daughter. It was October 1955: the same year that Diana (née Broughton) divorced her third husband, Gilbert Colville, and married the 4th Baron Delamere. Idina died, aged sixty-two, in Mombasa, in the country she called home.

She'd had a hard life in many ways. Money and material comfort cannot compensate for the lack of love and security, the emotional balm that eases our passage through hardships. Growing up should be a protected time, a happy process that creates self-confidence and teaches a child to love and be loved. Loss of that most vital ingredient for Idina probably began with her father's departure, worsening as she went through all her various husbands and lovers. Finally it manifested itself in the ultimate loss – that of her sons, the agony intensified as it would have been suffused with suppressed guilt. She'd never been able to give her children enough of her time, and although Dinan had been treated to a little more early mothering than her half-brothers, she'd been alienated from her mother for most of her life. Idina made her choices. Children, after all, are demanding, candid and tend to teach us lessons about ourselves we might not wish to learn. Idina's were neither seen nor heard. It must have been the final straw for Idina when, towards the end of her life, healing the rift with her only daughter and living child seemed doomed by events.

A few days in a coma and thus ended all hopes that Idina might divulge who'd murdered Joss – as she'd allegedly promised. Did she really know, or was this just another of Idina's elusive games? And if she had truly loved him, as some believe, how had that high-profile murder affected her? She was one of the few who didn't have fingers pointed at her over Erroll's murder. She was at home at Clouds at the time – although the lying, which seemed to come easily to the gin-soaked crowd of main players and witnesses, does make one wonder who was actually where that night. Idina could have hired a killer, of course, but there's no apparent motive: if it was a crime of passion then she would have done it at least thirteen years earlier. Frances Osborne doesn't draw any conclusions in *The Bolter*. But she does suggest that Idina always blamed Diana Broughton for this tragedy, irrespective of who'd fired the fatal bullet.

21

The Temptress and Murderous Thoughts

L ike Idina's, Alice's life and death continued to intrigue me. Like Idina, too, Alice used mood-altering substances, probably to negate an intolerable past. But it's also likely she suffered from clinical depression, the type which brought on moods dark enough to kill herself.

Suicide is an uncomfortable subject. Most of us avoid thinking about it too much – if we can. I regret not talking to my grandfather about his cousin's suicide – and I'd heard his grave somewhere on a hillside in Subukia didn't have a headstone. Alice didn't get one either, until her granddaughter came to visit her old home.

As well as clarifying many aspects of Idina's life, Frances Osborne's *The Bolter* added to the fund of stories about Alice. Frances believes that Alice and Joss had been enjoying intermittent affairs in Paris before either of them married. Idina then invited the de Janzés on their first Kenyan holiday – with ulterior motives: pregnant, she'd need somebody to keep Joss from straying. Better the devil you know, especially one so neurotic as Alice, and thus not a serious threat. In December 1925 the de Janzés stayed at Slains before they accompanied the Hays to Muthaiga Club, carousing their way through the festive season while awaiting the arrival of Idina's baby. Alice didn't fulfil her task – while Idina was in hospital having the baby, Joss met Mary.

When Idina returned home, she promptly left the baby with a nanny – as one did – to go on safari with Joss and the de Janzés. By the arrival of the long rains in April 1926, Frédéric's hopes of escaping this foursome arrangement were thwarted when Joss became ill with suspected malaria and ended up in Nakuru hospital. The de Janzés were left to hold the fort – and presumably the baby. While Idina was away from Slains, keeping faithful vigil at Joss's bedside, the nanny resigned, Frédéric had an altercation with a rogue elephant and broke a rib, and the farm accounts fell into a state of neglect.

When Idina and Joss finally came home in June, Alice had bought Wanjohi Farm. She and Frédéric moved there towards the end of 1926, but a peaceful married life was not on the cards – enter Raymond de Trafford. According to Frances Osborne (who also reveals that Idina was the owner of Mickey, Minnie's twin), on that fateful day in late 1941, Alice walked Minnie to the river bank, where she shot and buried the little dog immediately, before going back to her bed and shooting herself in the mouth with her revolver.

Paul Spicer had been in touch while writing Alice's biography, asking for information on distances and roads. He emailed me a photo of Alice's house taken in 1930. A pyrethrum cart was parked in front. The house was of dark wood, its light further blocked by surrounding farm buildings and groves of indigenous trees. There appeared to be five chimneys: fires must have been essential. A few creepers scaled the walls and there were some flower beds, but otherwise it looked sparse and bleak. It was nothing like so attractive or glamorous as some of the neighbouring houses – especially Clouds. I wondered how much time Alice actually spent there, with her social life in Nairobi to conduct – and a house at the coast too where she apparently added extra rooms when more guests were expected. Those cedar off-cut walls with a narrow veranda on the inner sides seemed unfocused, as if a veil of drizzle had been drawn across the camera lens. There was no telling from the black and white photograph if the sky was blue, and the house looked cold and secretive, as if tightly holding in Alice's pain and unhappiness: its sightless windows were like closed eyelids, completing the sense of privacy, even isolation.

*

Early in 2008 Alice's granddaughter, Angelique, was poised to come to Kenya, planning to stay with me, and we intended to visit her grandmother's old home to see the new grave. She also planned to restore the old manager's house, intending to provide funding to convert it into a school library. But Kenya was in the throes of post-election violence and tourists were cancelling their safaris. We didn't blame Angelique for going to Tanzania instead, with the rest of the world branding us a danger zone.

At the end of the year Solomon, now the proud owner of a mobile phone, phoned me almost in tears. 'They have broken the grave completely!' he told me.

'Who? Where?' I said.

'Harris's! It is all smashed. No stone now and no fence.'

I was shocked into silence.

'The new headmaster, he is angry,' continued Solomon. 'He says the white people promised to help them but they didn't. So now they have done this terrible thing!'

Early in 2009 I received a letter from Solomon on a torn-out page of an exercise book. He explained that the fence around Alice's grave and the gate had been 'taken'. He said the old wooden manager's house had been 'terribly destroyed' and would now be impossible to renovate. The new headmaster and chairperson of the school were selling the timber from the old house, he added, although some people were against it, notably families whose grandparents once worked for Alice. He gave me the contacts for the Kikuyu head and chairperson.

I wrote, but never had a reply.

Finally, in 2010, Paul Spicer's biography, *The Temptress: The Scandalous Life of Alice, Countess de Janzé*, was on the shelves, offering a new Erroll murder theory – one that implicated Alice. Spicer's enjoyable book certainly brings to light some interesting new stories, but also contained some anomalies, particularly what appeared to be the suggestion that Erroll's biographer, Errol Trzebinski, agreed with James Fox that Broughton pulled the trigger. The book also confuses people – Delap's first wife, Rosemary, with his second wife,

Bubbles (Maureen) – and places: Boy and Paula Long's farm Nderit with Delamere's. (Boy Long had earlier worked for Delamere on Lake Elmenteita, but their farm was beside Lake Nakuru.) The book states that Idina had moved to the coast before Alice's suicide, but later contradicts this claim. There's further confusion of identities: the book claims that Mary, who married David Leslie-Melville, was the granddaughter of Lord Portman, although it was actually her husband who was his grandson. I was surprised at the suggestion that the de Janzés could employ local Kikuyu farmers who had smallholdings in the area. In fact the only Kikuyu in the area at the time were a few labourers on neighbouring white-owned land. Today's smallholdings appeared in the rash of growth after 1963.

However, Spicer engagingly expands on Alice's character, offering new detail about her tragic, turbulent life. I read with interest how the young Alice's doting father threw her mother out of the house on a winter's night, causing her subsequent illness and death, then married her mother's cousin with whom he'd been having an affair anyway. When Alice was thirteen, her mother's family won their custody case and removed her from her father's indulgent influence. This estrangement was apparently devastating to Alice. She showed early tendencies to suicide and attempted to slash her wrists at school; Spicer believes she was already suffering from a mild strain of manic depression called cyclothymia. Despite having many suitors (including a gangster boyfriend in Chicago), he thinks Alice was probably a virgin when she married in 1923, but never really found sexual fulfilment with Frédéric. After the births of both her daughters, Alice suffered from post-natal depression; all efforts in France having failed, Frédéric tried the distractions of Kenya. Spicer says that although the Hays and de Janzés had met in Paris in 1923, Alice's affair with Joss began later, during their first visit to Kenya, in late 1925. Joss's alleged ability to bring women to orgasm easily would have instigated Alice's sexual awakening.

The de Janzés bought their 600 acres from Sir John Ramsden, helped by friendly neighbours Geoff Buxton and David Leslie-Melville. The small manager's house was already there and provided a home for Alice and Frédéric while they built their main home. Buxton introduced Alice to Raymond (or Raymund, the spelling Spicer follows some other authors in preferring) at a dinner party. Meanwhile, Alice still floated between France and Kenya, once naively taking a monkey back to wreak havoc in the Parisian apartment and drive the Portuguese nanny to distraction when it showed blatant disregard for valuable china. As if this wasn't inconsiderate enough – of the nanny and the African animals – Alice also added to the chaos in Paris by importing a crocodile and the rapidly growing lion cub. The unfortunate Samson ended up in a children's zoo, his story inevitably ending in tragedy after he was ill-treated in a circus and finally shot by mistake. History does not relate the crocodile's demise, but the monkey had a lucky escape back to Kenya with Alice.

After shooting Raymond at the Gare du Nord, Alice was pardoned by the President from serving her six-month sentence, and only fined 100 francs. Her second marriage to Raymond was, Spicer believed, for love. Her children did not attend the occasion, but her bulldog did. Alice then traipsed around Europe, funding her new husband's bad habits – including his gambling. Only after he had thrown a cocktail in her face in Paris did she pay for him to go to Australia. But later in 1933, the same year Alice had settled back in Happy Valley, Raymond reappeared. Frédéric, who had always been a true gentleman and remained a good friend to Alice until the end, died at the end of the year.

Although Raymond had a tendency to arrive drunk at Wanjohi, having driven all the way from his home at Njoro, Alice did her best to avoid him. She travelled regularly, including a courageous solo expedition to Congo. Raymond was deported from Kenya in 1939 for drunkenly striking and injuring an employee, but this didn't sober him up, as he was then convicted and jailed in England for drink-driving and killing a woman cyclist.

Alice would have been delighted when her old friend, society beauty Paula Gellibrand, came to stay, also with two failed marriages behind her. Paula was single again – but not for long: she met Boy Long at an overnight party at Idina's and married him soon afterwards. One way to avoid sitting home alone with morbid thoughts is to keep on the move. Alice had her beach house at Tiwi, south of Mombasa and a cottage in Muthaiga – close to Joss's Nairobi home and office. She would have busied herself, like Idina, throwing parties and keeping as many people as possible around her, in between having her many friends to stay at Wanjohi and the coast.

Meanwhile, as Lord High Constable of Scotland, Joss had to take part in the coronation procession of King Edward VIII. Edward's subsequent abdication because he wanted to marry divorcee Wallis Simpson would also have engaged Alice's sympathies: HRH was an old mucker from Alice's London days. In 1938, after the coronation of Edward's brother George, Joss was elected for Kiambu constituency and, according to Spicer, he was no longer supporting Mosley or the British Union of Fascists. Alice's contribution to the war effort was to look after Julian 'Lizzie' Lezard, an old friend of Joss, whom Joss had stationed at Wanjohi farm to do intelligence work: presumably he was offering the lonely Alice some company, although apparently Lezard was generously endowed enough to cause much delight at Idina's favourite after-dinner game. This involved several men standing behind a sheet, poking the necessary appendage through holes to get marked out of ten.

Lezard was a brief fling, whereas Dickie Pembroke was there for Alice when her father died and just after Joss was murdered. But then he was posted to Cairo. Alice was having health problems and, in early 1941, Dr Boyle performed a hysterectomy on her. Spicer writes that before Alice departed to Nairobi for the operation she gave her dachshund, Minnie, Nembutal – a barbiturate often used as a sedative. She preferred to put the dog down herself as it was experiencing panic attacks in the car. Alice felt she had murdered her dog, she revealed to Pembroke in a letter, adding that 'the length of our own lives lies entirely within our own hands (unless someone else gets at us first!)'

Lonely and probably suffering from clinical depression, Alice had focused all her affections on Minnie, ensuring the little dog didn't suffer. In spite of her irresponsible way of dragging wild African 'pets' off to inevitable sticky ends in foreign places, Alice always seemed more attached to them than to her children, making more effort to get the lion out of the zoo and back to Kenya than she ever did to take her children to Wanjohi. Animals are often easier company than people, their unconditional devotion comforting during life's 'downs'.

It is now generally agreed that depression is exacerbated by alcohol and drugs, as they further tamper with unbalanced chemicals in the brain. It is believed that substance abuse can actually cause depression, or advance it in someone who is already genetically predisposed to the illness. Whatever the cause, after the operation Alice was frail, depressed and missing Minnie. She sent her housekeeper, Flo Crofton, to excuse her from neighbour Pat Fisher's joint birthday party with Joss's former mistress, Phyllis Filmer, then took an overdose of Nembutal. There is no mention of how Alice was revived, but Spicer details how, a few days later, having sent Flo shopping in Ol Kalou, she took another large dose of Nembutal and shot herself in the heart. A servant broke in, but by the time Flo arrived Alice was dying. Dr Boyle borrowed a fast car from Dr Bowles and rushed from Nairobi to Wanjohi, but Alice was dead when he arrived.

Spicer records that Alice had left five letters: two to her children, one to Pembroke, one a suicide note and one to the police; all of which Boyle handed over to the police. The cocktail party Alice had requested at her grave was not held because many friends were away: only Pat Fisher and Flo Crofton attended the funeral, together with Alice's staff.

Alice's daughters, now in their late teens, were left to read about the death of their mother in the French newspapers, just as 15-year-old Dinan had read of her father's death eight months earlier. The will stipulated that to inherit Alice's farm her daughters must live there for a certain length of time: if they could not, the estate would go to the fatherless 8-year-old daughter of Alice's good friend Noreen Pearson. The war made it too difficult for Nolwen and Paola to take on the farm, then Noreen remarried an American officer and took her daughter to Washington. Thus Alice's farm was sold on the child's twenty-first birthday, which would have been in the 1950s.

Paul Spicer's mother, Margaret, had been a friend of Alice's. Spicer's interest in the elusive countess was further piqued by various coincidences, strengthening his conviction that Alice murdered Erroll. The book's epilogue enlarges on this: he spoke to Noel Case, who described Alice as an unpredictable employer, usually forgetting to make Noel aware of her movements, and dwelling on thoughts about her proposed grave site. Apparently she never spoke of her past or her children, and only once mentioned her father, whom she was keeping in an expensive home in America. Noel thought it highly probable that Alice had killed Erroll, given her belief in the afterlife. Ethnie Boyle, wife of Alice's doctor William, claimed she actually saw the letter in which Alice supposedly confessed all. Ethnie told her daughter, Alice Fleet, née Boyle (and later Alice Percival), who told Spicer.

Various others backed the theory that Alice was Erroll's murderer, including Lezard, Betty Leslie-Melville (who said so in her memoirs) and the latter's mother-in-law, Mary Leslie-Melville. A few years after Alice's death, Mary's headman had found the gun hidden under some rocks in the Wanjohi River just below Alice's house. Mary had said it was the exact make and calibre of the missing revolver used to shoot Erroll, but that there was no point in dredging up the case again as he and Alice were dead anyway. She'd even shown Betty the same gun, in the cupboard of her Nairobi home.

Spicer writes that somebody had written two anonymous letters to defence lawyer Harry Morris, saying Erroll's killer was a woman and a leading Nairobi socialite, spurned by Joss for Diana. Spicer also believes that Dickie Pembroke might not have noticed (or perhaps he ignored and later lied about) Alice's leaving their bed for over an hour: besides, she could easily have driven quickly and unnoticed from Muthaiga to Karen on roads that would have been empty in the small hours. Alice would have known Joss's movements, as she always did, stopped him on the road and shot him – not the first time she'd pulled the trigger on true love. In addition, Spicer agrees with Noel Case that, believing as she did in the afterlife, Alice would have anticipated her certain reunion with Joss.

Both Mary Leslie-Melville's and Ethnie Boyle's husbands were evidently great friends and supporters of Alice at different times. I wonder what their wives felt about such kindnesses, however innocent, shown to a woman who wasn't partial to nuptial fidelity even when she did have a man around. While it seems common knowledge that William Boyle was a lover, whether or not David Leslie-Melville partook of Alice's potent cocktails or sampled what went on between her expensive sheets is just another of many secrets Alice carried into her final resting place. And considering how even the Crown witnesses in court, supposed ballistic experts, confused guns, I'd be surprised if Mary Miller really knew enough about firearms to be so conclusive.

I do believe Alice would have killed herself at some point in her life regardless of whether Joss was alive or dead. I have observed a manically depressed friend's existence, as if permanently in a fog, unable to see any way out and seldom able to think straight. I don't believe that Alice, in her disturbed state of mind, would have been capable of planning such a well-executed murder. However, depression is a self-obsessed state of mind and engineering her own death would have been another matter.

Solomon, strangely enough, had never asked me my opinion on the murder. There isn't a Kiswahili translation of Errol Trzebinski's biography of Erroll or he, too, might have some political opinions on the subject.

Who did he think it was, then, I finally asked him, wondering if he'd dreamt up anything incriminating.

'Maybe Alice,' he said, adding with a smile: 'she was very naughty!'

After our initial visit to Alice's, Solomon had written down more of his strange dreams in his 'book of visions'. Now I read them tentatively, always slightly unnerved by his sixth sense. Solomon would have been burnt at the stake if he'd been born in England in the wrong century, but nowadays psychics are coming back into fashion. Indeed, here in Kenya, with lingering beliefs in ancestral spirits and the revered psychic powers of witchdoctors, he's nothing unusual.

Solomon wrote about how he'd 'seen' Alice in her car on the road we'd walked along to his brother's house – it had formerly been

Alice's private road through her farm. He'd stopped and talked to Alice about her farm workers, her children and her suicide. Amongst other revelations, Alice had told him she'd had gonorrhea, that indeed all the Happy Valley players had it. She'd also said she'd never been too worried about her children – they'd had rich relatives, while she, Alice, had died poor.

'Don't your dreams ever frighten you?' I asked Solomon.

'Oh no,' he said. 'I am always having these dreams – about Alice and other people.'

I remembered his 'conversations' with his son, Caleb, after he'd died and realised the comfort they must have offered to him at the time.

By now events in my life had forced me to think more deeply about suicide – my close friend's 16-year-old daughter, Jenny, had killed herself. This beautiful young girl's ashes had lain in my house while my friend went through a roller-coaster ride of emotional purgatory. Jenny had suffered from depression, but medical help had failed her. I read the bleak words from her diary, reproduced in a book written afterwards by her mother: 'People should be more afraid of the light than the dark. At least at night you can hide from all that is there.' Alice, as well as suffering from depression, had been through enough to unhinge anyone: her childhood was short, her father's behaviour appalling. Cocktails and drugs would have done nothing to improve any existing imbalances in Alice's brain. Regardless of whether she believed in an afterlife, perhaps she could no longer distinguish between light and darkness in the whirlpools of her mind. Or perhaps she had simply become too 'afraid of the light'.

When I revisited the area in 2010, the old wooden house once occupied by the manager was still standing, although strips of wood had been torn out of the walls, leaving gaps you could climb through. The inside was a splintering mess, but beside the door, the scarlet rose still bloomed defiantly. Alice's grave, actually only a dozen feet from the place Danson Mwaura had pointed out, was a tangle of nettles and broken stones. Even in death, it seemed, there was no peace or sanity for Alice. I glanced at it once more and noticed, beneath the mess, that a profusion of miniature wildflowers covered the jostled turf. The earth Alice had walked upon and loved was giving back a subtle token of appreciation.

We zigzagged home through the smaller valleys and hills, a dark-grey sheet of rain hiding the Aberdares. We gave a lift to a young man, who to Solomon's consternation had never heard of a colobus monkey.

As Solomon impatiently repeated the Kikuyu word for colobus: '*Nguyo . . . nguyo,*' I wondered about Alice. She killed herself – finally. She tried to kill de Trafford. Did she really kill Erroll? It seemed unlikely somehow. Behind us, a rainbow arched over Kipipiri, like a bright promise for the future. Its end dropped into a dark fold of foothill, exactly where Alice's old home must be.

Perhaps it touched her shattered grave.

22

An Unbroken Spirit

Early in 2009 we'd returned to Happy Valley after Kenya had been knocked sideways by the horrific post-election violence that had almost brought the tourist industry to its knees. But all was not bad, it seemed: Chinese labourers and engineers were finishing the smooth, wide tarmac road that wound through the hills and vales from North Kinangop, through to Ol Kalou and on towards Dundori. At last the struggling farmers of Happy Valley had a decent road on which to transport their produce.

But Solomon frowned when he saw the Chinese workers in their traditional pointed hats. 'Since they arrived in this area many colobus monkeys have been trapped. The Chinese are buying the skins,' he told us furiously, then with his voice cracking, 'and there was even an elephant killed, the tusks were gone, and it is the first time I see an elephant killed in this area.' Somebody else in the car pointed out that the Chinese had required 14,000 work permits, when as many unemployed Kenyans could have done the work. 'They are eating all the dogs in the area,' Solomon continued. This was a more debatable crime. Dogs are not spayed in rural Kenya – nobody can afford to have the operation done, or if they can they don't care. Thus dogs breed indiscriminately and the resulting puppies are likely to have a wretched life.

The story got worse. Solomon had been at the road camp near Miharati, complaining loudly about the group of colobus that had been killed. He was certain it was something to do with the Chinese road workers in the area. Later that week, back at the camp again, he was followed home: a car was shadowing his *matatu*, waiting when it stopped to collect more passengers. Solomon, in hindsight, had noticed it, but at the time he hadn't been intimidated. When he disembarked to walk the final stretch to his house, it was dark. There was no moon, just a sky full of stars. Solomon knew the way well – he'd often walked in the dark and it didn't worry him. But then he suddenly noticed a group of hooded men. Afterwards he realised that they had pursued him stealthily from the roadside, waiting until they were out of earshot of any possible witnesses.

'They broke my knee, they tried to twist my head so they could break my neck and they told me to stop interfering,' said Solomon, who'd ended up in hospital. 'I was saved by some dogs who began to bark. They stopped those men from killing me.'

'But were they Chinese?' I asked.

'No, they were Africans,' said Solomon, still limping two months later, 'It was the Chinese who hired these bad people.'

Nothing, it seems, will halt Solomon's determination to save wild creatures. Not long after this, he rang me. 'There is a big python near Ol Kalou. It lives by a dam and takes sheep and goats, so the people there – they want to kill it!'

'How big?' I asked.

'It is at least eleven feet long. But we could move it to near your house,' he suggested.

'Have you contacted KWS?' I asked, thinking how much the python would enjoy feasting on my chickens.

'Yes, they will come and shoot it!'

I agreed with Solomon – why kill an innocent creature? But I don't know how to catch, nor do I have the sheer physical strength required to hold such a large snake. Eventually I found a friend of my son's who was willing to come and catch it, bag it and bring it to me. I planned to release it somewhere safe, but not anywhere near my chickens.

It was a long day, a large area and they didn't find the snake.

This was after Solomon had to move home again. He'd remarried

– a kind lady called Grace. Then his brothers had decided to force him off the land he'd bought from one of them after another had burnt down his hut and driven away Esther and the children.

'But they can't, legally . . .' I began feebly.

Solomon sighed. 'I do not have title deeds.'

'But why are they doing this?' I asked.

'They have never accepted me,' he said sadly, 'because I am not from the same father. They always called me "roadside boy".'

Meanwhile he'd been attacked again, Grace had been threatened and their calf had been poisoned. They had a young child now and Grace was worried what Solomon's brothers might do next. She suspected his brothers were behind the death of the calf – and the threats.

I joined Astrid in trying to raise the equivalent of just over £1,200 to buy Solomon a small piece of land – just under 2 acres – near the Malewa River that runs down from the Aberdares, its waters swelled by those of the Wanjohi. The land was closer to Astrid's home and hopefully would offer a measure of security for Solomon, farther away from the 'bad devils' of Happy Valley.

Astrid helped Solomon find a lorry which came and took them and all their possessions away before Solomon's brothers realised anything was happening. The funds stretched to building a house too – a very basic wooden and tin affair, enough to keep off the heavy rain that had battered the area and swept away bridges.

I crossed fingers that Solomon would keep peace with his new neighbours, although before long he found a nest of barn owls in a school. Considering them to be birds of ill omen, a hysterical crowd of teachers, parents and students were determined to sentence them to death by stoning. Solomon, as usual, leapt into the fray. His admonitions that owls are important predators, vital to the ecosystem, fell on deaf ears. Even the teachers, it seemed, were influenced by superstition and the prevailing hysteria. So Solomon contacted local raptor expert, Simon Thomsett, and between them they rapidly engineered the moving process – although half the owl chicks had already been killed. The survivors were fed and cared for, then released when ready to hunt for themselves.

*

Meanwhile, in spite of all fundraising efforts and Solomon's pledge to do a sponsored walk, no more colobus had been moved out of the danger zones, and after decades of Solomon's frantic but fruitless efforts, there were very few left alive anywhere in Happy Valley. However, I stand in awe of Solomon's readiness to challenge the deeply ingrained superstitions and traditional beliefs that have such a hold on the majority of his peers. Most of the latter are avid Christians, although they don't always give up long-held practices and prejudices – such as the necessity to rid the world of owls. Solomon's religious views are unusual, like him, and they were revealed unexpectedly after one of our Happy Valley safaris. As we rattled into Captain, I suggested we stop for a cup of tea as it had been a long day and we hadn't eaten.

'I know a good place,' said Solomon. 'It is away from the road and so it is peaceful.' He directed me past Wanjiku's Happy Photo Shop, which offered 'colourful innovations', and after a few more lefts and rights we drove into the Kenyan equivalent of a piazza, albeit a dirty, scruffy one, where we sat on the veranda of the Hollywood Bar and ordered *chai*. The tea arrived promptly and we were enjoying a companionable silence, during which I was thinking that Captain wasn't such a bad place, when the peace was suddenly broken by what sounded like an explosion. It turned out to be bursts of very loud music, forcing its way through hissing, chest-high loudspeakers. The noise swelled around the Cheerful Kiosk at the far end of the square. We froze in horror and stared, dumbfounded, as a line of people, all dressed in red and black, began to bob slowly towards us, their curious, slow-motion gait keeping exact time with the agonised, contorted sounds from the loudspeakers. As the leader in the sinister line grew slowly closer, I could see another line had emerged from the corner behind us. In fact, all four corners of Captain's peaceful square were spewing out lines of grim-faced men and women, approaching a central point in a terrifying sort of war dance. Feeling somewhat targeted and totally trapped, we stared in transfixed horror at the converging lines as they gathered to continue their sinister, robotic dance on the spot. A crowd was gathering to watch, most of them dancing too now, while the furious noise from the speakers was becoming unbearable.

'What is going on?' I gasped into Solomon's ear.

'They are for Jesus!' he shouted back.

We left some money on our table and ran, leaving our steaming mugs of tea, although Solomon had the sense to grab the *mandazi* that had just arrived. As we somehow managed to get the car out from the melee without being massacred by the music or hypnotised into joining the dancers, the music stopped and somebody began to yell murderously through a microphone, the deadpan dancers still swaying as if in a trance.

We drove to the far end of Captain – until we could hear again. I stopped among the kiosks with their advertisements for drinks, cigarettes, malaria tablets, and ointment for aches and pains. If you listened to the Captain Christian brigade for any length of time you'd need the lot. *Matatu* touts were yelling, but even they were drowned out by the distant evangelists who had begun to sing now, if you could call it singing: it sounded aggressively ominous, as if bawling for revolution. It made my heart rate quicken, although women in headscarves, the babies on their backs sheltered by black umbrellas, walked by without looking particularly terrified. Men were leaning on bicycles. The Aberdares were smoky in the distance. Everything seemed very normal, almost peaceful – if you were deaf.

'Heaven help us,' I said. 'What are they shouting about?'

'They preach the word of God,' said Solomon.

I glanced at him and saw he was smiling wickedly. 'The Red Devils!' he added.

'But . . .' I said finally, 'they sound like . . . lunatics.'

Solomon nodded thoughtfully as he ate his *mandazi*. 'Yes, they get it all the wrong way. These churches, why are they not preaching conservation?' He sighed. 'My religion is to not hurt. My church is the forests. I worship with the birds and colobus monkeys in Happy Valley.'

23

The Valley They Called Happy

Solomon has always referred to Happy Valley with less facetious intonations than those disapproving settlers who pejoratively spoke of Happy Valley back in the days of its prime. He's right as it turns out. When I met Tobina Cole, she opened more windows on to bygone lives in Happy Valley, throwing light on how and why it was so named.

Geoffrey Buxton's siblings had included a sister, Rose, who came to stay with him in Kenya. There she met Algy Cartwright, whom she married in 1923, and Tobina was their daughter. Some years back I'd been given an address for her, when she was living in Edinburgh. I wrote, but received a terse reply saying she'd had enough of spelling out her life history to writers.

In late 2010, hearing she was back in Kenya, I phoned and, although Tobina was brief on the phone, received an invitation to visit. As I drove across Nairobi to the retirement home near Muthaiga, a scruffy young man at a road junction tried to sell me a bunch of mauve-blue water lilies, still dripping with water. I thought about Idina's water gardens, and the rivers and furrows at Buxton's Satima. I bought the flowers, even though, judging by the potent cloud of alcohol surrounding the vendor, he might not be likely to spend the money wisely.

Tobina, elegant and deceptively young looking, had tried to leave Kenya — like so many other descendants of former settler families — but failed to escape permanently, returning to the sunny country of her childhood like a migrating swallow, until she settled here again in her twilight years.

The sun was streaming through open doors and windows and lighting up her garden, full of English flowers. 'I shouldn't really have come back from Edinburgh,' she said after arranging the water lilies, 'after twenty years away. I hate Nairobi – there's nowhere to walk.'

A smiling maid dropped off some milk in the kitchen. A puppy jumped on to Tobina's lap, where it wriggled around gleefully. 'He's called Conrad,' she explained, 'because he's so black. You know, *Heart of Darkness*!'

Tobina told me the true connotations of the term 'Happy Valley'. It was her uncle who'd named it thus: he arrived on foot in this high, green land with its seven rivers. He'd come from the dry Rift Valley station with its meagre river and that relentless dusty wind that gave Gilgil its name. And so Geoff Buxton delightedly called this new haven 'my Happy Valley', despite the lack of drink, drugs and orgies on offer. 'He found his ideal farming country,' said Tobina. 'The name was nothing whatever to do with all the later shenanigans!'

My literary agent, Robert Smith, knew of another descendant of Sir Thomas Fowell Buxton. Edward North Buxton, who'd lived at Knighton in Woodford, Essex, had been pivotal in saving Epping Forest from destruction by local landowners keen to earn a fortune from property speculation. His efforts were rewarded by an Act of Parliament to secure the forest, which was opened by Queen Victoria in 1882. He even donated his own adjoining land to enlarge the forest for the public's enjoyment. This great philanthropic Quaker family from East Anglia had made their money from brewing (Truman, Hanbury and Buxton) and banking (later subsumed into Barclays). Robert found a postcard from the Edwardian period showing a picture of the scenic 'Happy Valley' at Westcliff-on-Sea in Essex, not far from Robert's own home. He wondered if that was where Geoffrey Buxton got the name.

Meanwhile, Tobina's family history is intriguingly intertwined with Happy Valley's earliest settlers, curiously full of connections and coincidences. Another Buxton sister, her 'Aunt Joan', had married Sir

John Ramsden. A generation later, Tobina married Arthur Cole, son of Galbraith Cole, former neighbour and relation of the Delameres; Galbraith's sister, Florence Cole, had married Hugh, 3rd Baron Delamere. (After Florence died, he'd married Gladys, who soon became a widow; she was another woman who'd adored – and some said killed – Lord Erroll.)

Galbraith Cole, Tobina's father-in-law, had been afflicted with the agonies of arthritis when only in his early forties – until, unable to bear the pain, accompanied by the gradual loss of his sight, he'd ended his life on a hill, looking across Lake Elmenteita towards Soysambu. His hand too weak and crippled to hold up the gun to his head, his faithful servant held it for him as he sat in his wheelchair and pulled the trigger, while Galbraith's wife, Lady Eleanor – Nell to friends – had taken the dogs for a walk. He's buried in the place where he died, as he'd wished, on a rocky *kopje* looking across Lake Elmenteita, where he can hear the zebra barking. A few miles behind the house, Nell built a delightful rough-stone church in his memory, which she called the Church of Goodwill. She was a friend of my grandfather's and he was sometimes a lay reader there. Many decades later I had got married in Nell's church, looking across Lake Elmenteita towards the place I was destined to flee to when my marriage came to an abrupt end. Every time I drive up to Gilgil and on to Happy Valley, I pass the obelisk on the hill commemorating Galbraith.

Tobina is also godmother to Tom Cholmondeley, great-grandson of the 3rd Baron Delamere. She visited Tom weekly in Kamiti maximum security prison when he was awaiting trial for a murder he didn't commit. 'He was a very good prisoner,' she said. 'Years ago I was a prison visitor with Margaret Kenyatta.' (Margaret was the English wife of Kenya's first president.) 'We went to check the kitchen and drains and things.'

Tobina spent many happy years of her childhood on Satima Farm. After her parents had split up, her mother came to live on Satima in the mid 1930s. Six-year-old Tobina shared a governess with Idina's daughter, Dinan, and Gillian Leslie-Melville. David Leslie-Melville had a pack of hounds, so on hunting days they were all let off school.

Learning polo was also part of their education. 'We did our lessons on the veranda of the Leslie-Melvilles' house,' said Tobina. 'I rode a horse to school, or went in the milk lorry.' Dinan would have had even farther to come, Clouds being the other side of Kipipiri mountain.

Tobina jumped up, still sprightly for a lady in her eighties, and found an old, heavy album the size of a small table. Her grandmother had been a photographer and developed her own photographs, and Tobina had old photos dating back to 1853. We looked at pictures of her mother and her eight siblings, until she found the more 'recent' photograph of two little girls: herself and Dinan Hay, who looked strikingly like the Idina I knew from photographs. 'Gillian and I called her Dina. She was about eight, older than me, but we were the same size. Then she went off to live with her grandmother in England and went to school there.' The girls had kept in touch ('more or less', Tobina said) until Dinan had died of cancer – relatively young, like her mother before her.

Buxton's Tudor-style house was 'such a dark house', Tobina said. But outside exotic plants flourished – almond trees and yellow arum lilies lining the Wanjohi River. Her uncle Geoff had also been one of the first to plant pyrethrum, getting the plants from Japan. 'Nowadays,' complained Tobina, who had a tendency to digress, 'the pyrethrum marketing is a disgrace. I went to the Nairobi Trade Fair recently to fuss at the pyrethrum board, to give them a lecture . . .' Her cook's wife had still not been paid for her pyrethrum, she said angrily. 'It's not fair on them – they depend on that income!'

Idina had first interested Tobina in pyrethrum: 'She was such a nice woman. She taught me to play backgammon. I planted pyrethrum with her – she showed me how to plant it – eighteen inches apart. My mother loved her too. They all had jolly good parties, just occasionally, but most of the time they worked hard on their farms – even Alice.'

'What was Alice like?' I asked, imagining her as less child friendly.

'She was so kind. She grew ducks, chickens and eggs for the Gilgil Hotel!'

These had been challenging times for farmers – the roads were deeply rutted, too muddy to negotiate after heavy rain. Tobina remembered oxen being chained to the car to pull them out. 'Money wasn't easy to make until the war,' Tobina added, 'although my uncle Geoff was old by then, and the altitude no longer suited him. Fred Chart, his manager, became his partner after the war. I think my uncle gave his share to Fred.'

Tobina Cole filled in more about the woman Solomon had referred to as Patricia Bowles. When living in Happy Valley she'd been Alice's neighbour, and was known as Pat Fisher. 'She was an actress from South Africa and she was the lead singer in some show. That's when Derek fell for her,' she said. Tobina had liked Pat, describing her as 'very doughty – she battled on'. After Derek died she ran her Pat Fisher Salon for Beauty and Hair in Nairobi's Mansion House, next to the New Stanley Hotel.

Tobina also mentioned a homosexual couple, 'Fabian Wallace and Graham Beech', who'd lived in a wooden house near the Fishers' 'black and white house' – which would have matched the farm buildings. Tobina told me how her mother had explained to her about homosexuals in the car once, on the way back to Gilgil. 'Fabian was a pilot, much liked by everybody, and Graham didn't do much. But they lived a very upright life with excellent food and wine.'

I puzzled over the houses: if Tobina's memory was totally reliable maybe the Fishers' original house had fallen down and the wooden house we'd visited in the Catholic school, which we'd then thought was Patricia Bowles's, had belonged to Fabian Wallace. But we'd passed another wooden house, not far from the one tucked inside the mission, which could also have belonged to Wallace and Beech.

Another elderly gentleman remembered Fabian Wallace living near Thomson's Falls. He said that Michael Lafone was Wallace's live-in lover then, although James Fox describes Lafone as 'a fierce womaniser with an eye-glass who was briefly and disastrously married in Kenya to Elizabeth Byng, daughter of the Earl of Strafford', also quoting the limerick that circulated, tarring Lafone with the same brush as de Trafford:

> *There was a young girl of the Mau*
> *Who said she didn't know how,*

She went for a cycle
With Raymond and Michael,
She knows all there is to know now.

Whether the dashing Michael Lafone batted for both sides remained to be surmised. Photographs reveal him as effeminate looking; in one he wears a silk dressing gown, and he stands very close to Joss, to whom he bears a slight resemblance. In the Happy Valley of their time, with all the drinks and drugs on offer, it can't have mattered much at parties who you ended up with for the night.

I also spoke to Benjie Bowles, who lives in Kilifi, north of Mombasa, and who was able to throw more light on Patricia Bowles. Benjie's father Dr Roger Bowles had married three times. His first wife was Evelyn, with whom he had a son and two daughters. Evelyn hated life in Kenya and fled back to England, leaving their three small children behind. Roger's second wife, Patricia, was known as Patsy Bowles. She inherited three stepchildren and meanwhile she and Roger had one son – Benjie himself – in 1941. But the marriage had not lasted. Roger's third wife was also called Patricia, which is confusing, although presumably it simplified things for Dr Bowles. She was Pat for short, and was the former Pat Fisher. Roger was her third husband; her first, back in the 1930s, had been Roddy Ward, who'd farmed near Thomson's Falls. Pat had then married Derek Fisher and they'd lived at Kipipiri, working for Sir John Ramsden.

'Both Pat, my stepmother and Patsy, my mother, were close friends of Alice's and Idina's,' Benjie explained.

Roger and Patsy Bowles happened to have bought a farm in the high and fertile Subukia Valley, not so far from Happy Valley – just the other side of Thomson's Falls – and also prime land, tending to attract wealthier farmers, although it doesn't quite have that giddy beauty of Happy Valley itself. The farm, Gemdin (or, as another friend formerly from the area insisted, 'Glendin'), had belonged to a Rowland Platt. 'He committed suicide,' added Benjie.

'He was my grandfather's cousin!' I exclaimed. 'Do you know where he's buried?'

'It was on a hillside. But I'm almost sure it was an unmarked grave . . .'

Patsy, Benjie's mother, had built a big house with a lovely staircase: Benjie recalled sliding down it on trays.

Meanwhile, up in Happy Valley, Pat and Derek Fisher had one son, Peter, who'd grown up with Benjie. 'We both went to school at Pembroke House in the early fifties,' Benjie added, 'and we used to go on our days out up to Idina's. I remember catching trout there!'

And who did Pat think had killed Erroll? She never talked about it, Benjie said. 'If she knew anything she kept it hush-hush.' Patsy, on the other hand, believed it was MI5 – and so does Benjie. But, as Benjie pointed out, living in Kilifi, as did Diana until she died, it had inevitably been a closed subject – out of respect for his neighbour.

When living at Kipipiri, Pat Fisher had evidently been a good neighbour and friend to Alice de Trafford. Benjie also explained that Derek had been cattle and forestry manager for Chops Ramsden and had remained there throughout the war, as some farmers did, providing food for British troops. Their son, Peter, was killed in a car crash in 1975 when his Land Rover rolled in Limuru.

I thought about how life in Kenya seems to involve so many tragedies, too many goodbyes, yet many white farmers and their descendants stayed on because of that special something about the country that is not easy to explain: a curious but powerful mix of intangible qualities – including a wonderful climate, stunning scenery, unlimited space and freedom, a thrilling lifestyle that allowed the shooting of the teeming big game on your own land, and of course plenty of cheap labour (including servants) – which first magnetically drew people from foreign climes. And thus they built homes close to the equator, in a land that wasn't truly theirs and would one day be handed back to the Africans, breaking many settlers' hearts when they had to leave. My grandmother was sent from the slopes of Mount Kenya to live in a home in England, after her doctor forbade her to live at altitude. Re-reading her poems and letters is heartbreaking. The people in England were strangers to her: she described them as 'dull and grey – like the sky'. She felt keenly that her sorrowful spirit had stayed on in her Kenyan garden, gliding beside the shadowed waters of a clear trout stream, watching her rose bushes trampled by goats as her lawn turned to dust.

24

The Secret Garden of Happy Valley

Driving to Gilgil, passing Galbraith Cole's grave on the nearby hill, I received a text from a number I did not recognise. 'They have destroyed the grave of Fraser Allen,' it read. 'It is very bad and he needs a decent reburial.'

I called the number, totally baffled.

'It's Wahome,' he said.

'Who did it?' I asked, 'and why?'

'It is a very bad thing,' Wahome said, 'and I do not know who did this.'

The Delamere graves had also been desecrated on Soysambu, with both the 3rd Baron's and Gladys Delamere's skulls stolen. Sometimes, I'd been told, the skulls of wealthy or influential people are taken to be used as tools of witchcraft. A similar thing happened to Diana Delamere's grave, which is not on Soysambu but on Ndabibi, Gilbert Colville's former farm. Curiously enough, when, after divorcing Colville, Diana ran off with his best friend the 3rd Baron, it didn't seem to affect any friendships. They remained a happy trio, regularly attending the races together, and Diana was ultimately buried along with two favourite dogs and between her latter two husbands. When we visited the tiny graveyard, atop a small knoll and circled by a hedge, it had been vandalised: stones were cracked, and although somebody had filled in the graves again, you could see they'd been dug up.

'Did they steal the skull?' I asked Wahome.

'No, I don't think they took the skull, they were after treasure.'

'What treasure?'

'They think you people bury their dead with valuables,' Wahome explained.

A friend from Europe was a passenger in my car. As Wahome and I had this conversation about skulls and treasure he began giving me nervous glances, as if I was a secret pirate.

'Can you find a relative of Fraser Allen?' asked Wahome.

'I'll try,' I told him.

Frank Daykin didn't have contacts for any of Fraser Allen's relations, nor did Janie Begg. I asked around among former settlers from the area: not many remembered Fraser Allen, but a few remembered his son, David, who they called *Mambo* – which means 'news', usually of a problematic nature. 'Mambo's father had been burnt alive in front of him,' another friend said, 'but Mambo is dead too now.'

Wahome had asked if I was visiting the area any time soon, but my Land Rover was going through a phase of expensive repairs and it seemed unlikely. But in early 2011, the renowned photographer Nigel Pavitt drove me up to Happy Valley as he wanted to take photographs of some old houses. We were accompanied by a friend, Veronica Finch, better known as 'Finchie'. As we sped up the new Chinese road, I realised I'd lost Wahome's number, as Solomon told us that Kruger's old farm had been grabbed 'by somebody high up in the forestry department'. He shook his head: 'Too many problems there now!'

On a crazy whim I persuaded my friends that we should make a detour to look for Morgan-Grenville's old place – although there were, of course, far more intact and accessible houses to visit and photograph. It turned out Finchie had been at school with his daughter, who'd later died of malaria, and remembered her arriving in 'swanky cars'.

Along the road towards the Daykins' old home, still rocky and rutted, Solomon stopped us to check on some donkeys. He'd been involved in worming them and cutting their hooves, part of his general work with animals in the greater area. A child, who looked less than three years old, clutched a bag of sugar and eyed us from the grassy verge. There were no houses nearby and the youngster would have been dispatched on foot to walk, probably some distance, to buy the sugar. It never ceases to amaze me how such tiny African children undertake daily chores that would defy many a British teenager.

A bright and sunny day, with the Aberdares clear and majestic before us, inspired our renewed search for Morgan-Grenville's. But although we could see where the road cut into the steep mountainside as it zigzagged its way up, we couldn't find the start of it. After we'd back-tracked repeatedly and done several five-point turns on the narrow road, a helpful lorry driver showed us how to get to it – through a fence. A farmer tilling the soil in the neighbouring field came over, pulled the fence aside and beckoned us in.

We were on the grassed-over track at last – climbing steeply in a series of tight bends, the drop below increasing dramatically as we reached an altitude of 8,500 feet. We stopped on one bend as Solomon felt sure we were close – we could see, above the densely forested slope to our left, a stand of tall eucalyptus. Excitedly, we abandoned the vehicle and ploughed our way through the undergrowth, scrambling up the slope, sticks tearing at our clothes and hair, until suddenly the forest thinned and there were signs of a former garden: cypress trees and clumps of agapanthus. 'It is here!' called Solomon from somewhere further up the hidden hillside.

Suddenly we were completely out of the thicket, stumbling on to the same road we'd abandoned lower down. Up here it faded into a stone footbridge over a stream. Further along the steep mountainside, two more streams also gurgled and tumbled down rocks. There were sudden unexpected piles of old foundation stones; then, as we climbed up through nettles, a concrete plinth. As we began to explore more, we found blackberries, acres of blue and white agapanthus and a tangle of garden flowers that included blue periwinkle, yellow broom, golden honeysuckle and pink roses. There was even a real English oak tree. Nigel's camera clicked constantly.

Mabel's legendary gardens had outlived her – here was a wild garden, flourishing untended as it wove through indigenous forest and multiplied. It was hauntingly beautiful, with the backdrop the dizzy heights of the Aberdares – so close you felt you could jump up and touch them – then below, chinks of a breathtaking view glimpsed through the thick undergrowth. When we stepped into a green, grassy glade, we could see far below the glimmer of rows of plastic greenhouses, where a Dutchman, newly arrived in the area, was growing flowers on the old Gillett farm, as well as the more pleasing shining expanse of Lake Ol Bolossat. I thought I could make out the roof of Fergusson and Bingley's former home, but then there were so many roofs. Once Morgan-Grenville would have been able to see their lights at night – one of the few pinpricks of light in the dark expanse below.

We turned back to the magical garden, festooned with garden flowers that had seeded themselves for generations, clambering at will over any rock, tree or foundation stone. There was an intoxicating feel of wanton abandonment in their wild loveliness. Yet apart from the tinkle of the streams and the calls of forest birds, it was wrapped in a deep peace: like a neglected graveyard. A shaft of sunlight beamed through the foliage on to Solomon's head as he said in wonder: 'How did this man Morgan discover this place and then think to build such a big house up here?'

'And build that road all the way up too?' I added.

Finchie had found a cluster of hydrangeas, their blooms bigger than a watermelon. She remembered Morgan-Grenville at the coast in his old age. 'He was tall and white-haired,' she said, 'but still a very attractive man.'

Solomon showed us how to suck the nectar out of a peach-coloured moonflower – 'copying the sunbirds', he added – as he had in his childhood. He suddenly said, 'I remember walking up here when I was young – over thirty years ago. It was such a big wooden house with a shingle roof and so many colobus monkeys, but nobody was living there.'

'Why destroy it?' asked Finchie.

Solomon sighed, 'That is Africa.'

The wind roared in the ancient gums like an angry sea as we came across more signs of Africa – a torn shirt, some shards of wood where a tree had been chopped, a smattering of charcoal. Suddenly a dog barked, higher up in the forest, and another answered. 'There are other people in the forest,' said Solomon, 'hunting the wildlife with dogs.'

It was time to leave, armed with clumps of white agapanthus for Finchie to plant at home in Karen. As we walked back down the road, we passed a golden ground orchid and she knelt in the grass to photograph it. Then she suddenly screamed, leapt up and began a manic dance, shedding all her clothes. She was covered in black *siafu*, or safari ants, which attack living flesh with their needle-like bites. They'll literally eat you alive. As she leapt about and I tried to pick them off her skin, her clothes and her hair, the men tactfully walked on.

'Morgan-Grenville's army,' said Solomon when we finally got back to the car, 'he set them on us because we stole his plants.'

We continued on to Gibb's house, still visible from the road and worth photographing to Nigel Pavitt's expert eye. Instead of it becoming dormitories, as the headmaster had told us it would on our last visit, some schoolteachers had moved in. It was Saturday and nobody was around, except one teacher's wife who was living in the old staff quarters. In the centre of a muddle of chickens, children and litter, she was hanging out copious quantities of washing that stretched from her doorway to the broken roof of what had once been the generator house at the other side of the narrow courtyard.

We walked outside again and around the southern side of the house, followed by a dozen children, with more materialising at every step to join the gathering throng. There was a smell of open drains and nobody had cut the grass, cleared the nettles or collected the unsightly litter that had been chucked indiscriminately around the former flower beds and lawns. The door to the long corridor swung open and we walked down it past locked doors – behind which, we were told, lurked the teachers when they were at home. The wooden floors of the corridor were soiled with cow-pats and decaying litter, while the walls were plastered with mud, grime and graffiti. Somebody had been practising their English down the far end, using a piece of charcoal, spelling most of the words wrong. One former bedroom at the back remained unoccupied, its filthy floors broken and sagging, its cupboards and fireplace still intact. Next door the bathroom had been gutted, except for the bath itself, which had lost its taps, so nobody – had they been inclined – could attempt to clean it of layers of litter and dirt. By now we had an entourage of about forty giggling children. Their feet were bare and their clothes ragged and dirty, but their eyes were bright.

'And this is their teachers, who are living like this,' cried Solomon afterwards, 'setting an example to those children!'

We drove on, photographing Slains, which had been swallowed up by acres of cabbages and maize, its few remaining mounds of mud wall barely visible. Finchie was intrigued by the ruin beside the Wanjohi River, just before Wanjohi town. A few years earlier, when we'd passed by with Frances Osborne, she'd wondered aloud if it could have been her great-grandmother Lady Idina Gordon's very first home. Now the house had undergone a facelift: a shiny tin roof, wooden shutters painted blue and an avenue of young hargenia trees heading up to it from a wooden, slatted gate. It had the air of an old French countryside villa.

Our final destination was Buxton's house, surrounded by a new flush of growth: emerald-green lawns surrounded the flower beds which bordered the house, the variety of surviving blooms including fat roses and opulent heads of hydrangea. A white bottle-brush flowered at the side of the house, the plum trees were heavy with fruit and the tangle of orange and yellow nasturtiums had climbed all the way up the back to the roof. But the years had taken their toll on the old house: a little more plaster had dropped from its sides, a few more windows were broken.

'My father, he was killed in Wanjohi town last Easter in a fight,' said the new young Kikuyu owner, Karanja, son of Solomon's former teacher. 'He liked to drink *changaa*.' A local brew, supposedly illegal, *changaa* can be made out of anything that will ferment. Often highly toxic, it regularly kills people.

Solomon later told us that Karanja had inherited his father's liking for local brews, which perhaps explained his persistent demands for money. We had brought tea and sugar, which we gave to Karanja's pretty young wife, as well as biscuits for the children, but Karanja

kept up his constant negotiations for cash as he showed us around
the garden, the fees he demanded for allowing us to photograph the
outside of his decaying house far exceeding any I'd ever paid at the
stateliest of Britain's National Trust properties. 'The roof is leaking
badly,' Karanja said gravely. 'We need assistance for the repair.' But
we were welcome to picnic in his field, he said, so we sat on a rug and
tucked into a deliciously elaborate picnic provided by Finchie. The
Karanja family joined our feast: the little girls trying apples for the first
time, but preferring the sugary biscuits we'd brought them. Karanja,
his younger brother, his wife and a delightful *m‡ee*, who just happened
to be passing, also sampled new culinary tastes, including olives (which
proved too alien) and roasted sunflower seeds (which were extremely
popular). They all expressed great mirth at our complicated picnic, not
to mention the fact that Finchie had packed plates, knives, forks and
various condiments. Solomon, used to European-style picnics, ate his
with a nonchalant air.

After the feast under the fig tree, sacred to the Kikuyu, Karanja
extorted a generous wad of money out of Nigel Pavitt. The financial
negotiations over, we laughed and joked like old friends, while Karanja
teasingly called Nigel 'Lord Egerton' after another colonial character,
albeit one who'd never lived in Happy Valley. During all this, a young
man with rakish looks, his cowboy hat at a jaunty angle, stopped to
watch. He'd lovingly decorated his bicycle from handlebars to pedals
with anything he could find – strips of cloth tied like ribbons, plastic
bottle tops threaded on strings, Christmas decorations, a gourd
and miniature flags, both Kenyan and American – the result being
colourful and eccentrically festive. But when we praised his efforts, we
discovered he was deaf and dumb.

It seemed ironic that Buxton's home, once so morally upright, now
sheltered a family partial to tippling; conversely the late *M‡ee* Nuthu
was teetotal, as were his family still living in the formerly gin-soaked
Clouds. Solomon had written that people in today's Happy Valley were
similar to their partying predecessors, but the old houses, it seemed,
didn't seem to retain any bad influences from the past.

*

Soon afterwards, Janie Begg gave me the contact details for Robert Morgan-Grenville's son, Richard, who was living in South Africa. He told me his father arrived in Kenya in 1933 and started building his house four years later. He also explained Fraser's death, using his mother's nickname for him: tractors in those days ran off parafin, but were started on petrol. Fraser turned the magneto, which sparked setting alight the petrol in his hand. Fraser was very badly burnt and died two days later. Richard didn't have any photographs of the house where he'd spent his childhood, but said if I visited their house on the coast at Blue Lagoon I'd find a painting of it. So I did – and there were several: the house, surrounded by flowers and shrubs, with a bench at the top of a green slope of lawn; a lovely stone statue in thoughtful repose; the view through the gum trees above a white-flowering border; a weeping willow over a pond. Although they were probably never great paintings, even before they'd faded, they still conveyed a sense of the lovely home.

I thought of the place today, a garden of remembrance, shedding a sense of finality and peace that would blow with the winds down towards Fergusson's old house.

25

A Picnic Under the Chandelier

Afew months later we were back in Happy Valley with two of Geoff Buxton's great-nieces, Jane and Libby, visiting from England. I was happy to take them, always eager to learn more about Happy Valley's curious past. It also meant good tips for Solomon, always gratefully received. Jane and Libby's grandmother, Olive, had been one of the seven Buxton siblings in Geoff's generation, so they were also related to Chops Ramsden. Linda Muir, née Cole, a relative of Tobina's by marriage, also joined us. It had been a long dry season, and the Nye-Charts' wooden house stood starkly in a bare and dusty wasteland. Next door in the main house, Karanja was intrigued by these relations from foreign climes – and welcomed us warmly. We stood on the front lawn, cropped short by cows and sheep, and looked at the L-shaped house. With a little imagination and some whitewash it could have been straight out of *Country Living* magazine. Jane and Libby were totally enamoured.

'It makes me feel quite peculiar,' Libby said.

'I could live here,' added Jane.

'You may see inside the house,' Karanja offered, knowing a fee would be forthcoming – I'd negotiated with him over the phone in advance.

We trooped around in the gloom: broken floorboards were sinking into the foundations, missing window panes were blocked up with cardboard to avert draughts, smoke-blackened ceilings were falling into the rooms, mouldering where the rain had leaked on to them.

There were two flights of wooden stairs to the upstairs bedrooms. The stairs were still sturdy, but upstairs flecks of blue sky peeked down through gaps in the wooden roof tiles. The former bathrooms were devoid of fittings.

Another man was accompanying us, although we never discovered where he fitted in. 'My name is Mwangi,' he said. 'I am an ABCD man!'

'What is that?' whispered Jane.

'I think he means he's literate,' I muttered back. Plenty aren't – even in modern Kenya.

Karanja's brother, who was missing school to meet and greet us, was using one of the old attic bedrooms. There was a bed with his very few possessions scattered over a threadbare blanket, but little else. He had chalked on his door: 'Actions speak louder than words'.

'Perhaps your family would like to renovate the house,' Karanja said hopefully to Buxton's descendants as we left. 'You can see we have no money for this . . .'

As we drove on to Kipipiri House, I heard more about their great-uncle, Chops. 'He was tricky,' Libby said. 'I was only about seventeen when I visited him, but I remember it was intimidating. I remember his old manservant who wore a stiff collar that had once fitted him when he was still size fifteen, but he was now a size twelve, so it rattled round his neck. Every day he ironed the newspaper and put it on a silver salver.' This had been at Ramsden's Scottish estate, Ardverike, where Ramsden had returned to retire when he left Kenya. When Libby visited he would have been well into his eighties.

At the gates of the flower farm beside Kipipiri House, I spun a long story to the lady on security duty, explaining how we'd been before and now here we were back again with long-lost relatives (*all* the way from England) of the long-dead white man who'd built the old house. She wasn't at all sure about us; and several lengthy Kikuyu phone conversations later, in which she'd evidently failed to explain why a bunch of white people – and Solomon – were at the gate and wouldn't go away, she handed me the phone. I spoke to a somewhat suspicious Kikuyu gentleman called Nganga, who finally agreed we could picnic

under a tree beside the house while waiting for him to arrive in about
an hour's time.

When we got to the house itself a beautiful Kikuyu woman called
Virginia graciously received us and insisted we picnic in the dining
room. She opened the carved door and welcomed us inside. As we
walked peacefully down a cool veranda lining the interior courtyard,
turning right into the dining room, I wondered about the mad woman
with the *panga*. Solomon kept looking at me with raised eyebrows, so
I knew he was wondering too.

Virginia seated us in the panelled dining room beneath the
chandelier. A picture of Kenya's President Kibaki watched us from
the walls, where once Ramsden's ancestral portraits would have hung.
Libby produced a treat – Scottish smoked salmon – while wryly
observing that it was amusing to be having a picnic 'in stuffy old Aunt
Joan's formal dining room – she'd have had a fit!' Virginia joined
us for lunch and explained how a young woman, claiming to be the
second Mrs Kanyoto, albeit merely a girlfriend, had arrived with a
bunch of heavies and a lorry, triumphantly led by the mad woman with
the *panga*. They'd forced their way in and made off with most of the
furniture, all the crockery, cutlery and linen and plenty of the fittings.
That, thankfully, was the last anyone had seen of her.

Just after we'd finished our picnic in such unexpected surroundings,
Nganga arrived. This soft-spoken, elderly gentleman took us round
the house and gardens.

'No waving *panga*,' Solomon said to me in an aside.

Thus, in a happier and more relaxed mode than previous visits, I
absorbed the tangible peace in the grand old house as we admired the
immaculate floors and polished wood panelling of the generously sized
rooms. The bathrooms, their original fittings intact, were pristine and
the old-fashioned chain flushes from the high cisterns worked perfectly.
There were six bedrooms, four with fireplaces, four bathrooms and
two living rooms – the larger L-shaped with window seats. The only
casualty was a door, broken by the imposter-wife on her mission to
take all the moveable assets.

The large kitchen with a Dover stove (New Crown, from Brisbane) extended into several pantries and stores, a walk-in meat safe, a wine store and serving room. Teams of white-jacketed servants would presumably have scuttled between them with silver salvers and bottles of the best wine and port. There was a long, covered veranda at the front – the first I'd seen in Happy Valley – which had doors into both living rooms and two of the bedrooms. The house, with all its rooms opening on to the inner courtyard, reminded me of Clouds. Idina had evidently liked Ramsden's house and had her own built to a very similar design.

The pond in the courtyard was empty and the rills dry, so Virginia turned on the taps to reawaken the cooling sounds of water running through and filling the pond. It was a hot dry day in February, so the fireplace at the back of the courtyard seemed redundant, but when the chill of night descended from Kipipiri behind, it would be a place to enjoy the stars, absorbing the open fire's warmth while sipping a glass of Champagne – although mulled wine might be more appropriate at this altitude.

The two nude statues that had once graced the courtyard, reminders of an unrestrained era, had been banished to a store at the rear of the house. Solomon was thrilled to find them. Perhaps the *panga*-wielding woman had hidden them, offended by their nakedness. We wandered on through the vast grounds, descending stone steps that cascaded into different parts of what once must have been a garden of breathtaking proportions. It was too soon for the central courtyard pond to have filled up, otherwise the water would have run beneath the house into the channels and ponds bisecting the sweep of front lawn with its majestic hedges rising either side. But although the grass was crisp and brown, it would only take a little imagination – and plenty of water – to green up those secret recesses of gardens and resurrect the withered flowers and shrubs running alongside the house in sun-baked beds. The cypress hedges remained green and well clipped.

'We have two gardeners,' explained Nganga as we headed for the shade cast by a couple of giant magnolia trees. From here we looked past the house to forest – deep green, apart from one ash-coloured scar on the side of the mountain left by a fire.

Kipipiri House and garden were crying out to be lived in again. I almost felt we were here on a mission.

'It could be a hotel,' said Virginia, echoing my thoughts.

'But would Mrs Kanyoto sell?' I asked.

'Mr Kanyoto loved this house – and the forest,' explained Nganga firmly. 'His wishes were never to sell it and to protect the forest. The forest is my job. But if somebody would lease the house for a hotel, that would be good. Nobody uses it now.'

A charming summer house at the side of the garden, shaded by a vast, gnarled bottle-brush tree, looked out on to the forested valley running up the side of the mountain.

'It was a court house,' Virginia said.

'Or a courting house?' Libby wondered.

'They used to watch the elephants from here,' Solomon recalled. 'They were coming to the salt lick.'

We climbed up Kipipiri on a path from the back gate, the hot sun striking our backs before we entered the cooler forest. Short of breath from the altitude, but inspired by the views, we scrambled up the steepening path until we came to three water reservoirs, fed by a mountain stream.

'They were the original ones,' Nganga explained. 'Even now they provide water for the house as well as the flower farm.' But the stone bases had cracked so somebody had lined them with less aesthetic black plastic.

On our previous visit, before being forced to flee from the mad woman, we'd intended to visit the grave of Count Gurienti. He had been a friend of Lyduska Piotto's: she'd told me how his Greek girlfriend, the late Elly Grammaticus, shot him dead, allegedly after discovering in his safe a sheaf of correspondence with a pretty 19-year-old girl. 'Greeks always have a tragedy,' she'd sniffed, adding that the young offender had actually been his niece.

'Oh, but Count Gurienti was a womaniser,' Bubbles Delap told me. 'Elly Grammaticus found out about one affair. She lay in wait, shot at his balls and killed him. He's buried up there in Kipipiri forest.'

'I knew Elly Grammaticus,' said Janie, who knows everybody, going on to tell a story that echoed Alice de Janzé's acquittal in Paris several decades earlier. Elly had also got off on the grounds of it being a crime of passion. A renowned Nairobi lawyer, Byron Georgiadis, handled her case – presumably he was Greek too. Janie said that Elly had only intended to maim Gurienti in the testicles, 'but somebody should have told her not to get so close with a shotgun.' She snorted knowingly, 'Of course it would kill him!'

'Did Gurienti rent the house?' I asked Janie.

'Ah!' she chuckled. 'I heard a rumour, from an unreliable source! The story is that he won it during a night of gambling . . .'

The grave had a mossy fence around it, and a wooden cross and stone, both inscribed. The stone had been pushed back and partly on to its side as if someone had tried to roll it away. I read that Piero Gurienti de Brezoni had been born in Verona in 1922 – the same year Alice de Janzé married, while Idina was already living in Happy Valley with Gordon. He'd died in 1972, almost a decade after independence, aged fifty.

As we descended again a group of at least a dozen men and women with axes and machetes melted into the forest. They'd seen Nganga and didn't want to be reported for illegally cutting these protected trees.

Janie Begg told me she'd found some old photos of Kipipiri House. I went to her new home, unusually situated on the edge of a very big African slum, an area most white people wouldn't venture anywhere near, but her pendulum had apparently advised her to buy it. 'And you can see Mount Kili,' she said triumphantly, before asking, 'Have you been up to Wanjohi recently?'

She heaved some old photograph albums on to a table and found the relevant pages, although none of the albums seemed to have any chronological order. Most of the photographs were of Ramsden's sheep: they were neatly labelled '2,000 ewes at Kipipiri' and '2,200 hoggets on the Kimuru'.

'Hogget?' I queried.

'A yearling sheep,' Janie replied.

There was a photo of Lady Colville and Lily Begg standing outside the Gilgil Hotel, taken in 1927; David Begg and Jimmy Bird on horseback in an empty landscape, taken in 1946; undated ones of Lady Joan Ramsden, and Gilbert and Diana Colville. There were also pictures of Kipipiri House looking much the same as it does now. There were pictures of Ramsden's other home, Waterloo House near Naivasha, and more of a small, stone house. 'That was Kimuru House,' Janie explained, 'which was built by Ramsden after we lived in the cave – some time after the 1930s.' There'd been no sign of Kimuru House when we'd gone on our caving expedition.

Another person with old photographs of Kipipiri House was Tobina Cole: she'd often accompanied her mother to visit her aunt Joan Ramsden. 'Chops wasn't friendly,' she told me, 'nor was Joan. But they were all good to us. Their daughter Joyce became my guardian in England.'

She looked askance at me for my interest in houses. 'I don't like houses,' she said, surprising me because her own home, although small, was attractive and had a pleasant ambience. She remembered that Ramsden's house at Kipipiri had been very dark: 'You couldn't see when you were inside the drawing room. I suppose people liked it after days in the bright sun.' She claimed it had been built after the war, 'about 1919', and that Chops had designed it.

Ramsden left Happy Valley in 1953: 'He had business in Malaya,' said Tobina curtly. 'His son John was shot there – by a Chinese crook. John was the farmer. So he sold Kipipiri and his other farms to Abraham Block – of Block Hotels – and returned to England, where he lived a long time – until 1965.'

Whether or not the Ramsdens had attended any of Idina's parties (some writers mention Chops attending the occasional wild event), Tobina's parents, she made it clear, had definitely not partaken in such decadence. 'My mother disapproved,' she said.

After looking at Tobina's fascinating old photos of Chops and his friends, as well as the wonderful garden in its earlier stages, it was time for me to leave. Tobina was walking next door to read to a blind friend. 'I read him the newspapers every day,' she said, 'and also we're reading about the early life of Hitler – up to 1936.' The time, of course, when Joss was involved with the British Fascist movement. I asked Tobina about his murder – after all, her uncle Geoff must have had his theories, as well as Chops – but she brushed it off with: 'There have been so many unsolved murders. Why do people carry on about this one?'

Tobina has no mobile phone or email, only an unreliable landline, which in Kenya is dependent on the weather. Too much rain and the lines usually go down, then it's anybody's guess how long they will take to fix them, if ever. But I could borrow her photograph albums any time, she said, ending our conversation as abruptly as she had over the phone, without ceremony or goodbye. She walked away without looking back and vanished behind a yesterday, today and tomorrow bush, with its scented mingle of white, mauve and violet blooms. It was as if a curtain had abruptly been drawn across the stage. I sat in my car a while before starting the engine, suddenly exhausted.

26

Polo and Terrorism

I had imagined my research was finally done, but then Bruce Rooken-Smith contacted me with more stories. My grandparents had known the Rooken-Smiths, a vast family who seemed related to everybody and were somehow, albeit confusingly, linked up with the Wanjohi crowd. Between Bruce, his brother Don, and their 95-year old mother, Marge Nye-Chart, who lived in a South African Frail Care home, they explained — at length — their baffling family history. It took time to understand who was who, who had married who and how they were all related. It was a bit like doing a vast, very difficult jigsaw, eventually becoming easier as pieces slotted in and the picture began to take form. Once again I was caught up in Happy Valley's constantly changing story, inspired by people whose upbringings were so similar to my mother's. These farming people I could relate to, having spent the happiest years of my early childhood on my grandparents' farm.

Alexander William Rooken-Smith had come to Kenya from South Africa in the early 1900s. He'd had three wives. Two of his children from his second wife were Violet (who married Bertie Case, son of William and brother of Noel) and Harold, Bruce and Don's father, who married Marge. Marge complicates the story: her father, Frederick Eeles, had come out from England and married her mother, Daisy, one of the nine Aggett children. When Frederick decided to return to England, Daisy refused to leave Kenya. She had an illegitimate son, Neville, with a white hunter, Posma, who planned to marry her after his next hunting safari, but it turned out to be his last: he was killed by an elephant. Daisy then married Lionel Griffin (who adopted her two children) and the couple had three more children. One of them, Marge's half-sister, married the half-brother of Marge's husband, Harold. Later on, after Harold had been killed in a car crash, Marge married Fred Nye-Chart. Fred's mother, Nellie, had been another of the Aggetts' nine children and a sister of Daisy Griffin (née Eeles, née Aggett), so Fred and Marge were actually first cousins. It made everyone seem remarkably interrelated in one small valley.

Daisy and Lionel's son, Ken Griffin, had taken over Satima as manager after the Charts and McLoughlins left, buying it just before independence and consequently finding himself bought out in the initial phase of the million-acre scheme.

The Rooken-Smiths were all polo players, keeping up a tradition Joss had begun on the first pitch at Slains. Solomon had pointed out the second polo field to me, near Buxton's house, still a flat open space, providing excellent grazing for cows and sheep. Don had been a teenager when Fred Chart ran the Wanjohi Polo Club on Satima Farm in the late 1940s. It closed down in the early 1950s when Chart left, but the show went on, using another rough pitch nearer Ol Kalou. Don meticulously recalled the names of players and horses – including Admiral Steve Arliss, 'who fought at the battle of Jutland and drove a Rolls Royce', and Billy Baldock (a woman), who called her home 'Much Bottle in the Marsh' and 'had a nice mare called Trial Trip'. All the neighbours played polo, including Dr Anne Spoerry, Alastair Gibb, John McLoughlin and the Gillett brothers. In late December 1952 the Ol Kalou Polo Club had a team playing in Nairobi for the New Year tournament, the same week Fergusson and Bingley were murdered. The polo went on, but the dedicated Ol Kalou players drove back and forth daily on the Friday, Saturday and Sunday. Bruce recalled: 'A round trip of some 200 miles each day – and then on the Sunday, still dressed in britches and boots, we did a sweep after a gang, behind our house!'

My interest was thoroughly awakened by Don's next story. Of all the tenuous links between me, Mary Miller and this more recent farming family, I never expected it to be a giraffe! Don Rooken-Smith had known Jock Leslie-Melville at Cirencester, but got to know him better years later, when Jock was translocating the threatened and last remaining herd of Rothschilde's giraffe from Soy, in western Kenya, to better-protected areas. The Rooken-Smiths had recently moved to Soy, so Don assisted in the cowboy operation: mounted on polo ponies they charged after the cantering giraffe, the aim being to herd them towards a man sitting in a bucket seat attached to the mudguard of a vehicle, wielding a noose attached to a giraffe-neck-length pole, which he planned to lower over their unsuspecting, spotted heads. The horses were terrified of the giraffe, high grass concealed warthog holes into which the horses frequently fell and after everyone had fallen off their mount (one woman's horse even somersaulted) they called it a day. However, eventually a number of giraffe were moved, some to the outskirts of Nairobi.

Coincidentally, in the 1990s I lived across the forested valley from the Leslie-Melvilles' Giraffe Manor, where Jock and Betty had started their sanctuary. The hand-fed giraffe, who'd happily stick their heads through the Leslie-Melvilles' dining-room window for a piece of toast and a kiss, spent their day entertaining schoolchildren and tourists at the educational 'giraffe centre' below the house. At night they were herded into the sanctuary, the forested foreground to my view of the blue knuckles of the Ngong hills. Forgoing all indigenous delights, the giraffe joined me every evening, heading straight for my bougainvillea bushes, beheading 'poisonous' plants like euphorbia and poinsettia. I would sit on my veranda looking up at multiple long, spotted legs, watching their owners drink the contents of my birdbath in several gulps. My children went to sleep listening to heavy giraffe footsteps and loud munching beside their open windows. If there was a moon they'd get a close-up of the spots.

These bougainvillea-fed giraffe bred madly and some were transported to Soysambu. One evening, after I'd moved there, I came upon a herd of giraffe. I froze as one of these giants strode gracefully over, bowed his long neck and kissed my outstretched hand. He was one of my old Langata friends.

*

I thought I'd closed my chapter on the enigmatic Mary Miller, but in early 2012, Solomon met some Kikuyu elders who'd told him some extraordinary – almost unbelievable – stories about her during Mau Mau. So I decided to go and listen to them first hand. Once again Happy Valley's history had churned up something totally unexpected, this time a matter I'd never heard of before and which even surprised my parents.

The tarmac road from Gilgil to Ol Kalou was broken and potholed. My Land Rover rattled at top volume. It was a cold, sunless July day and the Aberdares were hazy against a grey sky, their lower regions veiled by low cloud. My windscreen was blurred by drizzle, which my worn wiper rubbers failed to clear.

We stopped to collect 78-year-old Kamwambao in Captain. He had dressed up in an old grey suit, purple shirt, scarf and jungle hat, smiling toothlessly as he was assisted into the Land Rover. He didn't speak English, but spoke a little Kiswahili. Solomon had already warned me that this particular Mau Mau story was a delicate issue: we needed to avoid prying ears. Not all the elders Solomon had spoken to were prepared to talk. Mary Miller's former driver was still alive, but too old, immobile and forgetful. Githuku Githaiga, the man who had killed Fergusson and Bingley (and many other Europeans, according to Solomon) had also declined. 'He is feeling too much the blood of the white people,' Solomon explained.

Wanjohi had tripled in size in a decade, matched by the piles of roadside litter. People stared curiously as we stopped beside two more very old men and an elderly woman, who hoisted themselves into my Land Rover. Neither Solomon nor I fancied another trip to Mary Miller's former home, so we drove towards Delap's. The road had degenerated into a rocky quagmire. It had rained hard for months and the bridge over the swollen Wanjohi River had collapsed, although there had been some makeshift 'repairs'. On Solomon's assurance that it was safe, I drove tentatively across and continued along the road, realising that we couldn't go back now as there was nowhere to turn. We eventually stopped in front of a locked metal gate and a field of sheep. On trying to turn around we got stuck anyway, so it seemed a good place as any to talk, although there was nowhere to sit. I was aware this interview had to be quick in view of the ages of the interviewees.

Njuguna, who sported a cheap nylon suit and a tweed hat, was the youngster at seventy-two. He'd been a messenger during Mau Mau: messages were delivered by the fastest runners, relay-race style, but passed by word of mouth. Back in Wanjohi, when he'd first climbed into the Land Rover and shaken hands with Kamwambao, they'd suddenly recognised one another – although it had been well over fifty years: they'd known one another during Mau Mau.

Mugwe was eighty-three and the most forthcoming. He was clad in a thick sweater, gumboots and a faded sports cap, and was the only one who walked without a stick. He'd fled into the forests with other Mau Mau fighters in 1952, he told us. Wanjiru, seventy-six and almost blind, was reluctant to say too much. She wore a long cotton dress, a threadbare sweater and a headscarf, leaning on her stick after placing her umbrella and woven basket on the ground. She'd been one of the women responsible for taking food into the forest to the Mau Mau freedom fighters – including her husband, who'd been killed during Mau Mau. Solomon later told me she knew many things about Mau Mau which she was not prepared to divulge.

All four had taken the oath of silence, but now, nearing the end of their lives and with Mary Miller dead, they were prepared to talk, although Wanjiru's contribution was mainly nodding or an assenting 'eeeeh'. That same month, old grievances were being dug up in UK courts by three Mau Mau veterans, bringing cases against the British government. I'd heard and read of horrors inflicted by both sides, but I'd never heard or read any stories about white settlers actually siding with the Mau Mau.

Mary Miller had been a very good lady, these *wazee* agreed. During Mau Mau she'd helped and supported the freedom fighters, assisting them with food, clothes and medicine, and allowing secret deliveries of supplies to the men in the forest to be made directly from her home. They told me that Mary had actually allowed the Mau Mau to conduct their secret nocturnal oath-taking ceremonies on her property – she hadn't attended any oathing sessions herself, but she'd issued guards to warn them if any British troops or Kikuyu Home Guards were sneaking up. She'd even forewarned the Mau Mau of ambushes or attacks, often saving their lives.

Was she an eccentric old woman who hadn't really known what was going on, I wondered. Pro-self government, but a bit naive?

'She was good-hearted,' said Mugwe, 'she helped us because she truly liked us. She had no husband but she had one young son living at home with her.'

I asked if any of them had actually taken the oath at Mary Miller's home. All four nodded assent. They'd done so in the early 1950s: 'It was in her store – behind the house,' explained Mugwe.

'Those were very hard times,' said Njuguna.

'We took the oath again inside her house in 1969. By then she had left,' said Kamwambao. Solomon nodded – he remembered that too. They'd known Dedan Kimathi and confirmed he'd been a tailor and had worked for the Delaps. He'd also been a clerk and worked for many Europeans, including 'Lord Ramsden'. They named other white settlers who they claimed had helped the Mau Mau: 'Maran', 'Grace Hammerton' and 'Michael'. I later read in Tim Hutchinson's *Directory* that families with the name of Malan, Michel and Hamilton had all lived around Ol Kalou in the 1950s.

The *wazee* were tired and I didn't keep them long. Thankfully it only took Solomon and the two more able-bodied of the elders to push us out of the mud. Back at Wanjohi, Njuguna and Mugwe promised to meet again soon and we drove away, silenced once more by the road. I thought about these hitherto untold tales, acknowledging that although many of the white settlers genuinely cared about their Kenyan employees, they also cherished the homes and farms they had created. Many must have hoped to stay on after the inevitable advent of independence. Perhaps this explained why some had secretly assisted Mau Mau – to save their own skins, as well as to secure their futures. Back in Gilgil I ran this by Solomon.

'Yes,' he said, 'That is what I think too. Mary Miller, she lived alone by the forest. She wanted to stay safe.'

Mary had lived through the different decades of Happy Valley's chequered career. She would have known Idina as well, being a neighbour and friend to Alice de Janzé. Alice had not lived long enough, or who knows what she might have got up to during the time of Mau Mau?

Back home I was editing what I'd written about Mary Miller, thinking about her allegations that Alice was implicated in the Erroll murder, when I felt a cold, heavy weight on my foot. I looked down to see a very large lizard, stone still. I lowered my foot and it sluggishly moved itself on to my empty sheepskin slipper, where it took up a prehistoric posture, motionless yet threatening. It wasn't like any type of lizard I had ever seen before – if it resembled anything it was a dinosaur. Alice, my house help, was horrified: '*That* is the bad type of lizard,' she said, using a Kiswahili word I had never heard.

'It's not a chameleon,' I said defensively, imagining she was being superstitious.

'No,' she agreed. '*That* is the one that bites people! It is very dangerous.'

I was puzzled. 'Surely not . . . it didn't bite me.'

'You are lucky,' she said darkly. 'God was protecting you!'

More unexpected Mau Mau stories emerged when I was doing some research for John Heminway, who was writing the biography of Dr Anne Spoerry. She'd always been revered in Kenya as the legendary 'flying doctor', selflessly involved in humanitarian work in Kenya until she died in 1999. Then Heminway's article for the *Financial Times* had caused waves of shock and disbelief. He'd interviewed Dr Louise Le Porz, who'd known Spoerry in Ravensbrück. Spoerry had been sent to this concentration camp in 1944, under the supervision of Carmen Mory, who became Spoerry's lesbian lover. Le Porz revealed a very different side of Spoerry, a woman who'd murdered and tortured hundreds of Jewish women.

Heminway wanted to see Spoerry's first Kenya home near Ol Kalou. We found the house – a small and spartan affair. She'd lived there in the 1950s, then moved to Subukia in the early 1960s – where she learned to fly and became the fearless flying doctor who would land anywhere in the bush to help sick and injured people of any race or creed. What we weren't expecting was the rumours of her cruelty during Mau Mau.

Back in the 1950s many white settlers inevitably became frustrated with British policies, as had earlier politically minded figures, including the 3rd Baron Delamere and Lord Erroll. And now, during Mau Mau, a few angry settlers sometimes took matters into their own hands. Ol Kalou, it seems, had its share of such farmers, with whom Spoerry could rub shoulders with ease.

A week later I drove to Wanjohi, where Solomon had arranged for me to meet and interview – in a secret venue – several maimed Kikuyu elders to whom Dr Spoerry remained a hated name. One old woman wouldn't see me at all: she never wanted to set eyes on another white woman. The old men were victims of torture, which they claimed had been perpetrated by Spoerry and her Kikuyu assistant in her Ol Kalou clinic. One was missing an eye, another had bullet wounds, a third had a badly scarred leg. They told worse stories of fates that had befallen other Mau Mau fighters, many of whom hadn't survived to tell their tales of castration and lethal injections. My informants still remembered who'd been good to their African staff – and who hadn't. Morgan-Grenville had been generally liked, Delap too, but Fergusson, it seemed, was not. He was part of the group of white people, they said, who met with Dr Spoerry regularly.

Feeling I needed to hear some validation of such stories from the 'other' side, I found an elderly *memsahib*, who was initially reluctant to talk about it and didn't wish to be named. She remembered Spoerry, 'very mannish, but a character. And she got on with everyone up there – especially the men.' Anne Spoerry had regularly met up with some of the local men at settlers' meetings in Ol Kalou during Mau Mau, while the wives went for a drink and a curry at the Ol Kalou Club. 'My husband walked out,' said my informant, 'he told me he couldn't handle the shocking cruelty, it was so bad. They were very cruel to get information out of the Mau Mau. They killed terrorists by putting gas masks on them.'

*

At the start of Mau Mau, my father had just returned from an abortive trip across the Sahara where he'd watched two people die. Aged seventeen, he'd been rescued at the eleventh hour by the French Foreign Legion, hours from death himself. He returned to Kenya, now just eighteen, to find himself conscripted to the Kenya Regiment. There ended his job and planned career. He doesn't often talk about Mau Mau, except for the time he was charged in the Aberdare forest by a giant forest hog – probably the only highlight in those dark days. After I'd met the Mau Mau veterans, my father was in hospital with a broken hip and a weak heart. I was touched when, on hearing this, one of the Kikuyu elders continued to call me regularly, asking after my father and assuring me that he was praying for his recovery. Mau Mau was indeed ugly in its time, but the fact that many of those who fought in it and are still alive bear no animosity, is a tribute to Kenyans of all races and loyalties, highlighting their admirable capacity to forgive and move on.

27

An Italian Legacy

'd often thought about Lyduska Piotto's Mau Mau story, how narrowly she'd escaped death. She'd expressed her belief in fate, or some power greater than herself, no doubt brought into being by her extraordinary life story, which we'd only touched on when we met. Back then I'd been interested in Slains simply as Joss and Idina's home, part of a scandalous era. But now I'd been drawn gently, through a wealth of stories about an area which seems never to have experienced a stagnant moment, into a present that was changing faster than ever before. I yearned to know more about Lyduska, who had lived through such dramatic shifts in history. As an Italian, she was seen as the enemy during wartime. Like Idina she was a strong woman, who defied convention and survived an isolated existence at Slains. And like Idina, Lyduska's life and background were a book in themselves. I still had many questions about her, feeling that no story of Slains could be completed without the answers.

Then, suddenly and unexpectedly, almost as if Lyduska herself had granted my request, her third cousin in Canada contacted me, also trying to find out more. Linda Tomlin was able to tell me a little about their intriguing family. She'd tracked their kinship back to two brothers, sons of poor weavers in northern Italy; after Biagio and Pantaleone Lenassi had been orphaned in 1813, they made their way to Slovenia, then still part of the Austro-Hungarian Empire, living in the chapels of different churches. Pantaleone, Linda's great-great-grandfather, stayed near Postojna. Biagio, Lyduska's great-grandfather, made two lucrative marriages, thus ending up an extremely wealthy silk manufacturer near Gorizia in north-eastern Italy. Linda's emails, together with a poor online translation of an Italian article, 'The Countess who loved horses and Africa', by Paola Prizzi Merljak, helped me piece together more about the strong-willed, charismatic and beautiful Lyduska de Nordis Hornik.

She'd grown up an only child at her family home in north-eastern Italy, the Villa Nordis in Solkan (Salcano in Italian) on the banks of the Isonzo, near her great-grandfather's industrial complex. Lyduska's grandmother, Lidia Maria Lenassi, was born in 1861 and married off at the age of thirteen to 31-year-old Antonio de Nordis, moving to his family home, which dated back to 1830. They had two daughters: Eleonora was born in 1881 and Lidia Emma in 1888.

Lidia Emma later met Francesco Hornik – an Austrian officer born in Czechoslovakia and stationed at Gorizia. She fell in love and married him, in spite of her mother's disapproval of nobility marrying beneath them. They had one daughter – Lyduska. (I remembered her telling me that her parents' marriage had been sabotaged by her grandmother, who presumably had not married for love.) Lidia Emma's equally adventurous sister, Eleonora – known as Norina – wrote a book, *Giornale di Carovana* (1934), detailing her travels in East Africa, Malaya and Ceylon with her second husband, a keen big-game hunter, who is incorrectly named as Francesco, but who I later discovered was Paolo Dolfin Boldu. Lyduska called him 'Pula' – Sanskrit for 'great'. At some point Norina and Pula met Idina in Venice, presumably around the beginning of 1929 when Slains was up for auction, and it is likely to have been then that they bought their Happy Valley farm.

Lyduska came to Kenya to visit them before the war, although during the German occupation of northern Italy she was confined at the Villa Nordis. She would have been barely twenty, although she'd mentioned returning to Italy with a boyfriend. Meanwhile, back in Kenya, Italians were being rounded up and interned. With Italy now fully engaged in the war, attacks into Sudan and Kenya from the troops in the Italian colonies of Ethiopia, Italian Somaliland and Eritrea commenced in mid-1940. According to Lyduska herself, she returned to Slains in 1948, then stayed on after her aunt and uncle left.

On 1 March 1951 in Nairobi, as recorded in the *Kenya Gazette*, Lidia Hornik (Lyduska's real name), a 'spinster' from Ol Kalou, made application in General Notice 627 for the administration of the estate of Count Paolo Dolfin Boldu. It states that Count Paolo died on 1 December 1947 at Rosa, Italy, and the request was made by Count Francesco Dolfin Boldu, 'son of Paolo', to open up the estate and get it finalised. Norina, widowed at the young age of fifty-six, presumably stayed in Italy.

According to the Italian article, which was proving to be very inaccurate on many counts, Lyduska received a Kenyan estate as a wedding gift from her uncle, Francesco Dolfin, when she married the man she loved, 'bohemian' Nanni Piotto, who was neither noble nor rich. (In fact, she was not married to Nanni – real name Francesco –at this point and, moreover, Francesco Dolfin was not her uncle.) This in spite of her having a crowd of admirers belonging to the international jet set, for Lyduska spoke half a dozen languages. The writer further describes her as a fearless horse rider, often seen riding barefoot at all hours through the Italian mountains, in spite of suffering a fall as a child which caused chronic infection of the bone.

After the war, on learning of the redrawing of borders between Italy and Yugoslavia, Lyduska hastened back to Gorizia to determine the fate of her family villa, located right on the future border. The article states that she could even divert borders: these were forced to turn sharply, ensuring that her entire estate remained in Italy! Although Lyduska continued her life in Kenya, where she pioneered what are now described as organic farming methods, she was always the talk of her native town, the writer concludes, visiting annually with a glittering entourage. In 1970, Nanni died after a car accident in Latisana, not far from Gorizia. Lyduska remained in Kenya until her death in 2006. Her ashes were, as she wished, laid in the family tomb in Gorizia.

Count Cesaroni remained a mystery. The *Kenya Gazette* states that on 11 February 1941 under the act of The Trading with the Enemy Ordinance, 1939, Custodian of Enemy Property:

His Excellency the Governor has been pleased to order as
follows: 1) the farm in the Wanjohi Valley, Gilgil area being
the property of Anselmo Cesaroni and Adrianna Massaria
Cesaroni, which is set out in Schedule hereto, is hereby vested in
the Custodian of Enemy Property, subject to any encumbrances
which may have been created thereon. 2) The power is hereby
conferred upon the Custodian of Enemy Property to sell the
said farm either by public auction or by private treaty.

Then, later in 1949, A. Cesaroni is recorded as applying for water
rights on the Turasha River. This rises on Kipipiri and joins the Malewa
near Gilgil, going nowhere near Slains or the Wanjohi Valley.

I asked around Kenya's Italian community, hoping to discover more
about Lyduska, even learn her thoughts on the Erroll murder, until
I was given the mobile phone number of Lyduska's closest friend,
Signora Moretti, whose grandson happened to have been at school in
Scotland with my daughter. Giuliana Moretti, now in her nineties, gave
me directions to her Kileleshwa appartment on the edge of Nairobi.
After negotiating roadworks and snarled-up traffic, I finally stepped
into the elegant sanctuary of Giuliana's apartment, with its view over
a tranquil green garden, its verdant surrounds exploding with riotous
pink and red bougainvillaea and mauve jacarandas. Over a shot of
espresso coffee, the sprightly Giuliana talked about her own life and
her friendship with Lyduska.

In 1954 she was teaching at a very smart private school in Genoa,
armed with a degree in Italian literature and philosophy. But her life
took a dramatic turn when her brother sent her a ticket to Kenya, with
the ulterior motive of getting her away from an unsuitable boyfriend.
Brother and sister met at Mombasa, but the young Italian civil engineer
couldn't waste any more time showing his entranced sister the delights
of the exotically tropical port, for he was building a bridge in Tsavo.
Thus Giuliana, who spoke no English, found herself in the middle of
dry, dusty nowhere.

Back in Italy she'd read that Nairobi was 'paradise on earth'. This

seemed a far cry from such promises – no power and a long-drop
toilet. When she was attempting to get to the latter a large male baboon
threw stones at her: he'd learned that trick from the road workers.
Giuliana rushed to her brother in horror, but he was unsympathetic
and threatened to put her straight back on the ship, which was going
on to South Africa. But then he chanced upon a lift to Nairobi from
Mzima Springs and sent his sister off to find her earthly paradise. She
did – although on arrival in the city, she looked in a mirror with dismay:
her hair stuck out in all directions, dyed red by the dust. But Giuliana
quickly fell in love, with Kenya – and with a young Italian farmer called
Domenico Moretti. And both were loves, she told me, that had never
diminished, although she'd been widowed for some time.

Unfortunately, soon after she'd fallen in love with a new man and
country, her mother died, so Giuliana returned to Italy. But a year later
she was heading back to Africa, taking a free passage in a banana ship
to the Somali port of Kismayu. She was lowered out in a banana basket,
with her wedding dress in a box and a rose in a pot, a gift from her father.

The newly married Giuliana's new home was at Colobus Farm,
near Kipipiri, the old stone house – now a school – we'd visited some
years back. She described it as 'a lovely stone house with many glass
windows, built as a hunting lodge by an Italian architect. Every room
had a fireplace and the furniture was beautifully made, also by Italians.'
Here she was to experience a very different lifestyle: the bathwater was
brown, power only worked if the generator did and there was no phone.
But hardship was countered by exciting new things: when the *toto
jikoni*, the young kitchen apprentice, brought her a chameleon one day,
she was fascinated – especially by its changing colour. She laughed as
she told me that she'd adopted a chameleon lifestyle herself, learning
to change colour in order to fit into life wherever she was, whether on
Colobus Farm or visiting Italy.

The beautiful and sophisticated Italian girl was thrilled when her
new husband suggested a shopping trip to Ol Kalou. Imagining that
at last she'd sample some culture, she put on her chic designer two-
piece for the occasion. On the way they stopped at a South African
neighbour's house where the housewife was so drably dressed that

Giuliana began to worry she might end up looking equally plain if she spent too long on a farm. When she saw the woman's barefoot, feral-looking children, she couldn't get away fast enough, still hoping as they bumped along the dusty road to Ol Kalou that their local shopping town might offer some comfort. It didn't. Their first stop was the butchery where an entire carcass swung from the roof, to the delight of thousands of flies. At the one and only shop – known, she learned, as the *duka* – a few other white farmers were doing their monthly shopping. Giuliana glanced at a nondescript-looking man, but looked twice when she noticed the tiny, crocodile-skin shoes – this was Anne Spoerry. However, later she realised the worth of their local doctor, who would come at all hours along prohibitive roads to attend to a sick baby, and who was a godsend in times of need.

Then she heard another woman shouting and swearing. Giuliana sneezed politely and the woman whipped around. 'Is this your wife?' she said to Dominico, in Italian, with a snort of laughter. 'Oh dear! Well you had better bring her around!' This was Lyduska.

Domenico duly took his wife to Slains, where Lyduska declared that she would show the newcomer around – on a horse. Giuliana, who'd never been riding in her life, didn't dare argue: you didn't, with Lyduska. The small, slim Giuliana was kitted out in Lyduska's boots and trousers, which were several sizes too large. Lyduska rode Donnina, the beloved horse she had shipped out from Italy – 'Donnina always shows me the way to go,' she explained, as they embarked on a two-hour ride into the wilderness.

Domenico and Lyduska's boyfriend, Nanni, were beside themselves with worry – it was the middle of the emergency. But Lyduska, who'd always flouted regulations and authority, was immune to such 'fussing'. Giuliana explained that as a child Lyduska had polio and had thus been very spoiled by her grandmother. She grew up as the rebellious owner of a fierce temper, 'the family black sheep' who'd formerly delighted in shocking her aunt's smart friends – arriving filthy from grooming her horse, presenting herself to them without bothering to change. And now, here Lyduska was living the wild and free life of her choice, with her farm manager and boyfriend.

Lyduska was a great character and a true friend, but she had a fiery temperament, Guiliana explained: 'After an argument she would gallop away on her horse, leaving Nanni to fret and fume.' Once, after a row following one of Lyduska's typically extravagant shopping sprees in Nairobi, she'd ridden off in the dark. A frantic Nanni had to search for hours in the forests, worrying about her meeting up with terrorists.

Giuliana was often left alone on Colobus Farm with a gun, which she was supposed to carry all the time but lived in dread of using. On one occasion she was walking without the gun, but with a bottle-raised gazelle the tractor driver had brought her. It wore a bell around its neck so that she could keep tabs on it. When it suddenly ran into the forest, Giuliana chased after it. But her path was blocked by an African man with wild dreadlocks, who spoke to her in English. Giuliana asked him to speak Swahili (which her cook had taught her) as she knew no English, then for the next half hour she prattled away to him all about herself, where she lived and anything else he might want to know. Finally she retrieved the gazelle and walked home. Domenico later, after recovering from the shock of thinking about all the dreadful things that could have happened to his wife in the company of a Mau Mau terrorist who hated white people, told her that she'd probably saved her own life by virtue of being a chatterbox. She remained safer than the gazelle, which was subsequently taken by a leopard, breaking her heart.

Giuliana quickly discovered that as a farmer's wife in Africa, amongst all the other things she had to learn, she was expected to be a doctor. One morning when Domenico was out, the tractor driver arrived with a head injury, bleeding profusely. She was squeamish and terrified she might faint. Remembering she'd read somewhere about cognac reviving you after fainting, she poured herself a tumbler with trembling hands and downed it in one. Her husband arrived back later to find the tractor driver had been thoroughly bandaged, while his wife, who never drank anything, was snoring in bed in a haze of alcohol fumes.

One thing that had always puzzled Giuliana was her husband's preference for an old tin teapot rather than their lovely china one – a wedding gift. She eventually discovered that his teapot taste went back to his POW days, when six officers shared one tin teapot at tea time after work: a cherished part of the day. Her eyes shone as she told me proudly, 'I still use the tin teapot.'

After their first meeting, Lyduska and Giuliana became very close friends. The Morettis visited Slains every Sunday. Once when a rich American aunt of Lyduska's was visiting, she told Giuliana that she was living in 'merdo'. The younger woman was shocked at this liberal use of a word her grandmother would never even have heard of. One Easter Sunday, a priest visited Slains to take Mass. But Lyduska said repeatedly, 'I sleep here,' fixing him with her blue-eyed gaze, although he failed to understand that she was attempting to explain she was living in sin. Lyduska did eventually marry Nanni, in the early 1960s.

When Giuliana's father visited, then took Domenico to Canada to visit her brother, she took her baby, Dianella, and the *ayah*, to stay with Lyduska. It was during Mau Mau – nerve-wracking times for white women alone on farms – and Giuliana was disconcerted to find there were no bars on the large, low windows at Slains. 'Lyduska would never have approved,' she laughed, 'if she had known the *ayah* sneaked back in at night and slept beside the window. That was a great comfort for me.'

Giuliana also revealed a sadder side to her fearless and determined friend. Lyduska had many miscarriages and remained heartbroken that she'd never had children. 'Later in life, as a widow in Karen, she only had one fear, which was dying alone.' She asked her old friend from Happy Valley to be there to hold her hand when her time came.

Giuliana was in Italy and Lyduska was supposed to join her, but became too unwell. She'd fired Nyongo, her faithful old 'boy' who'd been with her for decades, and had been through endless employees ever since. Towards the end she'd been in a lot of pain and had become cantankerous and difficult. Her relatively new member of staff was taking the dogs for a walk when Lyduska died.

It was Giuliana who told me that Lyduska's adored uncle, who'd originally brought her to Kenya, was called Pula. He'd died before Giuliana arrived in Happy Valley, but she'd continued to speak of him very fondly. It seemed he'd also been very much an individual

— like Lyduska — and thus they had understood one another. Francesco, Giuliana thought, was a nephew of Pula's.

I asked about the mysterious Count Cesaroni. Giuliana had met him and his wife, although she never knew them well. She was aware there'd been a falling out, possibly something to do with their joint cheese-making business. She believed he'd been Lyduska's manager at one point, but said that he had not been good to Lyduska, unfairly bad-mouthing her.

I felt I'd settled old stories at Slains, rounding off Lyduska's many years there in my mind, while sitting in the afternoon warmth, enjoying such engaging conversation with her delightful old friend, somebody I hoped to see again. Before I left I asked if Lyduska had any opinions on the Erroll murder. But it wasn't a subject they'd discussed. Too long ago, Giuliana said.

28

Exit Happy Valley, Enter Diana and the Rest of the Entourage

Solomon and I had 'done' Happy Valley, some might say to death. I'd been visiting and revisiting the old houses for over a decade now, and had discovered unexpected layers of history concealed within those ruined walls. I felt I'd been on a long archaeological dig into tragedy, scandal and dubious legacy, beside which Erroll's murder almost paled into insignificance. I'd visited and revisited Clouds and Slains, explored more old houses than I'd ever intended to, and been drawn into more contemporary issues in Happy Valley, especially Solomon's conservation efforts. But none of that had totally extinguished the faintly glowing question at the back of my mind. Who did commit the murder – and why?

I needed a sabbatical, perhaps, and so did my Land Rover. After all, a brisk 40-minute walk would take me to one of Diana's former homes – and she remained a murderess in the minds of many. Needless to say, my thirst for the quest took over remarkably quickly and I was soon on the road to Nairobi and the Broughtons' first home.

All Diana's Kenyan homes have survived largely intact – far more so than those Happy Valley houses, apart from Ramsden's Kipipiri House. Solomon would doubtless put this down to Happy Valley's 'bad spirits', but judging by the poor state of the area's schools, roads and hospitals when I first visited – before the great road of

China – the Kenyan government hadn't bothered much to promote prosperity in the area.

Diana, although many mistakenly imagine she was one of Happy Valley's prima donnas, never lived there. She first arrived in Kenya after Happy Valley's heyday. It was late 1940 and the Second World War was well under way. For the brief time Diana's affair with Joss was conducted from opposite sides of Nairobi, between Muthaiga and Karen, she would have had no reason to visit Happy Valley. The area's ageing doyenne, Idina, had no time for the younger Diana, a glamorous and determined blonde who'd been openly conducting her affair with Joss in front of her new husband, Sir Jock Delves Broughton. After Joss died, Idina united in grief with his mistress before Diana, Phyllis Filmer, whose husband wouldn't have been in any mood to comfort her. Phyllis had supposedly been invited by Idina to come and stay at Clouds, which she did – for four years. Diana would have been less welcome than ever.

The subject of much gossip from the moment she arrived, the general consensus was that Diana had only married 'poor old Jock' on the rebound from her first, much younger and better-looking husband, whom she'd mistakenly married thinking he was rich. Jock offered her a wealthy lifestyle and a passage to Kenya, where she'd almost immediately met the irresistible Earl of Erroll, although their relationship had no time to grow beyond that infatuated first flush of new love before he was dead. Naturally it was Jock who was arrested as the prime murder suspect.

The Broughtons' Karen home, where Joss dropped Diana in the small hours on 24 January 1941, a short time before he was shot, is today owned by a wealthy Kikuyu businessman and leased out as office space. As it happens, Jock's former 'wing' housed the offices of a magazine I occasionally freelanced for. I drove up the long paved drive, which curved around to the far side of the imposing stone house, arriving at the front entrance. The trees had grown noticeably since the 1940s photograph and there were many newer outbuildings, as if someone had tried to expand it into a country hotel. The house had been enlarged since Diana's day, too, on both sides and at the front.

But the pond and entrance looked much the same, albeit framed in different foliage.

Entering through the original wooden front door into an entrance hall, I climbed the wooden staircase and turned left on the upper floor into the older part of the house. Heavy wooden doors led into panelled rooms with en suite bathrooms. There was an empty feel about the house, with certainly no vestige of a disturbed atmosphere or brooding secrets. It would be challenging to walk silently up these creaky stairs — a point discussed rigorously when Sir Jock was accused of descending them secretly in the dead of night to murder Joss, before later having to ascend them silently once again.

As I drove back on to Marula Lane, I looked at the many guesthouses that graced the large, treed grounds. Most of them were new, but it was still hard to tell which could have been the original guesthouse where the Broughtons' friend, Hugh Dickinson, stayed when in town. Eventually I decided it was probably the one nearest the gate, well out of earshot of the house. I turned left and headed to the murram pit where Joss's body had been found in his hired Buick, before dawn. It wasn't far in a car, but it had been suggested (at the trial) that Broughton, or (by others since) even Diana, had *walked* back from there after shooting Erroll — it would be a fair hike in the dark, lions aside.

Diana's next home was built by Cyril Ramsay-Hill in 1925. It has also survived beautifully — in the hands of the Zwager family, who grow flowers as well as involving themselves in conservation and tourism. The history of their unusual home was well recorded by Charles Hayes in his *Oserian, Place of Peace*: Ramsay-Hill bought 5,000 acres for £3,100 on the acacia-lined shores of freshwater Lake Naivasha and sketched out his 'dream palace', modelled on his grandmother's Seville home. He wrote of 'graceful arches and a fountain murmuring in a tiled courtyard'. The finished house did indeed have arches and a courtyard with Spanish tiles, as well as marble columns, domes, frescoes by Italian craftsmen and Indian teak floors. The farm was called Oserian, meaning 'place of peace' in Maasai. However, Cyril Ramsay-Hill's marriage didn't epitomise tranquillity: after his beautiful auburn-haired wife, Mary, ran off with Joss, she clinched Oserian from him. The house, better known nowadays as the Djinn Palace, became the marital home for the new Earl and Countess of Erroll. After Mary had died, Sir Jock contacted Erroll soon after his arrival in Kenya, wanting to rent the house at Oserian. This never materialised, although later Diana did end up there, having married the reclusive and rich landowner Gilbert Colville. Said by some to have been a manipulative woman, Diana persuaded Colville to buy her the house at Oserian as a wedding present. Colville, who himself had a Nairobi house in Muthaiga, opposite the golf course and conveniently close to the club, also bought Diana her Kilifi home, Villa Buzza, overlooking the turquoise Indian Ocean, where she spent an increasing amount of time in her latter years and which their adopted daughter has maintained to a high standard. Nobody has much idea about the welfare of the Nairobi pad, but as it's situated in one of Nairobi's most expensive suburbs, it's likely to have survived too.

Diana's home with her fourth and final husband, the 4th Baron Delamere, is now the home of the 5th Baron, Lord Delamere, and his wife, the Lady Delamere. A Kenyan citizen, he still owns his Rift Valley ranch over a hundred years after his grandfather bought it, albeit significantly downsized. Today's Soysambu encompasses the dry, rocky and waterless land adjacent to the alkaline Lake Elmenteita. Useless for agriculture, lacking in vital minerals and thus requiring livestock to be fed expensive supplements, the land is better suited to tourism – the direction in which Delamere's ranch, now a wildlife conservancy, has headed. Known to me as Hugh and Ann, the Delameres are old friends and have been my closest neighbours for over a decade. Their home is a sprawling but modest bungalow set atop a ridge overlooking the lake. Flamingos usually flock there, along with a variety of waterfowl, many of them rare; pelicans, which breed on the lake's rocky islands, fill the morning sky as they spiral up in air thermals before flying to neighbouring Lake Nakuru to feed.

Hugh's grandfather, a pioneer of note, slowly sold off his Cheshire

estate, sinking his fortune into the barren land. He was responsible for
— amongst many other accolades — Kenya's first pipeline and cold store,
developing successful strains of wheat and breeds of sheep, as well as
working out, with much sweat, trial and error, the mineral supplements
his cattle needed to survive, interbreeding them with local varieties
and learning much from the nomadic Maasai, expert pastoralists with
whom he enjoyed a genuine mutual respect.

Hugh, an avid historian and botanist, is also a farmer at heart,
periodically complaining about the dangers of the buffalo, which
he's not permitted to cull, not to mention all the zebra devouring
the water and grazing which he feels rightly belongs to his prize-
winning Boran cattle.

The Delameres' lifestyle is modest, with a regular but gentle routine.
They are generous and hospitable — all friends are welcome irrespective
of colour, class or financial standing. Dropping in before lunch finds
them on their covered back patio, which was open-roofed in Diana's
day. It's comfortable and unpretentious with plump labradors gracing
the black and white floor tiles, and a battalion of vociferous starlings,
doves and sparrows which perch anywhere they can while shrieking for
their lunchtime serving of croutons. Occasionally they'll engage in a
dramatically low fly-past. The original house was built by Boy Long,
who worked for the 3rd Baron Delamere between 1912 and 1927. Ann
showed me photocopies of Long's diaries: initially the 3rd Baron ('D'
to his friends) lived an austere and minimalist lifestyle at the far end
of the farm in a grass hut on the Meroroni River. Once the pipeline
had brought water to the dry country they were able to build stores,
cattle dips, boxes for horses and bulls, offices and the first version of this
house, which Long then occupied. Tobina Cole sums it up when she
wryly says of the 3rd Baron: 'He didn't live in a nice house at all – he
didn't believe in nice houses because you'd sit in them too much!'

Various people added to the original Boy Long house over the
years. Diana built the front drawing room, which overlooks the view
but is seldom used today. Diana and Tom, the 4th Baron, always used
it before dinner, changing for the occasion: he into a DJ and Diana,
according to Ann, 'flashing lots of jewels'.

Diana's friend, Lady Patricia Fairweather, had the cottage built so she could live in close proximity to Diana, on whom she allegedly had a crush – some say they were having an affair. She stayed for fifteen years. According to Ann, both Tom and Diana were heartily relieved when she left: 'She was an alcoholic and used to set her sausage dog on Tom,' Ann informed me. Inside the cottage hangs a portrait of Diana by Joyce Butter. It is not a particularly pleasant, nor flattering, picture. Not surprising, according to Ann, because 'they loathed each other'. It doesn't matter where you stand in the cottage's living room, those ice-blue eyes glare at you. I could see why it was banished to the guesthouse.

Near the cottage, Diana's former racing stables, once amongst the very first farm buildings, now serve as very basic staff accommodation. There's also a small shop selling tea, sugar and cigarettes, and a clinic where women sit patiently for hours on a bench, nursing crying babies, or lie in the dusty shade of a nearby pepper tree until the nurse, who has to make decisions that would alarm first-world doctors, can see them.

I never met Diana, but I ended up giving a home to one of her elderly racehorses, who was looked after by her now grey-haired Kikuyu *syce*, as grooms are called in Kenya – a word imported from India by the colonials. James Muhia is a great deal older than the racehorse and speaks highly of Diana. Hugh is less complimentary about her, but then she was his stepmother. Diana was always ambitious: she had elocution lessons, Hugh said, back in her young and single days when she ran a bar called the Blue Goose. 'She liked to be the only person talking,' he added. I asked Ann if she'd got on with Diana. 'We were never particularly cosy,' she replied, 'but of course we lived ten miles away . . .' But they both admit she was fond of Hugh's father, Tom. Ann showed me Humphrey Slade's eulogy, read out at the 4th Baron's memorial at All Saints' Cathedral, Nairobi in 1979. He describes Tom's latter years as his happiest, largely due to Diana, 'who was a wonderful wife to him'.

Hugh and Ann have had their own share of legal stress. In 2006 the Erroll murder was dredged up again, albeit obliquely: the onset of the

Kenyan murder trial of their son, the Hon. Thomas Cholmondeley, ignited the imaginations of the press. Tenuous as the Delamere links with Happy Valley are, decadent white-settler stories were gleefully dug up and wildly embellished, as foreign journalists — apparently indifferent to accuracy — made imaginative leaps from today's arid and dusty Delamere ranch in the Rift Valley, to the green, green pastures of Happy Valley where it was painfully obvious none of the frothing correspondents had ever been.

This was presumably due to the Diana connection: the fact she'd died Lady Delamere was enough to satisfy a panting press, in spite of the fact that no Delameres ever attended any Happy Valley orgies. During those years of decadence the 3rd Baron was too busy trying to raise cattle, the 4th Baron was in England and the 5th Baron — Hugh — was too young.

As Diana's step-grandson stood in handcuffs in that historic, high-ceilinged, wood-panelled Nairobi High Court, charged with murdering a Kikuyu poacher on his Rift Valley ranch, the world was watching. It remained a high-profile trial, dogged by claims that this assumed modern-day doyen of Happy Valley, father of two young sons, might hang. It was torture for Hugh and Ann, who had to make frequent trips to Nairobi, attending court and running up unwelcome bills at Muthaiga Club, battling the Nairobi traffic in their unreliable old Mercedes. Diana had given this to Delamere's father, who she nicknamed Bear. Today it still has Diana's silver bear on its bonnet.

Eventually it turned out Cholmondeley hadn't murdered anyone. Most observers of the court proceedings concluded he'd never even fired the fatal bullet that killed the Kikuyu poacher. Tough luck: he'd been stuck for over three years behind bars in squalid conditions while the Kenyan justice system waded through the evidence (or lack of it) in super-slow motion. (Back in the days of Diana, the 'long' trial of her husband had been over in as many weeks.) Today there are many Kenyans, black and white, who believe that the prolonged and often farcical trial of the 5th Baron's son with its exposure of police incompetence and corruption, not to mention the inflammatory remarks made by those in power, was a thinly disguised attempt by

Kenyan politicians to grab his land, particularly the smaller but more fertile Manera Farm near Naivasha, most of which has now been sold to pay court fees.

On another occasion I asked the Delameres if they remembered the tragedy of Buxton's Happy Valley manager, John McLoughlin, and his suicide. They did – although they were less certain about the date: probably in the mid or late 1960s, they thought, although they didn't see him often as he lived at the opposite end of the farm, about 15 miles away, 'and in those days we didn't have very good cars.' Nor roads, I suspected, and they hadn't improved as I'd almost got stuck in the mud driving a Land Rover to their house. Over cups of lapsang souchong, Hugh was complaining about the rain making it impossible to cut hay, not to mention the zebra breaking his cattle fences. I gently prodded him back into the past, although he went off at a tangent again, talking about his time at South Kinangop, not far from Kipipiri and Happy Valley, when he was the senior settlement officer during the early days of the million-acre scheme. He smiled: '£1,300 was the most any settler got for a house from the British government, so those with pretentious houses lost out!' Hugh's work was an interesting denouement to his grandfather's dream of Kenya being a self-ruling white man's country.

As thunder rumbled in the background, threatening more heavy rain, I steered the talk back to John McLoughlin's death. Hugh said, 'Well – Diana was not generous with her money.'

'Poor John McLoughlin – he had financial problems,' Lady Delamere conceded.

With McLoughlin's house some miles to the south, below the volcanic Eburru hills, and the rocky *kopje* where Galbraith Cole ended his life a few miles east, across the lake, I thought about these two men as I headed home. One had been desperately lonely and impossibly broke, the other crippled by a cruel illness. Why, I wondered, has suicide always been branded cowardly when it must take considerable courage to commit the act, even in the face of seemingly impossible challenges?

*

Diana's biographer Leda Farrant, whose book *Diana, Lady Delamere and the Lord Erroll Murder* was published posthumously in 1997, does not flatter Diana either, but gives an interesting account of her life. Diana Caldwell was born in 1913 (the same year Lady Idina married Euan Wallace and Muthaiga Club opened on New Year's Eve), her father seventeen years older than her mother. Blonde, blue eyed and a fearless horsewoman from a young age, Diana was adored by her father. A nanny prepared her for boarding school, where she proved more sporty than academic, leaving her mother free to enjoy her live-in lover in a *menage à trois*. With this role model before her, Diana didn't cling to her own virginity, going on a cruise at sixteen with her dog and two men – one of them a lover. She went on to enjoy a variety of lovers, many of them married, until she married Vernon Motion in 1937 – she was pregnant. It was a waste on both counts – he wasn't wealthy as she'd imagined and she miscarried.

One of Diana's many lovers during her farcical marriage was the already-married Sir Jock Delves Broughton, owner of Doddington Estate in Cheshire. In the latter years of the 1930s Diana also met and had affairs with Hugh Dickinson, who would follow her to Kenya, and June Carberry, who according to Farrant was one of Diana's lesbian lovers.

After divorcing Motion, Diana sailed with Broughton to Cape Town in 1941 – in wartime hardly a romantic cruise. They got married in Cape Town – Farrant claims that Diana could have entered the Kenya Colony as a single woman, but it probably appealed more to arrive with a title: that of Lady Broughton. As Farrant puts it: 'As well as men and horse riding, Diana loved money, jewels and titles.' Diana continued to entertain lovers, even during her honeymoon. On their arrival at Muthaiga Club, she met the 43-year-old Lord Erroll, incorrectly referred to by Farrant as 'Lord Josslyn Hay'. He was apparently deep in debt, but more obviously sexy, handsome and titled: a perfect dancing partner for the young Diana. Thus began their regular outings to Torr's Hotel (owned by Ewart Grogan), locally known as Tart's Hotel. Here people observed the couple dancing as if glued together, requesting songs like 'Let's Fall in Love . . .' Local gossip soon branded them lovers. Oblivious of wagging tongues, on to the Claremont the glamorous couple would breeze. The better-known New Stanley Hotel – not far from the bronze statue of the 3rd Baron Delamere – was too 'old' for such bright young things. Every night extended into the small hours of the following morning, yet Jock appeared to be turning a blind eye. After all, Diana was only twenty-five and he was old enough to be her father – plus they had a curious marriage pact, in writing, that gave Diana an easy get-out option.

It was all inevitable, perhaps, but doomed from the outset, Farrant believes: 'Joss was too similar in character to Diana. With their meeting, one or other had to change!' She asserts that Diana and Joss had a flaming row in the small hours of 24 January 1941, just after he'd delivered her home to Karen and shortly before he was shot. Farrant remained uncertain if the tiff was because Joss told Diana that Phyllis Filmer was about to return to Kenya, or because he made it clear he wasn't marrying Diana – he needed, after all, to be kept in the manner to which he was accustomed, as his previous wives, Lady Idina and Countess Mary, had done. This argument was supposedly overheard by Diana's husband and June Carberry – who'd both dined with Diana and Joss at Muthaiga the previous night – and the maid Wilks, from upstairs in their respective rooms. 'Nobody ditched Diana,' writes Farrant. 'Predictably she was savagely and uncontrollably furious.'

Diana's penchant for shooting any man brave enough to thwart her was later revealed: three of her many lovers – Peter Leth, Ron Watts and Peter Kennedy – claimed she'd fired shots at them, one when he was indiscreetly having sex with another woman in Diana's Kilifi beach house.

Farrant also quotes the managing director of the *Nation* newspaper at the time, who found himself playing bridge with Diana at Muthaiga Club and had to attempt an apology for a recent article by newcomer Stanley Bonnet, who had conducted 'in-depth' research and drawn his own conclusions. He'd incriminated Diana as a murderess in a piece that had slipped into an early edition of the *Sunday Nation* before anyone stopped it. But Diana had apparently waved the embarrassed MD aside with a breezy: 'Oh, everyone knows I did it.'

This confession, Farrant concluded, was sufficient to extinguish all former theories.

It proved hard to find someone who knew and liked Diana: the one woman who remained loyal to her wished to remain anonymous. This lady believed it was highly probable that Diana's comment was tongue in cheek, probably also a hint of her wish that everyone would just drop the subject. 'Print what you like,' she might have said to her grovelling bridge opponent, 'I've been tried and found guilty by the general public already!'

A fearless huntress and horsewoman who also piloted light aircraft and fished for marlin, Diana certainly wasn't a shrinking violet. But was she really capable of cold-blooded murder?

People had gossiped copiously about Diana – inevitably. Tongues had clicked when, less than three weeks after the murder, she'd gone on safari with Sir Jock and her old flame, Hugh Dickinson, and shot her first lion. That just added to the evidence that Diana had shot Erroll, they said.

Elizabeth Watkins, whose mother took over Erroll's seat in Kiambu constituency after his death, writes in *Olga in Kenya: Repressing the Irrepressible* that she, along with many others, knew exactly who'd killed him. Diana, she states, had killed her lover after being rejected by him: she'd told him she'd be free to marry him, but he didn't want to be 'landed with a penniless divorcee with expensive tastes'.

Even today plenty of people still believe that Diana finished off Erroll; after all, she was cold and calculating, usually toted a gun and, as her life panned out, it was very obvious she wouldn't hesitate to take shots at errant lovers. In mid-2010 I was at a lunch party, fittingly on Soysambu, listening to the Erroll murder theories of two middle-aged gentlemen. 'It was Diana, without any doubt,' they agreed, taking it in turns to expound their views over the well-spiced array of curries.

'She had a row with him and she shot him before they even got to the house. Then she drove home and made Broughton drive the body away.'

'I disagree: she was young and fit – she could easily have walked back from the scene of the crime!'

As we quaffed more fine wine on Diana's old stamping ground, I suddenly realised, with a chill of disquiet, that we were sitting on the exact veranda where John McLoughlin had shot himself. Happy Valley, still talked about almost a century on now, seemed to have extended its sinister, death-laced tentacles everywhere I turned.

'Who do you think did it?' one of the gentlemen turned to ask me. 'You've read all the books!' As if my interest would give me special insight.

I laughed it off – saying how all those women in such fierce competition over Erroll must have exhausted their stiff upper lips, with nobody letting on who performed the final deed.

It was tempting to imagine Erroll's women, including MI5 agents, with the addition of more than a few disgruntled men, lining up beside a dark and lonely road to do the angry deed, Agatha Christie style. Beforehand they would have drawn straws to choose who actually pulled the trigger to keep it from being too messy. But they all would have said angrily to him – in his last moments. 'That bullet comes straight from my heart . . .'

The conversation turned to shooting guinea fowl.

I was still smiling to myself, picturing an eclectic dinner party attended by all the writers about Happy Valley and any surviving descendants of the murder suspects. There might even be another murder – or they might just end up swapping wives and husbands.

It was doubtless my spending so many long hours in court during the years of Tom Cholmondeley's trial reignited my interest in that of Sir Jock Delves Broughton. The latter case had also attracted international attention, in spite of more serious matters like a world war. While we'd traipsed to the capital in old, faded farm clothes, Diana, parading her new outfits topped with black hat and veil, had worn diamonds. Many contemporaries had found this self-absorbed, even callous, although she did have the sensitivity – or squeamishness – to leave the court when Erroll's ear was handed round in a jar as an exhibit.

As Diana outlived the rest of the gang of Erroll fans, popular opinion was that she'd reveal all before her death. But when she died aged seventy-four in 1987, the *Daily Telegraph* titled its piece on Monday, 7 September: 'Femme fatale takes Kenyan murder secret to her grave.' Indeed she had – if she ever knew it.

29

Many Motives for Murder

J oss's murder once again had me in its grip. One night I even dreamt I was there, watching it all happen at that Karen road junction, but I couldn't see much through the early morning mist. Yet the gunshots of my imagination were so loud I awoke with a start, my heart racing. Totally awake now, I reached for a torch and the latest book I'd found on the subject. There were more suspects than I'd realised.

A comprehensive account of the murder and its aftermath is given by Rupert Furneaux in a 1961 volume of his *Crime Documentaries* series, *The Murder of Lord Erroll*. He points out that the defence didn't need to prove Broughton's innocence, only to make the Crown case fail. Top lawyer Harry Morris, hired from South Africa, started off by sowing seeds of doubt and ended up so confident he'd destroyed the case that he didn't even hang about for the verdict. Morris dwelt on Broughton's life story, emphasising his illnesses and disabilities to prove he was unlikely to have climbed down drainpipes, jumped on to the running boards of a moving car and hiked back through lion-infested bush very late at night. Morris also mentioned Erroll's possible Fascist associations, as well as the others who had cause to hate the late Earl. Broughton himself, when first told his wife's lover had died in a car crash, expressed his doubt that it had been an accident.

Although police investigations of the site and the car itself were poor, much was made of some white scuff marks found on the rear seat of the hired Buick, as well as the smell of Chanel No. 5, cigarette ends and 'wrenched off' arm slings in the rear of the car – which, it turned out, had been unscrewed. Then there was lengthy discussion over two Colt revolvers Broughton had reported stolen a few days before and cartridges found at his friend Lord Soames' firing range in Nanyuki. Examples of Broughton's 'suspicious behaviour' included his lighting a bonfire the morning after the murder, burning amongst other things a pair of new-looking white shoes.

Crown witnesses included Gladys Delamere, who had supposedly spoken to Joss regarding his relationship with Diana and who asserted in court, 'I was frightened for all three parties concerned.' Others were Soames and June Carberry (whose evidence contradicted each other); Erroll's 'boys' Musa and Waweru; the Broughtons' friend, Hugh Dickinson; Lezard of the Happy Valley 'hole in the sheet' game; and various ballistics 'experts'. Morris, however, was extremely clued up on ballistics, especially matters of powder, grooves and revolving directions. He ultimately got the Crown's 'pro', 34th Asst Supt Harwich, to agree that the bullet which killed Erroll was certainly not fired from Broughton's stolen guns. Broughton's supposed murder weapon, if it existed, would be an unlicensed .32, probably a Smith & Wesson, which had now totally disappeared. He also got Fox, a government chemist, after a long stint in the witness box, to declare that the crime bullets were not from the same gun as those found at Soames' farm.

June Carberry, when dining with Diana, Jock and Joss the previous evening, had witnessed a bizarre Champagne toast. At Erroll's 'last supper' Jock wished his wife and her lover 'every happiness' and an heir, before they went off to dance; he was left to spend the evening with 'Junie', as he called her. 'Junie' then accompanied Jock home and had to help him upstairs as he was drunk – or so she claimed: she was a heavy drinker herself. If she can be believed, they left Muthaiga Club at 1.30 a.m. (she looked at her watch) and arrived home at 2 a.m. Broughton then looked in on her, to check on her alleged malaria, at about 2.10 a.m. (in his dressing gown) and after a short time she heard a car. She claimed that Diana had talked (or possibly argued) with Joss for ten minutes and then, after another brief period, Diana came to her room – at about 2.40 a.m., she estimated – for half an hour. Broughton returned to June's room – to check she was all right – around 3.30 a.m., although he claimed to have no recollection of this. The Crown prosecutor pounced on Broughton's second visit to June as his guilty attempt to prove his presence in the house. At some point before, after or during these times, somewhere between the Broughton house and the gravel pit, someone shot Erroll in the head. And all of this evidence is dependent on the honesty of the only people at the Broughton house that night – Sir Jock and June – and the two never called as witnesses, Diana and the maid called Wilks.

For the accused to give evidence is a risky business, as case histories have shown, but Broughton did. After his examination, cross-examination and re-examination, Furneaux asserts, 'Broughton emerged from his ordeal with flying colours. He had proved himself an excellent witness and he had answered the Crown's 1,500 questions with apparent candour and sincerity. He was never shaken.'

There were only seven defence witnesses and, amongst his conclusions while summing up, Morris asserted his conviction that there had been two to three people involved in the murder. But it was his exposure of the ballistics flaw in the Crown case that convinced the twelve-man jury to come up with their verdict of not guilty. Furneaux also concludes that Broughton was certainly no murderer: 'He may have acted rashly, inexcusably, but if he killed to protect his marriage, he killed under grievous provocation.'

Meanwhile, Sir Jock's life – what was left of it – and reputation had been left in pieces in spite of his acquittal. He died the following year, six months after Diana had left him, in Liverpool's Adelphi Hotel, supposedly suicide – an act which some interpreted as an admission of guilt.

For various reasons, many writers have believed that despite the verdict, Sir Jock was indeed guilty. James Fox, in *White Mischief*, implicated Broughton as Erroll's killer. His co-investigator, Cyril Connolly, latterly interviewed June Carberry's stepdaughter, Juanita, afterwards heading his notes: 'The end of the trial.' Fox pursued this thread after Connolly's death in 1974: Juanita claimed that Broughton had actually confessed his guilt to her when he arrived at her parents' farm in Nyeri a day after the murder. Apparently he'd even told her he'd thrown the gun into the Thika Falls on the way. Only fifteen at the time, Juanita had always liked Broughton, saying he was kind to her. She felt sorry for the lonely old man, and thus kept his secret.

Sixty-one years after the murder, issue 579 of the *Weekly Telegraph* contained an article, 'Solved: Mystery of White Mischief Gun' by Neil Tweedie, supporting the Broughton theory again. The writer claimed to have had a moment of inspiration while talking to a Roger Beazley, who'd discovered the 'truth' from June Carberry. According to the article, Broughton had dropped the murder weapon (the absence of which would sabotage the case) into a shallow pool at the Thika Falls. It was the obvious place to stop and quickly dispose of the gun as he was on his way to the Carberrys' Nyeri home anyway. June, on discovering this, had instructed her servants to retrieve it. The gun ended up hidden in the roof of a workshop at the Carberrys' Eden Rock Hotel in Malindi. In the 1950s Beazley's cousin and her husband took over the workshop and found the gun. When they took it round to June's flat she apparently went white as a ghost, sped out to sea in a boat and dropped the offending 'evidence' over the reef.

The *Weekly Telegraph* took up the issue of the gun again in May 2007. 'Revealed: The White Mischief Murderer', by Judith Woods, told how Christine Nicholls, author of Elspeth Huxley's biography, was given a tape recording and witness statements by Mary Edwards, the wife of a former deputy high commissioner to Kenya. This tape was recorded by Dan Trench, whose parents had been business partners with the Carberry family. June Carberry, he claimed, had told his family 'the truth', but Dan hadn't wanted to repeat the story until he was old and frail: nor did he wish it to be made public until after his death. It was the same old gun story: June's servant diving into the Thika Falls to retrieve the weapon and the boat rushing it out to sea all those years later, this time to be disposed of by John Carberry.

Crime writer Benjamin Bennett – who in *Still Unsolved – Who Shot the Earl of Erroll?* incorrectly calls the late Earl 'Josh' – reconstructs conversations in and out of court, concluding that Broughton did the deed with a Smith & Wesson revolver nobody knew he possessed and which he could then hastily dispose of. Dismissing suggestions of political conspiracy, he believes that the Earl's brush with Mosley and the British Union of Fascists was 'a passing phase' during his impressionable younger days and that this murder was indeed a crime of passion. He points out that when defence lawyer Morris mentioned that Erroll might have been the victim of a Fascist plot, the Attorney-General dismissed the idea of political murder as 'absurd'. He concludes: 'In a mystery story Sir Delves Broughton would have achieved a unique formula for murder.'

Alf Smith, Assistant Inspector of Police at the time of the murder, retold in *White Roots in Africa* (1997) the events of the morning of 24 January 1941, including his interrogation of the night watchman in Kiswahili. The latter claimed to have seen Broughton get into the back of Erroll's car, later returning on foot. Smith recorded everything, but says that as Inspector Poppy, who was in charge of the case, did not speak Kiswahili the watchman did not tell him anything.

Some have argued that Broughton hired a Somali hit man to carry out the murder, a notion expanded by Colin Imray in the chapter titled 'Murder of the Century' of his *Policeman in Africa* (1995). Imray, who arrived in Kenya in 1948, confesses to having read *White Mischief* but never asked to see police files on the matter. Having spoken to Inspector Poppy, 'a highly competent CID man . . . with an excellent detective brain', he points out that Poppy was never in any doubt that Broughton was guilty. The evidence was botched by 'a series of absurd mistakes', but Imray maintains that Broughton was a good actor and had a very strong motive. He reaches his own 'speculative scenario', due to the absence of a proper investigation and 'in the light of a very inadequate trial', that it was Broughton's Somali 'boy', Abdul, who pulled the trigger; trained at the shooting range on Lord Soames' Nanyuki farm (where spent cartridges were found, later used in court), Abdul was then paid to disappear. Years later, the writer states, a corroded revolver was found in the bush near the crossroads.

Many people in the 1940s – and since – have agreed that there was no way 'poor old Jock' – unfit and walking with a limp, could have hidden in Erroll's car and done the deed, possibly, if anyone was to believe June, while very drunk. And how would he have walked back, suffering as he did from night blindness?

The Broughton theory also surfaced in Juanita Carberry's otherwise uninteresting autobiography, *Child of Happy Valley*. Her literary inspiration stems from a miserable childhood at Nyeri. Juanita was neglected by her stepmother, June, and abused by her father, John, the backdrop being the drunken parties of the Happy Valley set. Having watched them all frolic, Juanita wrote: 'They behaved as if the Africans and I were invisible,' further criticising the exhibitionism of the white people in front of those to whom sexual pleasure for women (who were traditionally circumcised) was an alien notion. 'What did the Africans make of the way these people, supposedly their masters, behaved?' asks Carberry. 'How they retained any respect for Europeans, I can't imagine.'

In 1980 she'd 'confessed' all to Fox in her Mombasa house overlooking the harbour, where those early white settlers had first glimpsed Kenya's exotic shores as they sailed into their new homeland, unburdening herself of a secret she'd long held on to.

Tatler ran an article, 'Silent Witness', by David Jenkins, soon after Paul Spicer had labelled Alice the murderess. The journalist interviewed Juanita, then living in London, to be told that Spicer's claim was 'bollocks'. According to Juanita, her stepmother was a drunk who once tried to sexually abuse her, while her 'father' (and it's debatable if he actually was) delighted in extreme mental cruelty, restricting his vicious tortures to Juanita's pets. Juanita had a lover at fifteen, was pregnant at sixteen (and miscarried) and although she married twice, never wanted children. After seventeen years as a merchant seawoman, the tattooed and ageing Juanita still held firm that Broughton murdered Erroll. She also claimed that when the police came to question Idina, she wore nothing at all apart from high heels, while wielding a cigarette holder. If it's true, perhaps Idina was mocking their blatantly inadequate investigations. Perhaps she suspected there was more to the story than the aggrieved husband or lover's tiff . . .

In the article Juanita comes across as somewhat unusual: she told Jenkins of her contract to have her body plastinated or preserved. Even if this doesn't portray her as attention seeking, verging on exhibitionist, I would also question the honesty of any teenage girl, especially one who'd been subjected to unkind (or worse) treatment and was, in all probability, more unbalanced than the average teenager. Wouldn't she be screaming out for attention – possibly all her life?

Other people had (and still have) their theories: Erroll's list of spurned female conquests and angry husbands was enough to invite speculation ever after. June Carberry had supposedly been having an affair with Erroll too – before Diana arrived on the scene – so some might have tried to point a finger at her. She had, after all, in a fit of what was presumably hellish fury at being scorned, smashed every gramophone record he had ever given her.

There were incriminating whispers about John Carberry: the owner of a vile temper can indeed be capable of murder. At the time he'd been away in South Africa but stories circulated about his jealousy over his wife's 'affair' with Erroll. Bubbles Delap remembers Carberry as 'very good looking – well preserved'. He was kind to her, she explained: once she had stayed at his Eden Rock Hotel for a month and gone on daily fishing trips with him, but then most men would be kind to a pretty younger woman. Initially Lord Carbery, he dropped his title and changed his name and its spelling by deed poll to John Evans Carberry. He divorced his first wife; his second wife, Maia, mother of Juanita, died piloting her plane. His third wife was June, whose claim to fame, as well as being a wicked stepmother, remains that she became a key witness at the Erroll murder trial. Their farm at Nyeri, ironically, was called Seremai, 'place of death'. Popular rumour was that it was Carberry who had hired the Somali hit man.

Few people I've spoken to believe that Alice de Trafford was Erroll's killer – even after Paul Spicer's *The Temptress* ricocheted into the market in 2010, stating emphatically that it was she who murdered Erroll. She wasn't hauled up before court, says Spicer, thanks to Dickie Pembroke, her bed partner on the night of the murder, who vouched for her. But really it's a wonder the authorities believed any of them.

Then there was Gladys Delamere – second wife to the 3rd Baron. Delamere's first wife, Florence, had died aged thirty-six and he'd only remarried much later, in 1928. He was thirty years older than Gladys and four years after their marriage he'd died. In 1938 she became Mayor of Nairobi, later becoming supposedly another wounded heart aching for the caddish Lord Erroll. Elspeth Huxley points out in *Out in the Midday Sun: My Kenya* that Gladys was sometimes painted in a bad light by contemporaries 'as a bossy, bitchy and emotionally unbalanced woman, endlessly carousing at Muthaiga Club with Happy Valleyites, and so possessively in love with Lord Erroll that she was even suspected of having shot him'. However, Huxley adds that even though Gladys may well have been one of Erroll's casual affairs, she doubts her involvement was that dramatic: 'When I knew her, while she certainly caroused quite often at Muthaiga Club, the Happy Valley was not her scene.' Gladys, formerly Lady Markham, is portrayed more kindly by Leda Farrant in *Diana, Lady Delamere and the Murder of Lord Erroll* (1997), who explains how she selflessly looked after Delamere in his twilight years. She was apparently highly popular and during the war she always made all ranks welcome at her Loresho home, unlike many more snobbish families.

Several others, including Broughton's lawyer Morris, mooted the possibility of a political assassination. Joss's political views are more understandable when seen in their historical context: plenty of other notables joined the British Union of Fascists in its early stages, seeing it as one way to keep communism at bay and 'save' Britain. It's possible Joss had remained involved in a scheme to bring about a negotiated peace with Germany, in keeping with the policy of the BUF. Some members veered away from Fascism later on, but Edward, Duke of Windsor's Nazi sympathies became an embarrassment after his abdication and marriage to the twice-divorced serial adulterer Wallis Simpson – one of whose conquests had been the German ambassador to Britain. Churchill tactfully sent Edward away to govern the Bahamas.

In 2000, Errol Trzebinski's biography of Erroll, *The Life and Death of Lord Erroll*, first went into the political assassination theory in real depth. Joss's background and early links with the Foreign Office had laid foundations for his future political career. Add to this a friendship with Oswald Mosley, going back to the 1920s, and links with the Duke of Windsor. At the time of his murder, Joss was thirty-nine years of age, ambitious, very talented when it came to making speeches and swaying the opinions of others, and possessed an incredible mind and memory. He was also liked and respected by many prominent settlers. In the context of wartime Britain, his political leanings and knowledge made him a danger to the British government.

From the outset, enough coincidences and clues became Trzebinski's way to inspire her research, aiming to clear the Earl's name as well as to reveal the real story. Her good friend, Mombasa-based journalist Edward Rodwell, had received several anonymous late-night phone calls telling him that a 1987 BBC documentary *The Happy Valley*, Fox's book *White Mischief* and a recent article written by Rodwell himself had all got it wrong: Erroll had been a full-blown Nazi, a threat to the British government and, according to the nameless caller, the real killer had left the country. Meanwhile, Trzebinski was given a 25,000-word document, known as the 'Sallyport Papers', compiled by former Intelligence officer Tony Trafford, revealing that Erroll's murder was a political assassination. This story had been told to Trafford by a retired naval commander who gave his name as Edmund and who'd served in Intelligence in the early 1940s. 'Edmund', diagnosed as terminally ill in the late 1980s, was distressed by the stories fabricated around Erroll's death. Thus he opened his heart to Trafford, who decided to make it public.

Using the above document, Trzebinski details the story of Joss's assassination. 'Operation Highland Clearance' involved two agents, one a blonde woman from South Africa, attractive enough to seduce Erroll and, via pillow-talk, to become au fait with his movements. 'Susan Melanie' (doubtless a false name) and her colleague, 'James Gregory', took instructions from Britain's Special Operations Executive (SOE), a war organisation with operatives worldwide. Following instructions from Cairo and Nairobi, the female agent pretended to be broken down on the road where she already knew Erroll would be driving at that lonely hour. After he'd stopped to give her a lift, the rest was easy. Plenty of people, Trzebinski points out, believed his killer was a woman and it wasn't difficult for MI5 to cleverly engineer the whole episode so that it looked like a crime of passion.

The police handling of evidence after this carefully managed, top-secret assassination was too poor to be accidental. Even Broughton's baffling behaviour can be explained, Trzebinski thought, as it's possible he was also in on the whole thing – and of course very few documents to do with Erroll survived either. SOE Cairo's files were burnt in 1945. There were further eliminations, including 'Susan Melanie' herself.

Joss was not popular with certain members of the Italian community according to the late Cynthia Salvadori, who in 2008 wrote an article, 'Anti-Fascists on the Equator', about her parents for *Old Africa* magazine. While Erroll was 'making speeches around the colony' to 'drum up support for the BUF cause', Salvadori's parents attended a meeting at Njoro Club at the end of 1934. Her mother wrote to her afterwards: 'I think I told you we were going to a lecture on "British Fascism". The noble Earl of Erroll made a rotten speech and didn't really answer any questions, and made personal remarks in very bad taste – a vulgar, fat, little bounder.' Salvadori concludes that Joss's murder was likely to have been 'a political assassination, engineered by the colonial government to whom he was an extreme embarrassment'.

Nellie Grant also wrote to her daughter, Elspeth Huxley, about the Njoro Club session: 'There were 198 people there, no less, and a very good-tempered meeting,' later adding, 'Whenever Joss said British Fascism stands for complete freedom, you could hear Mary Countess at the other end of the room saying that within five years Joss will be dictator of Kenya.'

Further corroborating Trzebinski's view that Erroll's murder was no crime of passion, *Old Africa* ran a story in August 2012: 'Lord Erroll Killed by MI6 Operatives'. The writer, Palle Rune, had met fellow radio ham Ray Cuthbert in 1974. The latter, now blind, had served in military intelligence in Kenya during the war, but would not comment on the subject of Erroll's murder, even when plied with drinks. Almost twenty years later, Cuthbert, now frail and in the UK, wished to speak to Rune, with whom he'd lost contact. They met and Cuthbert explained that enough time had now passed to relieve him of his oath under the Official Secrets Act. 'I want to tell you what happened at Karen the night of Lord Erroll's murder and why,' he apparently said, continuing to explain that Erroll, as Paymaster General in the British forces in Kenya, had knowledge of plans for the approaching campaign into Italian Somalia. His friendship with Mosley made this dangerous under wartime circumstances. Cuthbert confirmed that a male and a female operative were used, although he didn't know any details of what actually happened.

Cuthbert's story, as told by Rune, was well received by Trzebinski, who follows this up in the same issue in her article 'The Last Word'. She opens by pointing out that on the Saturday of Erroll's murder, he was 'to review the King's African Regiment Territorial Army on Eldoret Racecourse'. This never happened and their commander-in-chief, Colonel Barkas, an undercover military contact for SOE, ordered the troops back to barracks as the Earl had been in a car accident. Trzebinski goes on to detail the tightly planned assassination – all the relevant spots in Nairobi were bristling with intelligence operatives that night. Trzebinski also mentions that, before setting sail with Diana, Broughton had dropped into the War Office in England to ask how he could help. The insinuations continue that Broughton was in some way involved in Operation Highland Clearance. And thus was his Somali chauffeur, who flagged Joss down at the gate, requesting a lift to Nairobi as he had a day off the following day: 'This man, a crack shot, had been posing as Broughton's driver for roughly six weeks. In fact he had been handpicked, his presence vital, lest the female operative failed in some way.'

Joss was a threat, 'a loose cannon' as Trzebinski puts it. His connections with Mosley and the Duke of Windsor made his high position dangerous. Tanganyika had been German during the last war, while Mussolini was in neighbouring Abyssinia. She concludes: 'The subject may be threadbare, but now warrants a fresh look at the past.' She even suggests that perhaps Cyril Connolly was deployed

to write about the Broughton theory, resulting in *White Mischief*.
Letters continued to ignite the pages of *Old Africa*, between those
readers supporting the Broughton theory and those who agreed with
Trzebinski. Other Kenyan magazines continued to run stories too
– and it seemed that the subject would never wear out. As Nicholas
Best put it in 1979 in his entertainingly written book (albeit one with
a misleading title), *Happy Valley: The Story of the English in Kenya*:
'Everyone in Kenya knows exactly who did it – the only trouble is,
everyone's suspect is different.'

One puzzling detail emerging from several books is that Walter
Harragin, Attorney General, also the chief prosecutor presiding
over the entire affair, took little notice of the curious case of Hugh
Dickinson, an adoring friend and avid admirer of Diana's. 'Hughsie
Daisie', as Diana called him, had allegedly been allowed into her
bed, albeit occasionally, since the early 1930s. An officer in the Royal
Signals (as, interestingly, was the male agent Trzebinski describes in
Operation Highland Clearance), Dickinson secured himself a posting
to Kenya to coincide with the arrival of the newly married Broughtons;
this puzzled his family as it made no sense career-wise. He met the
newlyweds in Mombasa, taking custody of the marriage contract
between Broughton and Diana: this stated that she was to get £5,000
a year for seven years if the marriage was annulled due to her meeting
a younger man. Dickinson moved into the Broughtons' guesthouse
in Karen, which he used as a pied-à-terre when he was in Nairobi –
virtually every weekend.

In court Dickinson actually lied, saying he'd been at the coast
with a septic toe at the time of the murder. In fact, it turned out, he'd
been sent to Nairobi to recover from this affliction – Kenya's muggy
coastal climate is hardly conducive to the rapid and clean healing of
wounds. That the court was oblivious to this lie is puzzling, especially
as Dickinson was hardly a reliable witness, having previously been
embroiled with the Broughtons back in England in two insurance
frauds – paintings and pearls – engineered by Sir Jock himself.

Connolly and Fox interviewed Dickinson at the London Savoy
in 1969. He described Diana as 'wonderful', Jock as 'devious' and

'two-faced' but physically incapable of committing murder. He lied to Connolly and Fox too, saying he was in Nyali in hospital after a cactus spine had poisoned his foot. But Fox picked up Dickinson's 'slip' in the witness box. Dickinson had told Harrigan he'd been in hospital (at the coast) from around 17 January for about a month, but then told Morris he'd last seen Jock and Diana, he thought, on the last day in January – when they most definitely hadn't been at the coast.

Fox writes in *White Mischief*: 'Dickinson did seem nervous when the murder was mentioned.' He'd dined out on it that Christmas, though, according to Fox's informant. He claimed to all present he knew who'd done it but was sworn to total secrecy. 'He had not done it himself, he said, neither had Broughton, although Broughton, he said, had engineered it.' He claimed he'd been offered £25,000 for the story he refused to tell.

But if Dickinson could lie so easily in court, why indeed should anyone believe anything he said?

In late 2011, I visited my old friend, the much admired East African historian Monty Brown, who sadly died a few months afterwards. He was an octogenarian – probably the last person around who had attended Lord Baden-Powell's funeral. Monty had always been fascinated by the Erroll murder and was kind enough to show me his archives, saying he was unlikely to do much with them himself. His attic study, overlooking a tranquil stretch of the Nanyuki River, was an archive itself. The walls neatly displayed an intriguing array of material: photographs of one-year-old Monty beside a dead lion, and aged two and a half at 16,000 feet up Mount Kilimanjaro. There was even a list of members who attended the inaugural meeting of the Royal Geographical Society on 25 March 1909, for which Monty had found photographs of all present.

Monty sat at his father's old desk on the worn leather seat of a Uganda Railways chair, which Monty himself had rescued from the old Maktau station. He showed me a copy of an unpublished memoir by the late writer and historian Arthur Wolseley-Lewis, who points out that on the night of Erroll's murder, Hugh Dickinson had been staying round the corner from the Broughtons, with Wolseley-Lewis's aunt, Molly Parker. She confirmed that Dickinson returned that night in the small hours. 'So why on earth should he stay there when he had a guesthouse on the Broughton plot?' Monty asked. 'Because he wasn't meant to be officially in Karen at all!' Wolseley-Lewis believes that Britain's Secret Intelligence Service (also known as MI6 and which focused on foreign threats) recruited the Broughtons and Dickinson; Erroll, a known Fascist at the time the British were attacking the Italians in Abyssinia, was also Assistant Military Secretary to the East African Headquarters and thus 'was a great security risk'. Dickinson himself pulled the trigger and drove Erroll's body to the murram pit, then walked back. His exceptionally muddy shoes were noticed by Molly Parker's servant, who had to clean them. Wolseley-Lewis believes that Diana, even if she was on the payroll, probably didn't know Joss was going to be killed and had genuinely fallen in love with him, naturally arousing some jealousy on the part of both Broughton and Dickinson. The murder was actually a hushed-up disposal of a popular man who'd done much for the colony. Thus, Wolseley-Lewis believes, much was made of the playboy side of Joss and all his affairs, and 'many "red herrings" were dragged across the road intentionally'.

We were late for more than one delicious meal provided by his wife, Barbara, as Monty Brown explained at length his own Erroll murder theory. Having studied the relevant firearms and ballistics in depth, as well as visiting the Broughton house and the former murram pit to make meticulous calculations, he agreed with Wolseley-Lewis that Jock and Diana were highly likely to have been recruited by MI5 along with Dickinson: they were all crooks anyway, so they were ideal for the mission – to trap Erroll. Monty gave me another perpective on Errol Trzebinski's informer, Tony Trafford: he was seconded to British Intelligence in 1940 (his father had also been in the Intelligence Service) where he would have been enjoined to keep the Official Secrets Act. Monty also took issue with some of Trafford's details. He also explained that the 'Sallyport Papers' were incorrect on matters of ballistics. Susan Melanie, who Monty calls a 'nebulous creature', the woman whom Trzebinski details as actually shining a torch to blind

Erroll and then shooting him, used a Colt PT32 Special revolver, according to Trafford's informant. But, Monty pointed out, a detailed reading of the court proceedings show that the murder weapon was in fact a Smith & Wesson.

According to Monty, the team strategy was simple: Diana traps Erroll, Jock feigns tolerance and Dickinson ensures he's in Mombasa, although he actually comes back undercover, which would have been by road and which was why he stayed at Molly Parker's. After dinner, Broughton, pretending to be drunk, insisted Diana be home by 3 a.m. – although usually he simply accepted that she would be staying at her lover's Muthaiga house. As Diana detained Joss to bid her a fond farewell inside the house, Dickinson hid in the car – or possibly it was Broughton himself, the whitened shoes he would have worn accounting for the white scuff marks later found on the rear seat. At the junction where Erroll turned right to town, there would have been two cars. One, blocking the possible exit route to the left, would have been manned by African and European policemen; in the other would have been Dickinson – or Broughton, depending on who wasn't in Erroll's car – and another white policeman, who would have flagged Erroll down. Erroll would have stopped and wound down the passenger window; Dickinson would have appeared while Erroll was dazzled with a torch and pulled the trigger. On seeing the pistol, Erroll would have ducked and hit his head (accounting for the graze on his forehead), the first bullet missing him and the second hitting its target. There were plenty of men around to shove the body into the footwell, then drive and push the car through the mud to its final resting place. Broughton would then have driven home, burning the white shoes (seen by Juanita Carberry in the rubbish pit before the fire was started) the following day. The whole operation was arranged in London, while the pistol was buried somewhere in Africa.

Monty had known Diana and didn't like her – nor did he like what he'd heard of Jock. A female friend of Monty's had known Diana too and had told him that Diana was frightened of Jock: she'd had threatening letters from him. Monty believed this fear was founded in Diana's apprehension that he'd reveal her part in the murder. Monty further pointed out that while Jock's two Colt revolvers were 'stolen' a few days before the murder, he also must have had, illegally, a Smith & Wesson: 'You can tell by the ringing marks in the bullet which weapon it was fired from,' Monty explained to me, as proved in court by Morris. Monty also showed me his *Sporting Ammunition Catalogue* from the 1930s, showing that in 1936 the incriminated gun was still in use.

And thus we have an extraordinary conglomerate of murder suspects. There were those who might have killed Erroll out of jealousy, in some cases entangled with love. They included Broughton, Phyllis Filmer's husband, Phyllis herself, Alice, Gladys Delamere, Dickie Pembroke, June Carberry, Hugh Dickinson and Diana. If the hit had been put out for tender in the 1940s, doubtless many other names would have rolled in.

Or perhaps it was all engineered by British Intelligence, using any of Broughton, Dickinson and Diana, a combination of two of them, or all three – or none of the above. Would MI5 recruit people whose integrity was known to be dubious after the insurance frauds back in England? Or perhaps that would deem them perfect secret agent material – they'd already proved they'd do dirty deeds for money. The involvement of all three would make a lot of people partially right in their murder theories. It would also explain some of the more puzzling aspects surrounding the case – including the fact that Broughton remained so calm in court, almost as if acting. The last supper and the gun 'theft' would become deliberate red herrings, and this made sense of them too. The police investigations and the court case would have been intentional shams, the conclusion inevitable. Furthermore, most of the witnesses and players were dishonest. Some of them were drunks, who lied in court – some possibly because they'd been paid to keep a state secret, others (or all of them) because they were all trying to protect each other with absolutely no knowledge of who really did it.

Then there's the hired Somali idea. Hired by any or all of them – he could even have been back-up for a serious and tightly planned political assassination.

There was one other curious theory I stumbled upon, probably thanks to Monty Brown. I felt I'd been 'getting warmer' in the hunt for the murderer and now it was time to make my own mind up, but perhaps I needed a little 'help'. In Kenya a psychic or medium is often a *muganga* – the Kiswahili term for the traditional witchdoctor. Nowadays a *muganga* provides more services than damning – or killing off – people using potent curses, while offering those already cursed protective or healing charms. He (even she in these changing times) will often be psychic enough to see into the future – or past – and might even be a Christian to boot. Many of Kenya's top politicians apparently consult their witchdoctor to ask important questions, seeking predictions. Some respected historians use them to uncover further 'truths' about their subject. Monty Brown is one such: his *muganga* had sworn that Hugh Dickinson was guilty.

I knew of a few, supposedly powerful, *muganga* types and decided to ask the burning question. This *muganga* used 'the energy' from a photograph of Lord Erroll to come up with an answer, reached after my lengthy questioning. The curiously obtained verdict was that yes, MI5 had ordered the murder: a man and a woman had shot Erroll somewhere outside the Broughton gate, with the man pulling the trigger. Erroll had not recognised either of his assailants. Both agents had returned to the UK – with the gun. The reason for his assassination was political, and was also linked to the British royal family and somebody's illegitimate son. These last unexpected revelations startled me into remembering old rumours about Beryl Markham. Had Erroll known too much about something else, as well as matters of war?

Murmurings were rife in the 1930s about beautiful Beryl, who'd grown up barefoot in the Kenyan bush, trained many famous racehorses and been the first woman to fly solo across the Atlantic from Britain. It was said she'd had affairs with Edward, Prince of Wales, and Henry, his brother, Duke of Gloucester, then been paid off by Queen Mary to vanish back to Kenya.

Less than a week later a friend happened to have an elderly gentleman staying, and asked if she might bring him out to Soysambu: 'He's an interesting character . . .' When I realised how interesting, our meeting almost seemed fated. This man, whom I shall call Jack, had known Beryl very well, probably loved her too, like so many others, but it was a love that had remained unconsummated. Beryl had trusted him, he said, and thus he insisted he did not wish to be named.

'The only thing *she* cared about was if a horse was lame,' he insisted, 'but after a few pink gins she'd really talk to me.' As Jack sipped his gin and reminisced through a long afternoon, I could see how he'd shared and understood her world. He'd been as close a friend as Beryl would allow. She'd never let anybody come too close – an attitude probably rooted in having an alcoholic mother, who'd left her anyway when she was very young, and a father who'd basically sold her off to an older man to pay off debts. 'She was virtually a child herself and her first husband was violent with her,' Jack said.

I asked about the rumours regarding Beryl's royal affairs while married to her second husband, Markham. 'She had two sons,' Jack told me. 'Gervase was supposed to be Markham's, but if you saw him in the flesh it was obvious whose son he really was. The other son, born later, was Prince Henry's.' On the latter occasion Beryl had discovered she was pregnant after she'd returned to Kenya, so she'd taken a ship back to England where she planned to have the child. But, Jack said, she'd been intercepted: 'The royals got her off the boat in Marseille and she was whipped into a private clinic. That was the last she saw of her son.' Beryl's side of the deal was to keep off British soil and to keep quiet – permanently. Jack had seen the contract in which she'd been paid off – for life – by Queen Mary: £600 a year, which had probably sounded reasonably attractive to a woman with little education and who'd always been broke. Jack took a small sip of gin before making it clear that I could write what I liked, but he would deny everything he'd told me. 'I've been offered so much money by journalists,' he smiled, 'but I won't take it.'

There have been two biographies of Beryl: Mary Lovell's *Straight On Till Morning* (1987) and Errol Trzebinski's *The Lives of Beryl Markham* (1993). Beryl's own memoirs are recorded with poetic eloquence in *West with the Night* (first published in 1942). She doesn't mention any princes or sons in her biography and Trzebinski is adamant the dates don't support the royal bastard theory, although

Lovell's book does allow for speculation. The inter-war years had certainly been golden for the royal princes as they let rip in Kenya – pursuing women, married or not, in between hunting safaris. Edward, Prince of Wales, and his brother Henry, Duke of Gloucester, both came to Kenya on safari in 1928, the Prince of Wales returning in 1930. On that initial visit everybody was falling over themselves to meet and entertain royalty, with Muthaiga Club destined to become the perfect venue for wild royal carousing. Happy Valley wasn't the only place that tarnished Kenya's name, or indeed that of the British Empire. Between the wars, there was plenty of bad behaviour in the smart circles of England, as well as in the colonies – and the royals were often in the thick of it. Alice de Trafford was often seen in the Embassy Club in London with Edward and George: the latter, Duke of Kent, was also a lover of Kiki Preston's, an American lady notorious in Naivasha and partial to taking drugs. Greswolde Williams, the main supplier of Happy Valley's drugs, actually had to be ushered out of Muthaiga Club for offering cocaine to HRH.

The governor of the Kenya Colony, Sir Edward Grigg, declared the princes 'indefatigable'. Sir Derek Erskine described how the Prince of Wales had thrown all the gramophone records out of the window of Muthaiga Club's ballroom (assisted by Erskine's wife). Edward P, as he came to be called, proved himself to be spoiled and devoid of manners, happy to keep his entourage waiting for hours while he vanished with a blonde (who turned out to be Beryl).

The princes also knew Joss. Edward P and Joss had become even better friends during a ship voyage back to Kenya in 1930, with Beryl – now banished by the Palace – another passenger. As Earl of Erroll and High Constable of Scotland, Joss would later have to don his official robes to attend George VI's coronation in May 1937 after Edward's abdication in 1936. And of course Edward P and Joss were both old muckers of Oswald Mosley's.

Beryl slept around, as did plenty of beautiful women in the roaring twenties and thirties. She shared Denys Finch Hatton and Bror Blixen with Karen Blixen; Boy Long and Joss with Idina; and Joss and Tom Cholmondeley with Diana. Both princes shared her. Beryl's son,

Gervase Markham, had been born in England in 1929, but his birth was not registered for sixteen months. Back home in Kenya there'd been much speculation and Beryl apparently never denied any rumours. Trzebinski displays photographs of Beryl's husband of the time, Mansfield Markham, and Gervase on the same page, pointing out the family likeness, but then Jack had other, very firm ideas. Unless she'd had an eleven-month pregnancy, or a prince had managed to slip into Kenya without anyone knowing, it seems impossible. Nonetheless Henry cared deeply enough about Beryl to support her regardless of the child's parentage. It's equally possible that Beryl had no idea who her son's father was. She was 'no one-man mare', as Jack put it.

Gervase was brought up by the Markham family and saw precious little of his mother, who continued to live in London as royal mistress of the Duke. The Palace promptly removed him on an official visit to Japan – which he tried to resist – although he finally went at the end of March. By July he was back with Beryl, enjoying the good life with her in London until the end of 1929 when Queen Mary's agreement was settled. Mansfield wanted a divorce and Queen Mary wanted Beryl out of her son's – or possibly both her sons' – way.

After Beryl returned to Kenya in February 1930, Karen Blixen, who saw her on her arrival, wrote that the younger woman was 'very unhappy and depressed. I can hardly believe that everything is as she describes . . . she is stranded out here now, parted from her child . . . and feeling very lonely and miserable.' Karen then received a telegram at the end of April asking her to meet Beryl for lunch in Muthaiga and was astonished to discover that she was returning to Europe, and 'had to leave the same day for Mombasa to catch the Italian boat on the 1st'. As 'a stupid man' asked to join them for lunch she never discovered what on earth had made Beryl take this unexpected step. It's unlikely Beryl would have told her anyway, but she speculated: 'Perhaps it is the Duke of Gloucester who cannot do without her any longer, and in itself I suppose it is better to be at home in England . . . If he is going to support her for a lifetime, the way her miserable husband has arranged things, then at least they can enjoy each other a little.'

And thus until October 1930, Beryl was back in the UK, flouting the royal agreement, enjoying Prince Henry once again. But on 16 October he was firmly removed from her influence by the Palace. He was sent to Addis where he later contracted shingles — an illness caused by severe emotional stress.

It's possible that Beryl, on returning to Kenya in February 1930, was feeling vulnerable and unhappy because she was pregnant. On discovering this she might well have headed back to her lover in England, when she could have been forced off the boat in Marseilles. She could have been anything between three months on and almost full term: tall women can conceal it. Jack had no idea if Beryl's 'other son' had survived. Another woman, who also wished to remain anonymous, confirmed a second son, adding, 'he was called Miles'.

On the voyage to Kenya with Joss and Edward, Prince of Wales, Beryl might have been showing suspicious signs, or perhaps she just had morning sickness. She might even have confided in Joss, while Edward himself might have let slip a few family secrets. Errol Trzebinski comments: 'Naturally there would have been discussions about women.' She later says that O'Mara (his false name), a young officer in the King's African Rifles who supposedly had something to do with the cover-up of Erroll's murder, 'was convinced that Joss had some unpalatable information on the Duke of Windsor'. O'Mara wrote in a letter: 'Why were they determined to eliminate Joss completely? He talked too much, knew too much, wanted too much, for silence about the Duke of Windsor's doings and ambitions.' When Trzebinski asked by letter, 'Who do you think wanted him out of the way?' O'Mara responded: 'SIS — Lord E. had become an embarrassment.'

Even if Beryl was — in some degree — an unwitting player in the whole Erroll saga, she'd rocked the royal apple cart, as would Wallis Simpson six years later. A woman, possibly the mother of one, maybe even two, royal sons, had lived and died with very little money, and nobody cared — but then nobody really knew. As Beryl herself wrote in the preface to her own biography by Mary Lovell, she had benefited from sharing memories — 'But some memories I have kept for myself as everyone must.'

Once, when I was in my late teens, I was collecting my parents' post in Karen. Beryl Markham was collecting hers too. I knew who she was – everyone did. I watched her walking away – holding her head high to detract from a slight limp – then driving off in a beaten-up old car laced with bullet holes, from the time she'd driven through a road block during Kenya's abortive military coup. She'd had a don't-give-a-damn air and a faded but eye-catching glamour. A little like I'd imagine Idina to be, although Idina didn't end up alone and penniless. But she must have been another woman who kept many secrets.

Conclusions at Clouds

Having spent what felt half a lifetime pacing the dusty, broken floors and long-destroyed gardens of Happy Valley's homes, it was time to return to Clouds – the place where I'd started my search and where I now needed to finish it. I wanted to revisit a house that had come to feel curiously like a second home, but more important I still hoped to find out the truth about Erroll's murder. Maybe I'd become crazy enough to imagine Idina herself would step out from behind an apple tree and tell me what really happened.

'Do you know of anyone,' Peter Nuthu had asked me on a previous visit, 'who might like to repair this home and use some of the rooms for the tourists to come and stay?'

'But . . .' I began, and then didn't have the heart to tell him. 'It might be a bit difficult!' I ended lamely. The truth is that millions of shillings needed to be spent to make the house luxurious enough for tourist home-stays. Then there's the fact that this relatively densely populated country with its denuded hillsides might not have the same appeal to overseas visitors as viewing a tarted-up, traditional Maasai homestead on sun-kissed plains – and there isn't even the added attraction of elephants or leopards in the area any more.

Then, with that strange way my Happy Valley adventures had of slotting into place at exactly the right time, Solomon and I were asked to take up a motley group of interested friends, including two artists, Leonie Gibbs and Sophie Walbeoffe, who wanted to paint the old house. The new Chinese road was in use, even if the last few miles to Clouds were worse than ever.

The dark avenue of towering eucalyptus trees was now a row of fat stumps and you could see the house from the gate. It had been so long I'd lost Peter's number, if indeed they still lived here. But Paul came limping up to see why there were vehicles at the gate, and his face lit up when he saw who it was. Elizabeth, another brother, John, and the elderly but sprightly wife of the late *mzee*, Grace, rushed out and hugged us all. Even Leonie and Sophie were treated like long-lost relatives. Peter was away teaching, but his eldest daughter, Njeri, now had her own baby strapped to her back, a startling reminder of how much time had passed since my previous visit with Frances Osborne.

'Why did you stay away so long?' they all chided.

The wind hissed through the remaining gums – they were gradually removing those 150-foot non-indigenous trees, planted by Idina's servants. 'They are a danger in these winds,' Peter explained. One corner of the roof above the old kitchen had collapsed under a heavy fallen branch. As if in answer to Peter, and rage the forests that once acted as windbreaks had gone, a gust of wind blasted down from the mountains.

'This is the most beautiful place I have ever been in Africa,' cried Sophie, oblivious to the crumbling house. 'I could live up here!'

Leonie's sister Miranda is married to Peregrine, son of Diana Denyse Hay, or Dinan as she was nicknamed. The family called her 'Puffin'. Dinan had left her first husband, Iain Moncreiffe, father of Peregrine, who'd then married Hermione, Leonie's mother's half-sister. She and I had also discovered I'd met her parents in Fife, when at St Andrews University. Additionally, Sophie's driver, Saidi, found he knew Peter and Paul's sister in Nanyuki – and suddenly the whole day was taking on the surreal feeling of a reunion. Sophie knew the Erroll family too: at a heartbroken stage of her life she'd stayed with her great friend, Merlin, 24th Earl of Erroll, Dinan's other son.

We walked around the old house. Elizabeth's 'home' was now in the room beside Idina's old bedroom, leading off the bathroom where Idina supposedly bathed in Champagne. The tarnished lion's head tap above the bath still drily watched over the dust-cushioned seats. 'Idina's old water system is still in place and we still use it,' said Paul. 'We just don't bring the water in here.'

Bats still watched us silently from their inverted positions in musty corners, and in the long, large front room there remained that disconcertingly powerful feel of times past, as if its lack of present use had never expelled all those old ghosts. It was early March, and the end of Kenya's hottest, driest season, but it was cold up here at over 8,000 feet and the one little boy who wasn't at school wore a woollen hat. He was sick, Paul pointed out, but he wasn't going to stay in bed, not with something as exciting to watch as a motley crew of white guests.

In a corner of Grace's room, where she and *mzee* had lived together, there was an old wing chair with a cloth thrown over it. It looked exactly like the one Idina sat in beside the fire at Clouds, in her twilight years, pictured in *The Bolter*. Leonie gave Paul and Elizabeth her copy as a gift. She sat on the dusty, dark wooden window seat in a shaft of bright light that illuminated the floor around her feet, which was covered with dried maize cobs. She read aloud to them Frances's words near the end of the book about Solomon guiding us up to Clouds, 'raising his long, thin fingers to indicate left or right. A couple of times we had to give up and turn back, find another way. How on earth, I ask, did Idina drive her Hispano-Suiza along here?' Solomon wasn't listening – he'd gone outside to see if he could see any signs of colobus.

'Our father used to read *White Mischief* to us. We read it to our children,' said Paul delightedly. 'Now we can read this new book to them.' They didn't seem to have any other bedtime literature – buying books can hardly be a priority when it's tough enough finding funds to feed, clothe and educate your family. Dipping into *The Bolter*, Paul raised his eyebrows. John was reading over his shoulder. 'Do all white women behave like this?' he asked nervously.

We walked outside. The whole area around Clouds was desperately dry and even the lawn was brown, but the scarlet roses still bloomed behind the old house. 'And the pear, apple and plum trees in the back field have now been fruiting for almost ninety years,' Paul told us proudly.

'Do you make apple pie?' asked Leonie dreamily, leaning on the fence and gazing across her sister's grandmother-in-law's orchard towards the brooding bulk of Kipipiri.

There was a pause – pastry was not in Paul's vocabulary and proved difficult to explain.

'You cook the apples, with sugar,' I attempted, not very successfully, 'and then cover it with . . . something a bit like chapatti and cook it in an oven.' Paul was trying to be polite to the foreign guest, but didn't manage to look impressed at the idea. There was no longer an oven at Clouds anyway.

I noted sadly that even more forest had been shaved off the lower reaches of the mountain. Blue-grey plumes of smoke rose from its upper slopes, still dark with forest. Back around the front of the house the dams were dry and the stream was no longer running, with only a few soggy depressions between the rocks to hint it ever had. Solomon and Paul were intent on finding the caves in the narrow valley they'd told us about, but the nettles clinging to its steep sides put the rest of us off. We walked on into the neighbours' fields, past the concealing trees, suddenly coming into the open and seeing the view Idina would once have admired from her windows. The sun was now being replaced by heavy afternoon clouds rolling in from the Rift Valley below. It's usual up here to have sparkling mornings then afternoon rain. Standing there above the approaching clouds that inspired the house's name, it did indeed almost feel as if I was on a cloud. Given a glass of Champagne, a herd of elephants splashing in the dams in the light of the setting sun, a handful of dashing, vagabond men and a woman as entertaining as Idina to host dinner – it would have been cloud nine!

Later I studied an old black and white photograph Lyduska had given me: it must have been taken from the front door of Clouds. It looked over the water gardens, the backdrop the staggering view we'd just seen. I suddenly realised the figure I'd thought was a dog, was actually an elephant. In Idina's day many wild animals had trekked between the mountain forests above Clouds and the expansive plains beneath, pausing to drink at the dams below the house. Today all we saw were two Sykes' monkeys, and in the centre of the maize patch below them, a trap with carrots inside to seduce the 'pests'. Solomon was there already, embattled and ready to dismantle the structure, but Paul stopped him: 'That is not our land,' he warned.

'Come, Solomon,' I said gently. 'Come and paint the house with the other artists.' Sophie was already at her easel, creating a kaleidoscope of magic with colours that I felt would have made Idina laugh with delight. Leonie joined her, sitting on the grass, creating another delightfully impressionistic portrait of the old house, her brush strokes transforming it into that merry place where you could imagine much laughter and many parties. The figure of Idina moved across the foreground, ghostly, blue-tinged and mysterious. 'I had to put her in,' Leonie suddenly said. The altitude was affecting Leonie and she said she felt dizzy, suddenly falling asleep under a pear tree.

Sophie wanted to paint the living room. 'Will you sit on the window seat?' she asked me. Sitting there, I naturally thought about Idina. I'd looked up the meaning of the name. Evidently unusual – most sources didn't list the name Idina – there seems to be as much controversy about her name as literature about her life. One said it was a variant of the old English Edina, meaning 'rich friend', another said it came from Adina, meaning 'noble', while a third said it was a name from Israel meaning 'gentle'.

Frances Osborne's book had enabled us to gain new understanding of Idina. A heart wounded many times and an intelligent mind had – in the way of the old British stiff upper lip – forced down an accumulation of agony. One didn't speak of such things, so instead she indulged in escapism. Perhaps all the free sex Idina promulgated during Happy Valley's most hedonistic days was purely a bid to run from her feelings. It could have become an addiction. Psychologists have recognised a compulsive pattern of driven, insatiable sexuality as sexaholism. A sexaholic uses sex to narcotise deep-seated angst. Idina apparently died with Euan Wallace's picture by her bed and Osborne believes she had never got over him. Knowing her sons were calling another woman 'Mother' must have intensified that pain. A psychotherapist might say that Idina was, after Euan, subconsciously attracted to the 'wrong' men, so that she never again had to endure such heartbreak.

'Idina liked horrid men,' Hugh, the 5th Baron Delamere, had recently told me. 'Bird used to squeeze the dog's paw until it yelped.'

Idina's friends believed she truly loved Joss too — the only other man she had a child with. Perhaps she found it hard to ever completely leave go of the two men who had fathered her children. There would always be the pain of that twisting knife — however minuscule — somewhere inside. Idina must have steeled herself not to broadcast her suffering — or even show her daughter with Joss that she cared about her too — until it was almost too late. All the other husbands and lovers, including Gordon, Boy Long, Langland, Haldeman, Soltau and Bird, were perhaps just filling in gaps in her troubled heart. Like Alice de Janzé, Idina had not received much fatherly love either. Her father ran off when she was only four. Alice had been indulged until the age of thirteen by the father whose cruelty killed her mother. After that she was removed from his care. Both women seemed to have spent the rest of their lives searching for something they'd never had, while negating those uncomfortabe feelings with addictive behaviour.

They'd both been heartbroken at the death of their beloved friend and lover, Joss. But had either of them any idea who'd killed him?

I suddenly had cramp, as if Idina's pain had driven a knife into my abdomen. Luckily I didn't have to sit for any longer — Sophie paints quickly, but something was spooking her out. 'I can't go on,' she declared. I felt a little odd myself — as if I wasn't alone on that dusty window seat. I was glad to move across to the doorway where the easel stood among the floor's carpet of maize cobs. I looked at the picture — the figure in blue on the window seat drawing my eye, somehow shocking me: I was wearing blue, and the face was impressionistic, but I knew it wasn't me Sophie had painted.

'That's Idina,' I whispered into the silent space of the darkening room as I stared at the painting. Then Grace hobbled up, looked at Sophie's picture too and asked me in Kiswahili, 'Why has she not painted you? Why has she painted that white lady who used to live here so long ago?' It was as if she knew what Idina looked like, had met her spirit walking through the rooms, slipping sadly away into her neglected gardens.

I shivered. Back in the garden again we laughed about it. The others were ready to go and felt, perhaps, that some of us women were being affected too deeply by this place. Solomon was still out looking for the colobus or he would have felt spooked too.

I made one final visit to Clouds as my book neared completion. Needing to be alone, I wandered into Idina's old orchard, feeling that somehow I needed to share my thoughts with Happy Valley's first lady, who hadn't been among the drunken, dishonest and unreliable witnesses in court. I wished for the thousandth time I could have met her, asked her what she thought had happened to her wayward third husband — and why?

My thoughts replayed the Erroll murder. I imagined the Buick heading from Karen to Muthaiga — fast and furious. Perhaps the Earl was feeling irritated by Diana that evening, for whatever reason. Work was stressful, it was late, he was tired and possibly he was afraid he might be a political target.

It would make sense to pick an attractive woman to waylay him at the road junction, although there are plenty of ways to stop someone on a lonely road at night. Then it would all have happened fast: bright torches in his eyes would have prevented his recognising anyone he knew lurking in the shadows, so even if Dickinson was out muddying his boots, while the others were wandering between bedrooms and corridor-creeping in Karen, he wouldn't have showed himself to his victim. Nor would Joss have seen Broughton, or Broughton's Somali driver, if they were involved in the action. It wouldn't have been possible to get away, even if he'd tried, and in those last minutes as bullets were fired in rapid succession, Joss wouldn't have known much — or suffered for long. There would have been several cars, plenty of people who all knew exactly what they must do — and in a short time the car would have been placed by the gravel pit with the body stuffed into the footwell. Everybody would have got away quickly before early workers might pass and, meanwhile, a cloak of darkness hid all but the lights of the Buick, dimmed as it was wartime.

If Broughton was out that night, someone would have dropped him at the gate to lessen the chances of his being seen or heard. Whether or not he'd ventured out of the Karen house after Joss had dropped Diana, he'd reportedly been restless throughout that evening – maybe he'd known, without being sure of the details, that something 'bad' might happen. It's possible he reacted with genuine shock the following morning when told the Earl was dead, supposedly after a car crash. After all, Jock had immediately questioned whether it was really an accident.

Dickinson would have been useful as reserve hit man, even if he didn't pull the trigger. Perhaps he knew more than Jock and Diana about what was planned for that night. Assuming they were all in the loop to some extent, they would have followed orders and reported back as necessary, doubtless for a good fee.

Diana's reported emotions at the death of her lover, if indeed they were genuine, are harder to read. Her devastation (if it was) could have been worsened by her guilt over her own involvement – to whatever extent that might have been. The fact that the trio went away on safari immediately afterwards suggests they needed to be together, maybe to talk things through and prepare for the farce ahead in the High Court.

And when it was all over, either Jock's continuing guilt contributed to his suicide, or they needed to eliminate him too by then. Diana, regardless of how much she knew, proved herself emotionally tough enough to pick herself up again and carry on pursuing her own ambitions.

It is highly probable that with superior numbers of Italian troops to the north of the British colony, and the British invasion of Somaliland imminent, it would have been considered too risky to allow Erroll to continue to be so deeply involved in colonial politics. Those making the decision would have also taken into account his ambition, his intelligence and certain secrets he might have known – maybe including a few about the royals and a possible bastard son, or two.

Sir Isaac Newton once said: 'If I have seen far, it is because I have stood on the shoulders of giants.' I felt enormous gratitude to all the many writers on the subject, then sudden peace and a sense once again that I was not alone. I hoped I had exorcised something, if not laid Idina's ghost, finally, to rest.

*

A shaft of sunlight broke through a cloud, lighting my way back to the car. Elizabeth had filled a bag with pears for Solomon and me. For Grace and her family it was time to go back to the slog of tilling the land to feed and educate their many children and grandchildren, waiting and praying for the rains not to fail. Kenyans are eternal optimists.

'It is going to rain very soon,' John told us.

By that evening, the whole mountain seemed to have caught fire: from my home on the plains of the Delamere ranch far below, I could no longer see Kipipiri or the Aberdares. The horizon was hung with smoke, shrouding Happy Valley and the hill which held Clouds in its folds – as if they didn't exist any more. There were, I now knew, thanks to Solomon, more urgent issues than an unsolved murder. While colobus monkeys and ancient forests were being removed from Happy Valley, the slaughter of elephants and rhinos for their ivory and horns was happening on an escalating scale all over Kenya. Securing the future of Kenya's wildlife, integral to its tourism industry, as well as protecting and replanting those vital and valuable forests, needed urgent and immediate action. I thought of the people I'd met, and hoped for a miracle; that they and the rest of Happy Valley's present inhabitants might be able to improve their lives, while preserving, even one day restoring, the area's natural beauty.

After the fire came the cleansing rain: from my house the following day, I watched the dark clouds pouring a grey veil over the distant mountains and gave silent thanks, hoping it wasn't too late to save some of that Kipipiri forest. It would have washed away all traces of our footsteps in the garden of Clouds by now.

Bibliography

Books

Aschen, Ulf, *The Man Whom Women Loved: The Life of Bror Blixen*, St Martin's Press, New York, 1987

Barnett, Donald L., and Njama, Karari, *Mau Mau from Within*, Modern Reader Paperbacks, New York, 1996

Barry, Jenetta, *Full Circle Rainbow*, Lulu, 2011

Best, Nicholas, *Happy Valley: The Story of the British in Kenya*, Secker & Warburg, London, 1979

Bewes, Canon T.F.C., *Kikuyu Conflict*, The Highway Press, London, 1953

Blixen, Karen, *Out of Africa*, Cape, London, 1964

Bolton, Kenneth, *Harambee Country, A Guide to Kenya*, Geoffrey Bles, London, 1970

Carberry, Juanita, *Child of Happy Valley*, Heinemann, London, 1999

Corbett, Jim, *Tree Tops*, Oxford University Press, New York and London, 1955

Cox, Richard, *Kenyatta's Country*, Hutchinson, London, 1965

Dinesen, Isak, *Letters from Africa 1914–1931*, Weidenfeld & Nicolson, London, 1981

East Africa Women's League, *They Made it Their Home*, East Africa Women's League, Nairobi, 1962

Farrant, Leda, *Diana, Lady Delamere and the Murder of Lord Erroll*, privately published, Nairobi, 1977

Fox, James, *White Mischief*, Penguin, London, 1984

Furneaux, Rupert, *A Crime Documentary: The Murder of Lord Erroll*, Stevens, London, 1961

Glyn-Jones, Richard, *Still Unsolved: Great True Murder Cases*, 'Who Shot the Earl of Erroll?' Benjamin Bennett, Secaucus, NJ, 1990

Hamilton, Genesta: *A Stone's Throw: Travels from Africa in Six Decades*, Hutchinson, London, 1986

Hayes, Charles, *Oserian: Place of Peace*, Rima Books, Kenya and Canada, 1997

Henderson, Ian, with Goodhart, Philip, *The Hunt for Kimathi*, Hamish Hamilton, London, 1958

Hewitt, Peter, *Kenya Cowboy*, Avon Books, London, 1999

Hutchinson, Tim, *Kenya Up-country Directory*, 2nd edition, privately published, Kenya, 2006

Huxley, Elspeth, *White Man's Country*, vols I and II, Chatto & Windus, London, 1935

Huxley, Elspeth, *East Africa*, Collins, London, 1941

Huxley, Elspeth, *Forks and Hope*, Chatto & Windus, London, 1964

Huxley, Elspeth, *Nellie: Letters from Africa*, Weidenfeld & Nicolson, London, 1980

Huxley, Elspeth, with Arnold, Curtis, *Pioneer Scrapbook, Reminiscences of Kenya 1890 to 1968*, Evans Brothers, London, 1980

Huxley, Elspeth, *Out in the Midday Sun: My Kenya*, Chatto & Windus, London, 1985

Huxley, Elspeth, *Nine Faces of Kenya: An Anthology*, Collins Harvill, London, 1990

Imray, Colin, *Policeman in Africa*, Book Guild, Lewes, 1997

de Janzé, Frédéric, *Vertical Land*, Duckworth, London, 1928

Kenyatta, Jomo, *Facing Mt Kenya*, Martin Secker & Warburg, US, 1938

Leakey, Dr L.S.B., *Mau Mau and the Kikuyu*, Methuen, London, 1952

London School of Hygiene and Tropical Medicine, *The Preservation of Personal Health in Warm Climates*, The Ross Institute of Tropical Hygiene, London, 1951

Lovatt-Smith, *Kenya, The Kikuyu and Mau Mau*, Mawenzi Books, UK, 2005

Lovell, Mary S., *Straight on Till Morning: The Biography of Beryl*

Markham, Hutchinson, London, 1987

Lovell, Mary S., *The Sisters: The Saga of the Mitford Family*, W.W. Norton, New York, 2001

Markham, Beryl, *West with the Night*, Houghton Mifflin, Boston, MA, 1942

Migel, Parmenia, *Titania: The Biography of Isak Dinesen*, Michael Joseph, London, 1968

Miller, Charles, *The Lunatic Express*, Futura, London, 1972

Murray-Brown, Jeremy, *Kenyatta*, George Allen & Unwin, London, 1972

Osborne, Frances, *The Bolter*, Virago, London, 2008

Owen Weller, Henry, *Kenya Without Prejudice*, East Africa Ltd, London, 1931

Parker, Ian, *The Last Colonial Regiment: The History of the Kenya Regiment (TF)*, Librario Publishing, Kinloss, 2009

Plaice, Edward, *Lost Lion of Empire: The Life of 'Cape-to-Cairo' Grogan*, HarperCollins, London, 2001

Smith, Alf, *White Roots in Africa: The Experiences of a White African*, Janus, London, 1997

Spicer, Paul, *The Temptress: The Scandalous Life of Alice, Countess de Janzé*, Simon & Schuster, London, 2010

Stonehouse, John, MP, *Prohibited Immigrant*, The Bodley Head, London, 1960

Trzebinski, Errol, *Silence Will Speak: The Life of Denys Finch Hatton and His Relationship with Karen Blixen*, Heinemann, London, 1977

Trzebinski, Errol, *The Kenya Pioneers*, Heinemann, London, 1985

Trzebinski, Errol, *The Lives of Beryl Markham*, Heinemann, London, 1993

Trzebinski, Errol, *The Life and Death of Lord Erroll: The Truth Behind the Happy Valley Murder*, Fourth Estate, London, 2000

Vere-Hodge, E.R., and Collister, P., *Pioneers of East Africa*, The Eagle Press, Nairobi, 1956

Watkins, Elizabeth, *Olga in Kenya: Repressing the Irrepressible*, Pen Press, London, 2005

Magazine and newspaper articles

'Kenya's Clouded Future: Can the European Survive?', Elspeth Huxley, *Daily Telegraph*, 1 March 1963

'Kenya on the Brink', Parts 1 and 2, *Sunday Times*, 10 and 17 August 1975

'Femme Fatale Takes Kenyan Murder Secret to her Grave', *Daily Telegraph*, 7 September 1987

'Solved: Mystery of White Mischief Gun', Neil Tweedie, *Weekly Telegraph*, August, 2002

'Revealed: the White Mischief Murderer', Judith Woods, *Weekly Telegraph*, May 2007

'Silent Witness', David Jenkins, *Tatler*, 2010

'Lord Erroll Killed by MI6 Operatives', Palle Rune, and 'The Last Word', Errol Trzebinski, *Old Africa*, 42, August 2012

Various articles on Solomon's conservation work in *The Nation*, Nairobi

Index

Index

309